CHILDREN OF THE EMPIRE

Also by Gillian Wagner

BARNARDO

Gillian Wagner

CHILDREN OF THE EMPIRE

WEIDENFELD AND NICOLSON
LONDON

First published in Great Britain in 1982 by
George Weidenfeld and Nicolson Ltd
91 Clapham High Street
London SW4 7TA

ISBN 0 297 78047 6

Printed in Great Britain by
Butler & Tanner Ltd, Frome and London

Advertising the advantages of emigration
(from *The Christian*, 1882)

Innocentium injuriis maxime obnoxium esse

HENRY PEACHAM, *Minerva Britannica* 1612

CONTENTS

LINE DRAWINGS AND ENGRAVINGS IN TEXT

The author and publishers are grateful to the following for permission to reproduce illustrations: 1, The Shaftesbury Society; 2, Victoria and Albert Museum; 3, National Museums of Canada; 6, Thomas Groom & Co., Inc., Boston, Massachusetts; 7, The Middlemore Homes Committee; and the Barnardo Archives for the others.

ILLUSTRATIONS

All pictures without attribution are from the Barnardo photo library

INTRODUCTION

Children of the Empire is the extraordinary story of how tens of thousands of children left the shores of Britain, sent overseas unaccompanied by either parents or friends, to start new lives mostly as farm labourers or domestic servants in Canada, Australia, New Zealand and South Africa, countries which then formed part of the British Empire. The children, sometimes sent away while still mere babes, were mainly aged between five and seventeen. Some were orphans, but more often they had either been neglected or abandoned by their parents or were the children of parents so impoverished that they were unable to provide adequately for their families; a few were sent overseas because they had committed crimes, others to remove them from an environment where lack of opportunity and example must lead them to the workhouse or to a life on the streets.

What must surprise is how long the policy of emigrating children endured and the speed with which Britain made use of her overseas possessions for this purpose. It was a mere decade after the first British settlements in Virginia and New England had been established that the Aldermen of the City of London sent a hundred pauper children to the newly founded colony. Their action was to start a long tradition of child emigration which was to last for over three hundred years, ending only when the New Zealand cabinet brought the final Child Migration Scheme, only begun in 1949, to an end in 1952, and Barnardo's and Fairbridge changed the focus of their work in Australia.

It is impossible to know how many children were sent overseas in the seventeenth and eighteenth centuries, probably relatively few compared to the numbers emigrated during the course of the nineteenth and early twentieth centuries, when the figures twice peaked at between three and four thousand a year. It is known that between 1870 – when juvenile emigration became a recognised movement – and 1930, Canada received more than 100,000 children whose descendants are now thought to number over a million. Alone among nations, the British seem not to have thought that there was anything unnatural in removing children from familiar surroundings and shipping them thousands of miles overseas to set them down among strangers in a strange land. Britain alone had unpopulated and unsettled lands to which children could be sent in the expectation that they would benefit from being given a fresh start and improved opportunities. For most countries the dangers of war and revolution are generally seen as the only acceptable reasons for parting children from families, friends and country, a reason which in 1940 induced Britain to send thousands of her children overseas for safety.

It is only recently that research has started to be done and more is becoming known about the reasons for and the effects of this strange phenomenon, juvenile emigration. Since Canada received the largest number of emigrant children, Canadians have been the first to consider the economic and social consequences of child migration in their country. Joy Parr, in her pioneering book, *Labouring Children*, was the first to look critically at the juvenile emigration movement and to analyse its causes and consequences for the children. She has been followed by Phyllis Harrison who published a selection of letters from former emigrant children, relatives and friends in *The Home Children* and Kenneth Bagnall, whose book, *The Little Immigrants* deals with the subject in a more general way.

Children of the Empire is an attempt to trace the history of the juvenile emigration movement over three centuries and to look at the movement, which sent tens of thousands of children to Canada, in a wider context. The subject is too large, the canvas too wide and the actors too many for this to be a comprehensive study, but it does pose a question. Can the special circumstances in which Britain found herself, a small island, unable to support a rapidly growing population and at the same time controlling territories needing settlers, be sufficient explanation for her uniquely different behaviour toward a small proportion of her disadvantaged children? There seem to me to be so many different factors involved that no clear answer is possible. By telling some of the amazing and fascinating stories of these children, by giving some understanding of the despair which allowed families to accept separation from children as the lesser of two evils, and by looking at the reasons which motivated those involved with promoting emigration, I hope to show how a nation came to persuade itself that by sending these children overseas in the name of God and Empire it was doing its best for those children; and how finally it came to realise, albeit long after it should have done so, the dangers to which some children were exposed and how damaging such an experience could be.

Children were first sent overseas because they were unwanted: they might have committed a crime or merely have become public nuisances through destitution. Removal overseas was seen as an appropriate response to the problems they posed, and when it was no longer possible to send children to the North American colonies following American Independence they were sent first to Australia then to South Africa and Canada. Until the second half of the nineteenth century the numbers of children sent overseas were relatively small: the various initiatives started by individuals like Shaftesbury and organisations like the Children's Friend Society or the Reformatory and Industrial Schools did not receive much public support and were in consequence short-lived. Nevertheless their underlying philosophy was similar to that which motivated the juvenile emigration agencies of the nineteenth century: if a child was given a fresh start, removed from the environment which had caused the problems, it would be able to take advantage of the opportunities available to it in a new young country.

Two letters written in 1869 mark the real start of juvenile emigration as a recognisable movement. As a result of these letters, one written to *The Times*, the other to an evangelical journal called *The Revival*, two parties, one of girls and one of boys, sailed across the Atlantic to start new lives in Canada. They were the forerunners of many thousands more who were to make that journey and start an experiment in social engineering which was to ramify and extend itself in ways which could not then have been foreseen.

Throughout the entire period, child emigration was justified on economic grounds and never more so than during the second half of the nineteenth century. The surplus of destitute, homeless and unemployable children in Victorian Britain's urban centres was matched by the need in the Dominions for labour. There was a continuous demand for hands to work on the land and for domestic servants to work in the homesteads of Canada, Australia, and to a lesser extent South Africa and later New Zealand. But during that period child emigration was not only encouraged for economic reasons; there was strong religious and moral pressure to remove children from the evils of city life to the pure wide open spaces which the Dominions possessed in abundance.

The second evangelical revival which swept over the British Isles in 1859 not only strengthened religious attitudes; the development of many charitable missions and voluntary organisations can be directly traced to the influence of the new evangelicalism which was such a feature of Victorian Britain. Evangelical philanthropists had been quick to see that only to preach the Gospel of salvation to people so poor that their energies were entirely taken up by the struggle to keep body and soul together was to fight a losing battle. Nowhere was this more obvious than in the case of children. The big children's voluntary organisations that came into being at that period to care for the homeless and destitute all had a strong religious basis. The majority of the children's homes, like Barnardo's, the Methodist Children's Home, and Quarrier's, were evangelical in outlook, but all of them, Church of England and Roman Catholic children's homes included, saw in emigration the answer to both a social and a moral problem. Out of the hundred thousand children sent to Canada between 1870 and 1941 almost a third went out under the auspices of Barnardo's, making them the leading organisation involved in the emigration of children overseas. Thus Christian social concern enabled juvenile emigration to be seen also as sound policy from an economic point of view.

By the turn of the century another argument had come to be increasingly used to promote and popularise the idea of juvenile emigration. As the influence of evangelicalism waned, so the ideas of the social imperialists became more dominant. Queen Victoria's Diamond Jubilee in 1897 marked what can perhaps now be seen as the peak of British imperialism, but to advocates of Empire it must then have seemed to mark but a stage in its growth. The need to settle the untenanted lands of the Dominions with emigrants from Britain was one of the imperialists' prime objectives. Thus those involved in the work of juvenile emigration came to be seen in a new light, not just as philanthropists, but imperial philanthropists. Children were now no longer merely being rescued and given new opportunities, they were seen as the bricks with which the Empire would be built. Nor were the emigrating agencies slow to make use of this new form of appeal in their struggle to collect funds to continue their work. In their publicity material children were referred to as 'precious freight', the young colonists of the future who would help to consolidate the Empire and form a living link between the Dominions and the mother country. Child emigration was confidently presented to the public as 'an investment in Empire'. For nearly forty years the needs of disadvantaged children and the demands of Empire settlement were linked together until the demise of the latter and a better understanding of the real needs of the former brought this strange alliance of ideas to an end.

In my study I shall be looking at the history of juvenile emigration through the eyes of a small number of people: Shaftesbury, Maria Rye, Annie Macpherson, Andrew Doyle, John Middlemore, William Quarrier, Thomas Barnardo, J. J. Kelso, Margaret Bondfield and Kingsley Fairbridge, men and women whose work and beliefs affected the lives of thousands of children suddenly and dramatically. I have had the privilege of looking through the record books of many of the emigrating agencies. It is impossible not to be moved by the stories they contain. I have read many of the letters sent home by the children, both published and unpublished and I have had the pleasure of meeting many men and women who went overseas as child emigrants. They too have a story to tell and a point of view to put. The histories of some few hundreds of the many thousands who sailed across the seas are known. Among them there is evidence of both physical suffering and mental hardship, but others tell stories that show they found fulfilment and happiness in their adopted countries. When only a fraction of the whole story can be known is it possible to make any real assessment of the consequences of emigrating children to new lands?

Perhaps the only people who are in a position to pass judgement are the children themselves and their descendants. They are the ones who knew what it was like to be torn from family and friends, to leave familiar surroundings and to suffer the loneliness and depression that being alone in a strange country bring; some of them knew the joy of finding new families and new friends. I have tried through their letters and stories to give some idea of their feelings and I am immensely grateful to all those who have talked to me of their experiences. Many have deliberately covered their tracks not wishing it to be known that they were once juvenile emigrants; others are interested and proud of the fact. To them all I dedicate this book.

ACKNOWLEDGEMENTS

Without the generous co-operation of Dr Barnardo's, the Church of England Children's Society, the Fairbridge Society, the Middlemore Homes, Quarrier's Homes, the Salvation Army, the Shaftesbury Society and the Thomas Coram Foundation (Foundling Hospital) this book could not have been written. I am greatly indebted to them all for their helpful interest.

The Barnardo organisation is not only responsible for its own unique collection of children's records and photographs, but also for those of Annie Macpherson's Homes; the history books of the Marchmont Homes and the records of the Liverpool Sheltering Home are also in their custody. In making use of these records I have been very conscious of their private and personal nature. In nearly every case where the records are less than a hundred years old I have altered the names of the former child emigrants, except for those whose stories have already been made public. I am extremely grateful to the late Mr Jo Tate of New Zealand, to Mr Charles Zakharov, to Mr John Greenwood and to Mr Charles Davies for giving me permission to make use of their stories. I would also like to take this opportunity of thanking the many other former child emigrants from all over the world, whose names do not appear in this book, but who have given me a very great deal of valuable information.

I am also indebted to the Barnardo Council for allowing me to make use of the unpublished letters of Stuart Barnardo to his father Dr Barnardo. Mr Roy Clough and his assistants in the After Care department have been unfailingly helpful; Mr Roy Ainsworth's enthusiasm and knowledge have made the selection of the Barnardo photographs a particular pleasure. To them and to all those who work with and for the Barnardo organisation and who have encouraged and helped me by giving of their time and knowledge I am deeply grateful. In recording my appreciation of the help I received from Barnardo's in Australia

I would like to thank the Committee of Management, Col Peter Smeaton, Mr Philip Hart and Mrs Marie Macmillan for arranging a meeting with former Barnardo boys and girls and for many other kindnesses. I am equally indebted to the Committee of Management of Barnardo's New Zealand and to Mr Ian Calder, the National Director, for all that was done to enable me to take advantage of my short stay in New Zealand.

I was able to visit the Fairbridge School in Pinjarra, Western Australia, thanks to the courtesy of the Fairbridge Society and I thank the Chairman, Sir Peter Garran, the Director, Mr Ivan Vincent and the Principal of the School, Mr Line for making this possible. I had the privilege and pleasure of going to Pinjarra with Mrs Barbara Rowley, Kingsley Fairbridge's daughter and special thanks must also go to Mrs Daphne Briggs, secretary of the Old Fairbridgians who arranged for me to meet old Fairbridgians Mary Rowley, Millie Lander, Bill Newberry and David Buck at a most enjoyable and instructive luncheon.

I would also like to thank Mr Bowie, Director of the Church of England Children's Society, Dr Minto, Director, Quarrier's Homes, Mr Heaseman of the Shaftesbury Society and Mr Masters, Director, Thomas Coram Foundation, for their help.

It was to Canada that the majority of the child emigrants were sent, but none of the child care societies involved in juvenile emigration to Canada now have organisations in that country. The Public Archives of Canada have a rich and comprehensive collection of records on the subject and I am deeply indebted to the staff of the PAC for the help I was given while in Ottawa. My particular thanks go to Mrs Grace Campbell, whose unfailing interest and helpful guidance made the task of finding my way through the mass of material a great deal less arduous. Professor Joy Parr's generosity in allowing me to make use of her own research material and notes leaves me greatly in her debt. I recall with pleasure the day we spent driving through Ontario talking 'juvenile emigration'. I am grateful to Mr Michael Wilson, Professor Wesley Turner and Mrs Peter Spokes for making the day I spent at Niagara-on-the-Lake so interesting.

In dealing with the 1940 wartime evacuation of children overseas my grateful thanks go to Mrs Elspeth Davies for all her help. She not only went through the papers of the Children's

Overseas Reception Board, now deposited at the Public Record Office, on my behalf, but shared her personal knowledge of the CORB scheme with me. I am also grateful to Mr Tony Richardson of the Foreign Office.

Very many people have given me help in differing ways. I am indebted to Professor Laurence Lerner for permission to quote his poem, 'To Sarah Burge'; to Mrs Yvonne Lacey for help with the Zakharov papers; I thank Mr Kyril Zinovieff, Miss Betty Askwith, Mrs Joan Ambrose, Mr John Ruffles and Mr Les Field, Miss Eve Soar and Lucy Wagner; also Mrs J.S. Smith for help with the Middlemore family papers.

I thank the staff of the British Library; the British Library, Newspaper Division, Colindale; the London Library; Mr Nowell, the Barnardo Library; Mrs Margaret Metcalf, Chief Librarian, Battye Library, Perth, WA; Miss Anne Robertson, Manuscript Librarian, the Mitchell Library, Sydney, NSW; the staff of the Turnbull Library, Wellington and the National Archives of New Zealand; Miss Roberta Routledge of Archive Arrangement, London; Mr Murdo Macdonald; Mr Philip O'Shea, *New Zealand Herald*. To my husband I owe much, not only for his specialised knowledge of genealogy, but for the help and encouragement he has given me during the preparation of this book. I am also indebted to Sally Mapstone and Barbara Gough for help in the preparation of the manuscript and to my publishers for sharing my enthusiasm.

One

EARLY CHILD EMIGRANTS

'I conceive that London has got too full of children.'

ROBERT CHAMBERS, London Magistrate, 1826

IN 1607 five little vessels – the *Sarah Constant*, the *Discovery* and the *Godspeed*, all from Blackwall, together with the *Mary and John* and the *Gift of God* from Falmouth – left the shores of England carrying emigrants from all over the country to found a colony on the coast of Maine in North America.[1] They were the first passenger ships to cross the Atlantic and can claim to have begun the Atlantic passenger service which was, in the next three and a half centuries, to transport millions of men, women and children across the Atlantic to start new lives in North America.

Eleven years later, in 1618, the City of London agreed to send one hundred unwanted children across the Atlantic to Virginia and thus could effectively be said to have inaugurated the movement to emigrate juveniles overseas, a movement which was to last until the Second World War and which would affect the lives of tens of thousands of children.

Little is known of the unaccompanied children who were sent overseas in the seventeenth and eighteenth centuries. Apart from cases of penal transportation we have only the occasional record and tantalisingly brief references which tell us little except that throughout the period those in authority did not think it wrong to send unaccompanied children overseas, although legislation was enacted to prevent children being actually kidnapped and sent overseas for their labour.

Until 1700 the ships that crossed the Atlantic were built for freight and not for passengers and arrangements for emigrants were rudimentary. The journey lasted from six to ten weeks and sometimes took up to three months. We have no record of how those early pioneers endured the discomforts and dangers, tossing in small vessels on rough and stormy seas, drenched by waves whipped up by gale-force winds, or becalmed for days. For the passengers, exposed to the constant danger of diseases like scurvy and smallpox, provided with unwholesome and unappetising food, inadequately clothed and huddled together with livestock, furniture and provisions, anything other than sheer survival must have been an impossibility. Imagination boggles at the thought of conditions on board during prolonged bouts of stormy weather when all were kept under hatches.

It is a wonder that under such conditions women and children ever made the crossing. We know from records that two of the earliest emigrants, Thurston Raynor and Richard Kimball, both from Ipswich, took their wives and their eleven children with them; two of the children were babies and six others were under ten.[2] At the request of the Virginia Company a shipload of 'young and uncorrupt maids to make wives to the inhabitants and by that means to make the men more settled and less moveable' were sent over to Virginia in 1618.[3] One wonders how willingly the 'uncorrupt maids' went and where they came from! The Company promised to pay all the costs of transportation if the maids married 'public farmers', that is tenants of the Company's lands. If a private farmer wanted a wife she would cost him a hundred and fifty pounds of tobacco, which would certainly have provided the Company with a nice profit. In the same year the *Virginia* magazine recorded that the need for wives for settlers had resulted in young girls being kidnapped to be sold in Virginia.

Extreme measures had to be taken by the Virginia Company. In spite of all their previous efforts to settle men on the land in 1616 there were fewer settlers than in 1611. Three hundred emigrants had returned to England and if the settlement was to survive the Company had to take drastic action. Besides the girls the Company also sent over a hundred young apprentices and three hundred tenants for the Company's lands and gardens.[4] It was in this year, 1618, that the Company made application to the City of London to furnish one hundred children 'for the better supply of the colony'. The decision taken by the Aldermen to ship children for whom they were responsible overseas set an important precedent, one which was to be followed by others with similar responsibilities.

As with the movement in later years, the underlying reasons were economic: the children constituted a nuisance to the authorities and were a burden on the rates, while the newly settled plantation owners were desperate for labour. London at that time was swarming with homeless waifs, orphans and foundlings. The sixteenth century had seen a vast increase in the number of vagrants and beggars. Among the dispossessed and vagrant there was not unnaturally a fairly substantial criminal element which terrorised both town and countryside and caused all vagrants to be feared and treated harshly. The causes of poverty were roughly recognised and a man was either 'poore by impotency and defect' which included orphans; or 'poore by casualty', which included a man with a large number of young children, or idle and dissolute vagrants.[5]

The first poor law in 1531 took no account of children and merely dealt with the licensing of begging for the old and impotent and defined a range of punishment for sturdy beggars. But by 1636 the realisation that the vagrant child was growing up only to swell the ranks of the adult vagrants and criminals resulted in the Poor Law Act authorising the parish to take healthy idle begging children between the ages of five and fourteen and apprentice them to masters in husbandry or other crafts so as to enable them to earn their livings when they came of age. Very severe punishments were to be inflicted on such children who refused service or returned to their idle ways. The Poor Law Act of 1572 is notable in that the State for the first time came to accept the need for a compulsory poor rate, but vagrants and idlers were still to be severely punished. Young children were, for the first time, treated differently from adolescents over fourteen years and though they were to be dealt with by whipping and stocking, young adolescents were, if convicted of a 'roguish and vagabond's trade of life', to be punished in the same way as adults. By 1601 Church Wardens and Justices of the Peace were required under the provisions of the Act for the Relief of the Poor to set to work and apprentice not merely vagrant and destitute children, but children whose parents were unable to maintain them. It was but a short step for such children to be apprenticed overseas.

The fate of children apprenticed to mine, factory or mill owners was often one of terrible hardship, while it is known that many who went to the colonies in the early days as servants or apprentices later acquired land, property and position.[6] When the request for children for Virginia was received by the City, Sir George Bolles, the Lord Mayor, was more than ready to accede to the petition fearing that the 'overflowing multitude of inhabitants should, like too much blood, infect the whole city with plague and poverty'.[7] A meeting of the representatives of the hundred parishes of London was held in St Paul's to see how best the matter could be dealt with and how each parish should be assessed to accomplish the object. Thus in 1618 a hundred children were transported to Virginia. As it is only after exhaustive researches by genealogists that the names and fate of even some of the early emigrants to the New World have been uncovered, it is hardly surprising that nothing is known about these children or the successor party who went out in 1619. Shipping lists did not exist at this date and the accounts of the various Church Wardens show only the amount of money paid to the Chamberlain of London for this object. All we know about the 1619 party is that many of the children were very unwilling to be thus transported and it was only after some difficulty that the City managed to assemble a hundred children, keeping them at Bridewell until the party was complete.

It was not only the City that was troubled by idle young people. King James wrote to Sir Thomas Smyth, the Treasurer of the Virginia Company in 1619 saying,

> Where as our Court hath of late been troubled by divers idle young people, who though they have been twise punished still continue to followe the same havving noe employment; we have noe other course to cleer our Court from them have thought fitt to send them unto you desiring you att the next opportunitie to send them away to Virginia and to take sure order that they may be sett to worke there, [otherwise] they will never be reclaimed from the idle life of vagabonds.[8]

On receiving this letter Sir Thomas Smyth wrote to the Lord Mayor saying the Company had no ship and begged that the young people be detained at Bridewell until the next ship should depart for Virginia. It is not clear from this account whether the King, the City or the Company paid for the transportation of these unwanted young courtiers, or whether they formed part of the second party sent by the City, but we know from the Virginia Company Records that they sailed in the ship *City* later in the year.

The Council for New England was not long in following the example of the Virginia Company and in 1622 they too asked the City of London to send over poor children. In 1623 they widened the field considerably by securing from the King a letter to the Lieutenant of every shire 'for the setting forth of their poorer sort of people to New England'.[9] It is not known how far this vast new demand affected the fate of poor children. Some, certainly, were sent overseas, as scattered records show. The coffer books of Winchester record that on 30 December 1625 sixty shillings were spent 'for the apparelling of six poor boys that went to Virginia' and the Barnstaple account books note 'ten shillings and four pence paid for shoes for three boys sent to Virginia'.[10]

If the majority of these early young emigrants remain anonymous, their histories unknown, the sad story of the three children who sailed on the *Mayflower* in 1620, Ellinora, Jasper and Richard More, is well documented.[11] They were sent overseas, not because of poverty but because of personal and complicated territorial considerations. Samuel More, their father, was a substantial landowner. He married in 1610, when only sixteen, his cousin Catherine who was seven years his senior. She had inherited the property of Larden and the marriage had been arranged to keep the property in the More family. Unknown to Samuel, Catherine was leading an adulterous life with one Jacob Blakeway 'a fellow of mean parentage and condition'. Four children were born to the couple before Samuel suspected anything, but when the affair became known to him he petitioned the Lord Chief Justice of England for 'the disposing of the fower children of Catherine More by Samuell More'. Catherine appears to have abandoned and ill-treated the children and Samuel had had them placed in the care of a tenant of his father. Four years later, Samuel, who was seeking a divorce, brought them to London. There an agreement was made with 'one Mr Weston, an honest and sufficient merchant' and two associates 'to transport them to Virginia and to see that they should be sufficiently kept and maintained with meat, drink, apparel, lodging and other necessaries and that at the end of seven years they should have fifty acres of land apiece in the country of Virginia'.

Weston was the leader of a group of merchant adventurers and it was through his vision and enterprise that the famous voyage of the *Mayflower* took place. Only three of the four More children mentioned in the petition sailed in her: Ellinora aged eight went in the charge of Edward Winslow, Jasper aged seven in the charge of John Carver and Richard aged six was apprenticed to William Brewster. Richard was the only one who survived both the voyage and the hardships of life in New England. There he became the retainer and servant of Richard Hollingsworth, whose daughter he married as his second wife. He is also described as a yeoman and a mariner. Three of Richard's five children themselves had children, and, although there is no trace of the family in the male line after 1707, his daughter Susannah left a daughter 'through whom it is said the blood of Richard More was carried into many northern New England families'.[12] When he was seventy 'or thereabouts' Richard made a deposition simply saying that in 1620 he had been living in the house of Mr Thomas Weston and from there had been transplanted to New Plymouth in New England. One cannot help but wish that he had added to that statement some description of the voyage of the *Mayflower* and some details about his early life in New England.

John Winthrop from Groton in Suffolk, a Puritan and Governor of Massachusetts, was one of the most active promoters of emigration. On one voyage which he and his wife made to Boston on the *Abigail* in 1635 the names of fifteen unaccompanied children aged from three months to fifteen years are recorded on the list of passengers. As the ship arrived in Boston infested with smallpox it may be wondered how many of these children actually survived the voyage. Although after 1641, migration to New England in particular died down, it does seem certain that children continued to be sent to the other mainland colonies and to the West Indies. Winthrop records in his journal in 1643 that 'one of the ships, the *Seabridge*, arrived with twenty children and some other passengers out of England ...

and those children, with many more to come after, were sent by money given one fast day in London and allowed by Parliament and city for that purpose'.

The fact that Parliament in 1645 passed an ordinance for the 'Apprehending and bringing to condign punishment all such persons as shall steale, sell, buy, inviegle, purloyne, convey or receive any little children' presupposes that an organised traffic for the transportation of children for commercial profit existed. Between 1654 and 1685 it is said that more than ten thousand servants sailed from Bristol alone to the mainland colonies and to the West Indies, which had been settled in the 1620s and 1630s.[13] It has been argued that not only were individual pauper children transported overseas, but that there was an organised export to New England and to Virginia from London and Bristol of pauper children and foundlings.[14] Among the servants who sailed from Bristol there were doubtless many children shipped across the seas for their future potential usefulness. Some well-intentioned philanthropists certainly believed that life in America was to be preferred to a life of vagrancy. Anthony Abdy, a citizen and Alderman of London, and his two sons each left £120 in their wills for the clothing and transporting of twenty poor boys and girls vagrant on the streets of London to Virginia, New England or any other of the Western Plantations.[15] We know nothing of how these children were treated nor how many of them were sent overseas. It is said that English captains kidnapped Irish boys *en route* to America and sold them to Puritan planters under conditions of virtual slavery disguised as apprenticeship. We do not know if any distinction was made between the unfortunate child kidnapped and illegally shipped overseas and the vagrant child sent legally, but equally helplessly, overseas by those in authority.

There are far fewer references to children being sent or taken to North America in the eighteenth century. It would seem that this was because there was a decline in the practice and not just because there appear to be fewer records in existence. With the development of the system of deporting convicted felons to America, however, the word 'transportation' began to take on a new meaning. The word first appeared in a statute of 1662 and the idea of transportation as a form of punishment for juveniles was made explicit by the act of 1717 which permitted penal transportation of young people between fifteen and eighteen years of age to the plantations of North America provided they consented to go. If children only went to America by agreement, the same could not be said of those sent to the penal settlements that were founded in Australia as a result of America's refusal to accept further shipments of convicts after the Declaration of Independence in 1776. Australia, recently discovered by Captain Cook, provided a ready-made alternative to America for the placement of convicts, and a convict settlement was started in New South Wales in 1788 at Port Jackson. Captain Phillips, who was in charge of the settlement, regarded it as the direct successor to the old Empire lost in North America and indeed it was less than five years later that the first free settlers arrived and were given free grants of land. For the next fifty-two years convicts poured into New South Wales and when that province would no longer accept them they were sent to Van Diemen's Land. But six years later, in 1846, when the settlers of Van Diemen's Land (now Tasmania) protested in their turn at the numbers of convicts being dumped on them, Western Australia alone continued to accept those sentenced to penal transportation, until the whole system of transportation came to an end in 1853.

It is hardly surprising that among the convicts sent to Australia there were many children. A child above the age of seven was held to be an adult and therefore responsible in the same way for any crimes. Until 1780 there were over two hundred different offences punishable by death by hanging, a fate which befell many hapless children. Transportation would appear a mild form of punishment by comparison. There is no record of the total numbers of children who sailed on the convict ships to Australia, but the number of juveniles who sailed in the three years between 1812 and 1815 has been put at over a thousand, and the average number of children on each convict ship has been put at forty-three.[16] By the 1820s the evil effects of mixing the young and adult convicts had become evident and special ships began to be sent out for juveniles. On one such transport, the *Frances Charlotte*, which sailed to Van Diemen's Land in 1836, the authorities were sufficiently enlightened to provide teachers, so that while a third of the children were at school, a third would be on deck playing games, while the remaining third made music.

By the end of the eighteenth century attitudes toward the care and treatment of children were beginning to change. Public unease at the iniquities of treating the hardened criminal and the young delinquent alike was becoming more vocal and the dangers of keeping the two classes together more apparent. The increase in the numbers of juvenile delinquents caused the more thoughtful to look for the reasons behind the increase and to question a system which allowed children with no means of support to roam the streets of the cities. There were those who saw emigration as a positive step toward the rehabilitation of such children and not merely as an expedient to relieve the country of a burden or as a punitive measure.

The Philanthropic Society was one of the first to concern itself with the protection of poor children and the offspring of convicted felons. It was founded in 1788 by Robert Young and had the support of an influential group of nobility and gentry. An asylum was founded which also accepted and attempted to reform children who had themselves engaged in criminal practices. From its modest beginnings the Society grew rapidly and acquired more houses. They had to deal with a great variety of problems in trying to cope with the type of children they were admitting and inevitably they came to specialise. By the time the farm school at Redhill was opened in 1849 the Society had changed from a rescue society to a specialised organisation dealing with delinquent boys. In so doing it had been the first to attempt reformation rather than punishment as a means of dealing with juvenile delinquency. At the end of their period of training the boys were helped to emigrate under strict rules of apprenticeship and Redhill had become part of a growing movement which saw the emigration of juveniles as sound policy.

Peter Bedford, a Quaker, also known as the Spitalfields' philanthropist for his work among the distressed handloom weavers of Spitalfields, was another who fought to change a penal code which could condemn children as young as six to the gallows. A young boy, John Knight, had been condemned to be hanged for pickpocketing a watch from a man in Hoxton. Bedford, spurred on by a fellow Quaker, William Crawford, collected irrefutable evidence of the boy's innocence which he sent to the Home Secretary, Lord Sidmouth. Bedford's evidence was ignored and John Knight was hanged. Bedford's righteous anger led him to call together a group of people whom he knew to be interested in the subject of juvenile delinquency. Although money was subscribed for an asylum the committee were more concerned to investigate the cause of the increase in juvenile delinquency than to make any practical attempt to alleviate the plight of the children on the streets. The Society for Investigating the Causes of the Alarming Increase of Juvenile Delinquency in the Metropolis was set up. Twelve months later, in 1816, the society produced a report packed with information and detailed case histories.

From the patient recording of case histories like that of a boy, identified only by his initials, E.F., Peter Bedford's committee produced a list of the five most significant causes of delinquent behaviour.

> E.F. aged 8 years. His mother only is living and she is a very immoral character. This boy has been in the habit of stealing for upward two years. In Covent Garden market there is a party of between thirty and forty boys who sleep under sheds and baskets. These pitiable objects, when they arise in the morning, have no other means of procuring subsistence, but by the committing of crime. This child was one of a number; and it appears that he was brought up to the several police officers upon eighteen separate charges. He has twice been confined in the house of correction and three times in Bridewell.

Not surprisingly the improper conduct of parents, the want of education and the want of suitable employment were highlighted together with the violation of the Sabbath and gambling on the streets as contributing to the growth of delinquency among the young. The report also criticised the severity of the criminal code and the lack of discipline in the police force. Bedford and his friends advocated the setting up of schools and reformatories, but public opinion was not yet sufficiently alive to the need for such measures and Parliament did nothing until twelve years later in 1828 when a select committee was set up to investigate Criminal Commitments and Convictions and six years later another committee reported on the State of the Police in the Metropolis. By this time Bedford had his own Refuge and his superintendent gave evidence to the 1828 committee on the results of the work of his Refuge. He said that of the 282 children who had passed through the Refuge 117 were doing well for certain and maintained that this represented an advance on any other method yet tried. The Refuge trained boys in some basic skills such as tailoring, shoemaking or basket making so that they could be apprenticed to a trade on leaving. Some did become apprentices, some went to sea and some were helped to emigrate to South Africa.

The loss of the American colonies seems to have overshadowed the potential benefits of sending children as emigrants to Canada at this time; emigration to Australia was inescapably linked with penal transportation so that during this period South Africa and particularly Cape Colony, came to be seen as the most desirable destination for those wishing to send children overseas. The Government had become anxious to encourage more settlers to go to the Eastern Province of Cape Colony, both to strengthen the colony's eastern defence against the Kaffirs but also to counterbalance the influence of the Dutch and to relieve distress in the United Kingdom. In 1819 Parliament had approved expenditure of £50,000 for this purpose, free passages were provided and a grant of a hundred acres of land was given to each person or family able to deposit £10 in cash. The original party of emigrants, known as the 1820 settlers, numbered three and a half thousand, half of whom were children.

When the boys left Bedford's Refuge they were each given a suit of clothes and £5 in cash. Obviously some boys read and believed the glowing reports that were put out about the South African scheme and opted to try their luck in the colony. However, so great were the hardships of the early settlers that the Government had to help for several years by the issue of rations and advances in capital. One of the settlers' greatest needs was for domestic and farm servants, mechanics and farm labourers to help cultivate the land. For a boy willing to try his luck in a new country his desire to emigrate was doubtless encouraged both by the Refuge and by those in need of his labour.

Edward Brenton, a retired naval captain, was another social reformer greatly interested in the problem of juvenile delinquency. He was a passionate advocate of separate prisons for children, but not in conditions such as obtained in the

Bellerophon, an old hulk moored off Sheerness which had housed 320 boys for two years until she broke up and was replaced by the *Euryalus*. But neither was the *Euryalus*, which was moored further upstream off Chatham, what Brenton had in mind when he petitioned Parliament and humbly prayed that children of either sex under the age of sixteen years 'may no longer be committed to the common prisons of the land, but be carefully guarded and educated and kindly disposed of, either at home or in colonies of His Majesty'.[17]

What makes Brenton and his ideas so interesting in this context is that he is the first man to have given children a specific training which was designed to enable them to take up apprenticeships in the colonies, chiefly in South Africa, mostly as farm labourers or house servants.[18] Brenton had wanted the Government to establish a 'floating asylum' for delinquent boys where they would live under a system of kindness, conciliation, firmness, restraint, privation for faults, but very rarely punishment. When nothing came of these efforts to stimulate reform Brenton published a violent attack on the conditions on board the *Euryalus*:

> Who would have believed in the existence of such a ship for such a purpose, as the *Euryalus* at Chatham: 417 boys, between the ages of nine and sixteen, confined as convicts for seven years, each to cost from £70 to £100. A floating Bastille; – children pining in misery, where the stench is intolerable ... and while unfortunate girls are starving for want of needlework, these boys are confined in dungeons making shirts for convicts.... I denounce this system as atrociously extravagant, cruel and vindictive and I challenge any man to come forward and justify it.[19]

There is no lack of evidence as to the horrific conditions which obtained on board *Euryalus*, for when children will resort to self-mutilation to escape the tyrannical behaviour of the older boys and the guards and gain admittance to hospital, where at least they had regular food and a respite from crushing boredom and bullying, little more need be said.[20] They would break their own arms by holding on to a form and letting the edge of the table drop thus causing a fracture; sometimes they would get an older boy to do it for them and then they would pretend that they had fallen down a gangway. Another method was to heat a copper button, press it into the skin and after rubbing soap into the wound bind it up so that it turned septic. Yet, in spite of the conditions on board the *Euryalus* being known and publicly reported on, it remained at its mooring, bringing untold suffering to its unfortunate inhabitants for a further twelve years.

Brenton's Society – which was first known as the Society for the Suppression of Juvenile Vagrancy and later as the Children's Friend Society – had as its aim to collect the most destitute and forlorn of vagrant boys, who were wandering about the streets of the metropolis, without any home or means of subsistence, but living from begging or thieving; to assist parishes to manage and dispose of their refractory boys; and to aid respectable families whose children had been entrapped by receivers of stolen goods and 'seduced by some of the numerous gangs of young depredators' in the metropolis. The Asylum was to be run by a Master who was to bear in mind that 'gentleness and kind treatment must be the rule, punishment and severity the exception'. There was to be 'strict discipline, prompt obedience and perfect regularity', but flogging or blows were strictly forbidden and solitary confinement from six to seven hours for stealing the only form of punishment. An example of Brenton's enlightened approach to his work was his ordinance that 'no task was to be given from Scripture as a punishment'. Brenton opened his first home, the Brenton Asylum, in 1830. His well-publicised attack on the training and education of the children of Great Britain brought him not only public support but royal patronage, as the title of his home for girls, The Royal Victoria Asylum, testifies.

The rules of the Brenton Asylum stated that the boys were to be employed in field labour for three hours every morning and when the weather made outside work impossible, among other trades, they were to be taught to grind their own corn in hand mills, to make their own bread and cook their own meat, all necessary skills for a future colonial emigrant. Brenton was one of the first to recognise that children sent overseas needed supervision and by 1835 a committee had been got together in Cape Town to receive the boys on their arrival, to oversee the preparation of indentures and to ensure that they received proper treatment. After the opening of the girls'

Asylum a committee of ladies was also recruited to look after theirwelfare.

However, towards the end of the 1830s rumours had begun to circulate that all was not well with the children who had been sent to South Africa. An apprentice named Trubshaw claimed that he had been ill-used and mistreated and his complaint sparked off anxieties about the welfare of the children generally. On the basis of Trubshaw's complaint it was rumoured that the apprentices had been sold as slaves for money. This sudden anxiety about the fate of the children was occasioned more because, in 1838, the remaining slaves in the colony had been emancipated, than because of a single report of ill-treatment. It was feared that the apprentices might find themselves not only taking over the duties of those recently freed, but being treated in the same way. Alarm was also expressed at the thought of English children on isolated Afrikaner farms forgetting their native language. Although Trubshaw would seem to have been a rather unreliable witness – for upon his return to England he was promptly convicted of theft and sentenced to be transported – the damaging rumours continued to circulate. Brenton, who was dependent on public support, could not allow the rumours to grow unchecked. The Children's Friend Society asked the Government to conduct an official investigation.

Lord John Russell, then Colonial Secretary, instructed Sir George Napier, the Governor of Cape Colony, to institute an inquiry. Because of the vast distances to be covered, four magistrates were appointed to undertake the work and it took them six months to complete their reports which were extremely detailed and thorough. 434 apprentices were visited, more than half the total number in the colony. They were asked about their general treatment and whether they were taught a trade; they were asked to comment on their food, clothing and bedding, their weekly allowance, their education, their religious instruction, what opportunities they had for church attendance, what facilities there were for communicating with relatives, and finally if their treatment had been different since 1 December 1838, the date of the emancipation of slaves in South Africa. The apprentices' masters, 232 of them, were asked as to the regularity, industry, obedience and moral habits of their charges and each inspecting magistrate added a general report which included an assessment of the probability of the apprentices obtaining a livelihood in the future 'in situations of comparative comfort and respectability'.

The reports provide a fascinating glimpse into the conditions of life in the colony and the manners of the time. Some children were obviously much better off than others, little cruelty was discovered and the report was on the whole favourable. In the words of the Governor, 'I have now the honour to transmit the reports of the four Commissioners of Inquiry ... which will, I trust, satisfy your Lordship that the apprehensions of the Society were in a great measure groundless....'[21]

Walter Starkies reported that he was fifteen years old and that his parents lived in London.

> I cannot read or write; I never go to church or receive any religious or school instruction; I have not heard from my parents since I left them a year ago; I am employed in all kinds of farm work, digging in the vineyard etc. I and my fellow apprentices sleep in an apartment by ourselves. We do not get enough to eat on Sunday; only breakfast and supper, but no dinner; I do not like my situation, the work is too hard; we are kept at it from daylight till dark; I have only got sixpence pocket money since I came here.

His master, Mr Vander Merwe of Wagonmakers Valleys said he had no complaints to make of his four apprentices and said the reason the boys had no dinner on Sunday was because they themselves did not take dinner on that day. The magistrate noted that Walter appeared healthy and well clothed, but 'diminutive for his age and not happy, I fear'.[22]

The comment that the children were small for their age is a recurring one and reflects the impoverished conditions in which they spent their childhood. Although there were exceptions, the report reveals that many children felt lonely and depressed on the isolated farms to which they had been sent. Thomas Grimes and Edgar True, both fifteen and apprenticed to a neighbour of Vander Merwe told a different story. Grimes said he was able to read and write and correspond with friends in England; he said he was learning shoemaking, that he was kindly treated and happy in his situation, having good clothes and enough to eat. He simply reported that he did not go to church. Edgar True also said he was 'happy and contented with my situation' but that although he could read and write 'he had not written to his friends yet'. The magistrate commented that the boys appeared 'in perfect health, quite happy and are, I believe, most kindly treated in every respect; they are both small for their ages'. Some boys had no complaints to make but simply didn't like being in South Africa. Gibbens said, 'I have no complaints, I should like to go back to England; I do not like the black people here.' Keefe put it less strongly, 'I do not like being here; I have no complaints to make against my Master, I get enough to eat and am learning to spell.' Both boys were reported as being 'small for their age and evidently unhappy and anxious to change their condition'.[23]

Sarah Piper, a stout, well-grown girl of fifteen, whose parents were still living, appeared to be quite happy and contented with her situation. Although much troubled with scrofula in her neck, she had no complaints to make; she slept in the same apartment as her mistress and was employed in nursing and housework. She was one of those who had surprisingly quickly lost all knowledge of English, telling the magistrate 'I cannot speak English now.' An unexpectedly large number of children had forgotten their native tongue and the magistrates had to talk to them through an interpreter.[24] Although Sarah Piper seems to have been found a suitable home, it was obviously more difficult to provide for girls, and the Society was cautioned about sending out too many female emigrants and 'certainly none of intractable dispositions and headstrong character, there being fewer means of apprenticing them out respectably than of providing for the boys'.

It is perhaps not surprising that the Governor, Sir George Napier, should seek in his covering letter to give a reassuring picture of conditions in Cape Colony. A more penetrating analysis came from one of the magistrates, H. Piers. He thought the children were, with few exceptions, healthy, well clothed and well treated. But in so far as education and religious instruction were concerned this was 'if not totally disregarded, certainly very much neglected'. Most of the farmers were Afrikaners living in remote country districts so that even had they been willing they were unable to comply with that part of the indentures that stipulated that the children should go both to school and church.

The consequence of this failure ... unfortunately, is that these children are fast losing both their religion and their language, and gradually, I fear, falling into the immoral habits and customs of the coloured population with whom in common they labour daily throughout their apprenticeship. The result must inevitably be, when out of their indentures, that, having learned nothing that can procure a comfortable or respectable living, they must continue in the same degraded, hopeless position of farm labourer, on wages varying from 12s to 20s a month, without a chance, that I can perceive, of their ever rising higher.[25]

However, the children who had the good fortune to be indentured to tradesmen were very much more happily situated, having 'no necessity nor even excuse for intimate intercourse with the coloured classes, and have always the advantage of residing in or near a town or village where religious and school instruction can be obtained. When out of their indentures ... they cannot fail to procure a comfortable and respectable livelihood.'[26]

Napier was furious that the colony had been exposed to the indignity of having to undertake the investigation which inevitably called into question the bona fides of the settlers who had taken the apprentices. While hoping that the report had exonerated the colony he declared the inquiry had 'created the strongest disinclination on the part of the Local Commissioners to receive or take charge of any more of the Society's children'. Though he himself regretted overthrowing an institution 'which promised well as regards the Cape of Good Hope', he said, 'if many people in England were determined to believe every foolish report or misrepresentation to its discredit, I cannot but hope that the Colony will be spared the pain of encountering any further enquiry through the continued operation of the Children's Friend Society'.

Although Brenton had sent children to New Brunswick in Upper Canada and to Western Australia, the Cape had received the majority of his young apprentices, and with this outlet closed, the Society's work came to an end, and Brenton himself died the following year.

But three years before he died Brenton had the satisfaction of seeing the cause which he had championed triumph. Parkhurst, the first separate prison for juvenile offenders, was established in

1838. In December of that year the first boys came to Parkhurst from the metropolitan prisons and from hulks like the *Euryalus*; among them were some who had been sentenced to transportation. The boys, who when they first came wore leg irons, were taught a trade and farm work as part of a judicious course of moral, religious and industrial training. Between 1842 and 1853, when the transportation of juveniles was stopped by Act of Parliament, nearly one and a half thousand boys were transported to New South Wales, Western Australia, Van Diemen's Land and a few even as far as New Zealand.

During that time the idea of transportation as a drastic punitive measure had begun to change and the Parkhurst prison authorities began to hold out the prospect of removal to the colonies as an incentive to good behaviour. Since no occasion arose which necessitated the holding of an inquiry we know little about the subsequent careers of the boys in Australia. In the early years the transported child was treated in the same way as an adult convict and could receive a maximum of fifty lashes for quite trivial offences. When the Government appointed a guardian of juvenile immigrants to look after those sent to Western Australia it is obvious that the boys were, by that time, regarded as ordinary apprentices. Their labour was much needed and in time the boys became popular with the settlers and worked hard on the farms, although they were never accepted in the same way in New South Wales or New Zealand.

By the end of the 1840s the boys from Parkhurst had been joined by boys sent out by the Philanthropic Society's farm school at Redhill which sent over an annual contingent of fifty boys for many years. Children from the reformatory schools, which had become established all over the country owing in large measure to Mary Carpenter, whose interest in the problems of juvenile crime led to her impassioned belief in their efficacy, also joined the emigrant route to Australia. They continued to provide one of the more controversial types of juvenile immigrant to both Australia and Canada long after Parkhurst had ceased to exist.

Two

OPPORTUNITIES IN AUSTRALASIA

To seek for employment
Where work can be found,
To meet with enjoyment
On less crowded ground,
We cross the broad ocean
With gladness and glee;
And when in devotion we're bending the knee,
This, this shall our Prayer be
At the close of each day,
God prosper the people
Who sent us away.

Ragged School Union Magazine, 1857

AUSTRALIA was now emerging from its initial role as a convict settlement into a prosperous land, attractive to emigrants with money. New South Wales had grown into a successful and enterprising colony. The district to the south, known as Port Phillip, had claimed independence from New South Wales and would become the new province of Victoria. Melbourne, which had been no more than a collection of huts on the River Yarra, was a busy and important city. Adelaide in South Australia was growing almost as fast, and only Western Australia, cut off from the rest of the country, progressed more slowly.

New Zealand had only become a British colony in 1840 and its development was much influenced by Edward Gibbon Wakefield's ideas. Wakefield had a chequered early career and perhaps because of this became interested in colonial development. It was while he was serving a jail sentence for abducting and marrying Ellen Turner that he started to study colonial affairs. He was the first person to advocate that settlement should be carried out on scientific principles. He did not believe in free grants of land which made everyone a landowner before he had any farming experience; he wanted the money raised by the sale of land to be used to bring out carefully selected emigrants and he was totally opposed to 'the shovelling out of unwanted persons, especially paupers'.

When the South Australian Association was formed and a bill passed through Parliament establishing the colony, it embodied two of Wakefield's most cherished principles: the sale of land at a fixed price and the application of the proceeds to an immigration fund. The introduction of convicts was also forbidden. Wakefield, to his great disappointment, was not appointed one of the commissioners entrusted with the administration of the colony. He severed his connection with Australia and spent the remaining years of his life developing and guiding the colony of New Zealand. It is hardly surprising, therefore, that when a party of boys from Parkhurst arrived in New Zealand in 1842, only a year after Wakefield had won legal status for his New Zealand Company, their arrival was greeted with dismay.

When John Malcolm, who had been sentenced in 1838 at Edinburgh, and John Whitehead and George King, both sentenced at the Central Criminal Court in 1839, received pardons provided they went to New Zealand, they were considered to be among the lucky ones. Queen Victoria was only twenty-three when she signed their pardon.

> We, in consideration of some circumstances humbly represented to us are graciously pleased to extend our Grace and Mercy unto them and grant them our pardon for their said crimes on condition that upon a passage being provided and their proceeding to our Colony of New Zealand and on arrival there, this our pardon shall have full effect. Given at our Court at St. James, the 24th May in the fifth year of our reign.[1]

They were among the second party of Parkhurst boys to go to New Zealand and travelled out on the ss *Mandarin*, arriving in December 1843. Notwithstanding the Queen's pardon, the boys, along with those who still had their sentences to work out, were received with less than rapture. The editor of the *Southern Cross* wrote, 'We can scarcely think of anything more heartlessly cruel or infamously immoral and unjust than the conduct of the Home Government to this colony.... They have sent the seeds of crime and immorality to be scattered over the length and breadth of New Zealand in the shape of young convicts from the penitentiary of Parkhurst.'[2]

In the face of such a welcome it was much to the boys' credit that more than a third of them were said to have done well. They appear mostly to have gone into the tailoring and boot-making trades, a few only going on to the farms. Fifteen apprentices absconded into the interior where the native Maoris were said to have treated them kindly, and eight landed up in jail. It was difficult to find masters to take the boys and even when they did the results were said to be far from satisfactory. The Guardian of the Boys, in his third report, noted that 'the generality of masters have not attended to the moral and religious welfare of their apprentices ... nor have the apprentices appeared to appreciate the Benevolent intentions of Her Majesty's Government in giving them an opportunity to become useful members of society'.

In Western Australia the Parkhurst boys had a less prickly reception. The first group arrived in 1842 and by 1849, when they ceased coming, 231 boys had joined the colony. There were difficulties in finding sufficient masters to take them on, not so much because of any stigma attaching to them but because of local competition from parents who were prepared to pay to apprentice their sons and 'because they were too small in size and delicate in appearance, so small indeed as to create doubt ... as to whether they could really be of the respective ages set down'.[3] Schoeles, who was the first Guardian appointed to watch over the boys, obviously tried hard to help the boys and reported that the 'juvenile emigrants give very general satisfaction, but these lads do need close attention'.

One particular lad gave Schoeles a great deal of trouble, so much so that he was obviously at his wits' end when he wrote to the Colonial Secretary about him:

I much regret that my duty demands me to make a special report of the repeated misconduct of Government Juvenile emigrant James Nimmo who arrived on the *Simon Taylor* in August 1842. He was apprenticed as a harness maker in September and absconded in November. There were extenuating circumstances so punishment was foregone – a reprimand only, payment of expenses and indentures cancelled. James Nimmo was then apprenticed to myself and absconded. He was given three months hard labour in Fremantle. After two months, urged to try kindness I had him back, but he was taunted by fellow servants so I apprenticed him to Mr Grade but he returned him as incorrigible.

Nimmo is a notorious liar, insolent and idle, cunning and hardened to punishment and I fear very dishonest. Indeed to such an extent has a system of petty robbery been carried on in my house since his arrival that I am at a loss as to know how to treat this boy – he is case hardened to corporal punishment. To cancel his indentures and set him free would be a signal to his comrades to disengage themselves by bad conduct and could put a premium on misbehaviour. . . .

If a boy has to be sent to jail who will take him on afterwards having had contact with felons? Under the act my only alternative is corporal punishment, but this would be very obnoxious. Many of the boys are of an age too advanced to render it politic to administer such chastisement. Therefore with Nimmo, no one will take him, it would be equally vexatious to keep him in confinement or to turn him adrift, not to mention the bad example the latter course would set to all the other boys. . . . It is high time some course, well defined and planned, was marked out for my guidance.[4]

When Schoeles retired as Guardian he was succeeded by Wittenoom, an altogether tougher character. He wanted the Guardians to have the power to send a boy for the unexpired term of his indentures, if he was incorrigible, to a penal settlement. He said the power would be seldom used, but *in terrorem* it would have a most salutary effect.[5] He wrote to one lad, '. . . to those lads who behave well I shall endeavour to be a kind guardian, but you may rely that to those who refuse to listen to reason and persist in behaving ill I shall prove a severe one'. It is hard to imagine him being put upon by Nimmo as poor Schoeles had been. Wittenoom complained that Schoeles had issued clothes to boys who had no money in the bank because they had not worked long enough, and it is clear that under him a stricter regime was enforced.

His first letter to the Colonial Secretary was, however, on a different subject. Someone had had the unhappy idea of getting one of the boys, Weight by name, who was serving a twelve-month jail sentence, to carry out the execution of a murderer held in the same jail in return for a free pardon. Wittenoom wrote anxiously to the Colonial Secretary asking him to veto any such action 'which would not fail to create horror and prejudice in the minds of the settlers against the admission of these lads into their houses'.[6] When another draft of boys arrived soon after that Wittenoom felt that the prejudices against them had softened and the scarcity of labour made it almost certain they would all find work. Indeed when the first fourteen became free none went back to England, 'most comparing the high wage to be earned here with the accounts received of the sufferings and want of employment of the people in England'. Joshua Strickland, the first lad to be discharged, had been convicted in Worcester in 1838 when he was twelve. He had been sentenced to seven years' transportation and came from Parkhurst to Western Australia in 1842. He had been apprenticed to a baker for five years and at the expiry of his term was paid £18 5s. 'On the very day of his discharge he entered as journeyman the service of the principal baker in Perth at the wage of £3 a month besides which he boards with the family and has comfortable lodgings.'

By 1850 Wittenoom was very satisfied with the majority of the boys: some were working on the roads, some were shepherds and some farm labourers. A number had landed up in prison and two had been sentenced to transportation to the interior. Two had stolen horses and arms in an attempt to escape on an American whaler, but had been recaptured and sentenced. Only one boy is recorded as having escaped: he too saw the American whalers as the only means of gaining freedom and succeeded in being taken on by the master of one such ship. Wittenoom was not a man with many illusions. He did not give much credit to the system itself but thought rather that the boys were reformed only because they had the opportunity of earning good wages.

Emigration was not to remain the sole preserve of those dealing with the problem of juvenile delinquency. The collapse of the Children's Friend Society did not deter for long those who favoured emigration as a solution to the increasing problem of providing for the destitute and pauper child. An unexpected conjunction of events triggered off the next experiment in juvenile emigration.

The desperate shortage of young unmarried women in New South Wales coincided with the fearful overcrowding of the workhouses all over Ireland following the famine of 1845. By mid-December 1847 there were 15,000 children under fifteen in the workhouses, many of them orphans.[7] Fitzroy, the Governor of New South Wales, had been pressed to take up the question with Earl Grey, the Colonial Secretary, but Grey at first was doubtful. He had been told by the Emigration Commissioners that it was difficult to persuade single females to undertake the journey. The speaker of the New South Wales Legislature had written to Lord Monteagle, an Irish peer in more urgent terms:

> We wish to receive emigrants; we are willing to pay for them. There are millions among you dying of hunger; let us have those starving crowds; here they will find a superabundance of the necessaries of life. Instead of importing Indian corn to starving peasants, export the peasant and his family to where the Indian corn grows.[8]

Grey was anxious to accede to the request from New South Wales. Upon inquiry he was told by the Emigration Commissioners that there were a large number of orphan workhouse girls who would be suitable to send to Australia. New South Wales and South Australia were advised that steps were being taken to find them suitable girls. Stanley, the secretary of the Irish Poor Law Commission, wrote to all the Irish Boards of Guardians. In both Ireland and England some parishes were united to form poor law unions and guardians were elected by the ratepayers to oversee the government and administration of relief. One workhouse might serve several parishes in such a union. The Irish Boards of Guardians responded eagerly to the suggestion, although there were one or two dissenting voices. *The Tipperary Vindicator* saw the scheme as a form of white-slave traffic and said that the girls were being exported to Sydney like Circassian beauties to Turkish towns to pander to the vices of the rich settlers.[9]

Notwithstanding such colourful criticism, Boards of Guardians from sixty-eight unions were quick to provide lists of children for emigration: 2,500 girls were selected initially and twelve ships made ready to take them to Australia. The unions had to provide each girl with six shifts, two flannel petticoats, six pairs of stockings, two gowns and two pairs of shoes at a cost of about five pounds. The girls were sent to Plymouth and from there put on board separate ships.

The welcome extended to the Irish orphans was less enthusiastic than had been anticipated. Unfortunately for them, a ship bringing girls – mainly from England but which also included some former inmates of the Dublin Foundling Hospital – had preceded them and the disorders on board which had taken place during the journey out necessitated an immediate investigation. It appeared that the master had kept the passengers short of food at the same time selling quantities of spirits to the girls so that the Irish Foundlings were often drunk and mixed freely with the officers. One had died at sea as a result of a failed abortion and several immediately took to a life of prostitution when they landed at Sydney.[10]

The *Earl Grey* with the first contingent of Irish orphans arrived in October 1848. To the consternation of the authorities the surgeon superintendent who had been in charge of the girls asked the local committee to carry out another investigation, reporting that some of the girls were but prostitutes and beggars. The committee found that fifty-six of the girls, all from Ulster, were undesirable immigrants: 'Their violent and disorderly conduct on the voyage, the habits of pilfering, and their grossly profane language were such as to admit of no other conclusion than that they had mixed with the lowest grade of society.' Among the troublemakers were some who had long since left girlhood behind them and two were married women. But once these undesirables had been separated from the rest and sent into the interior the remainder of the girls quickly found jobs.

Strict instructions were issued to the Irish Poor Law Commissioners that they must be more selective. In their defence they said that it was unfair to accuse Belfast factory girls of immoral conduct on account of their bad language; such language was their natural manner of expression and ought not be construed as meaning that they were immoral. The 'Belfast girls' later gained the dubious distinction of a mention in *Hansard* when the question of emigration of orphan children was discussed two years later in the House of Commons.

It is obvious that more care was exercised over the later selection of girls, and, if all the Irish orphans did not have unblemished moral characters and sound health, at least there was no further cause for investigation, and the adverse publicity died down as the girls became absorbed into the community. Most gave satisfaction, although complaints continued to be made about their lack of training and their behaviour. The Irish Poor Law Commissioners were all in favour of the scheme continuing, but among the 4,175 girls who had been sent out, too many failed to adapt from the stultifying life and discipline of the workhouse to the very different social conditions of colonial life for there not to be adverse criticism by those opposed to the scheme. Their failure reminded the colony that these orphans were workhouse girls. Transportation of convicted felons had not long ceased and it was only natural that the colonists, their immediate need for domestic servants satisfied, wished to encourage a superior type of settler. Although the equipping and transporting of over 4,000 girls to Australia at the rate of 2,000 a year was a remarkable achievement, in the context of the overwhelming problems facing the Irish Poor Law Commissioners with their overflowing workhouses, the scheme made disappointingly little impact.

Shaftesbury (he was still Lord Ashley in 1848) was the next to talk publicly of emigration as a solution to the problem of child destitution, and he unfolded his plan for transplanting 'at the public expense' a thousand children from the ragged schools to Her Majesty's colonies in South Australia in an elegant and masterly speech to a poorly attended House of Commons.[11] He had learnt many of his facts from the city missionaries and from personal investigation. He said he thought the number of 'naked, filthy, roaming, lawless and deserted' children exceeded 30,000 in London alone and quoted Dr Aldis as saying that 'the children are diminutive, pale, squalid, sickly and irritable; I rarely saw a child in a really healthy state'. Shaftesbury's description of a visit to a lodging house was all the more graphic for being personal – 'within minutes of entering vermin were dropping on my hat like peas'. A filthy bed in one of these lodging houses was a luxury many children could not afford, and Shaftesbury described how many slept at night under 'dry arches of bridges and viaducts, under porticoes, sheds and carts; in outhouses, in sawpits, on staircases, and in the open air'. The children's daytime experiences were hardly better, many playing in courts where three privies served three hundred people: 'It is impossible to convey an idea of the poisonous condition in which these places remain during winter and summer, in dry weather and wet, from the masses of putrifying matter which is allowed to accumulate.'

Quoting the figure of 4,000 children under fifteen taken into custody in 1847 Shaftesbury implored the House to 'consider the temptations to which poor children ... are exposed by the reprehensible carelessness of this commercial city'. He stated that many thousands of children had never obtained a meal except by begging or stealing and he assured the House, that there are 'amongst the children, guilty and disgusting as they are, many thousands, who, if opportunities are given them, will walk in all the dignity of honest men and Christian citizens'.

Shaftesbury had learnt much about the behaviour and psychology of these children from his close association with the ragged school movement. Ragged schools came into being in the early 1840s and the advertisement which Shaftesbury saw which brought the movement to his notice exactly describes their function and purpose: 'Opened in 1840 for instructing (free of expense) those who from poverty or ragged condition are prevented from attending another place of religious instruction.'

Shaftesbury became President of the Ragged School Union in 1844 and his association with the Union was not only beneficial to ragged schools. It gave him an understanding of the children who attended them which was rare in a man in his social position. His description of the children and the methods employed by the schools to attract and hold their pupils, showed his awareness of how early experience affects later behaviour, and reveals a compassionate and sensitive understanding of the problems involved in their training: 'These children are not accustomed to ordinary rules; they have never been subject to domestic discipline, they have no notion of being forced. They may be invited, they may be soothed, they may be gained by attention, but in general they will have their own way.'

The dedication of those who taught in the ragged schools is well illustrated by Shaftesbury's description of what the opening sessions of one such was likely to entail:

I have heard teachers who have undertaken to open such schools on speculation – I do not mean money speculation, but by way of experiment – I have heard them describe the roaring and whistling, the drumming on the doors, the rattling at the windows, which signalise the commencement of the academical course. The boys, when admitted, often break everything, forms, slates, tables, intermixing their sport with occasional fighting.

He described a school where the teachers were compelled to barricade the doors and escape through the windows over the roof. Such, he said, was the character of most inaugural meetings of these schools, and a fortnight or more must in general, elapse before order could be maintained. Emphasising the high degree of patience needed by all who taught in such schools, Shaftesbury described the misfortune endured by one teacher, which, although comic to read of, illustrates just how enlightened were the methods used by ragged school teachers to assert their authority. This particular teacher had been tried beyond endurance by an especially disruptive boy and when his patience finally gave out he had seized the boy by the neck and given him a good shaking. The incident appeared to have passed off with little being said, but three minutes later the teacher found himself prostrate at full length on the ground:

The boy, it seems, was determined to be avenged for the insult which he considered he had received, got upon the floor, and passing between the legs of the teacher, suddenly expanded them, with a shout of joy; and then having thrown the gentleman upon his back returned to his seat. Now, had the gentleman given way to his anger and punished the boy for his offence, the result would probably have been that the school would have been broken up, but exercising correct judgement, he took no notice of what had occurred. He saved his dignity by assuming that he had fallen down. The boy having obtained his redress was fully satisfied – the school is now in effective operation and I believe the boy is become a diligent and obedient pupil.[12]

It was the graduates from the ragged schools that Shaftesbury wanted to send to South Australia. He saw the removal of the children as a reward for good conduct since imprisonment for them was no matter for shame, they regarded it merely as the ordinary lot of humanity and 'look upon it as a grievous act of oppression, and when they come to school they speak of it as one gentleman would tell his wrongs to another'. Shaftesbury believed that removed from vice and temptation after a decent training, the children, none of whom were to be under fourteen years of age, would conduct themselves like honest citizens.

He was in no doubt as to the need for their services in the colony. The depression of 1842 was over and there had been steady growth and expansion during the second half of the 1840s. Labourers were a select group, much cosseted by employers who were desperate for their labour. Henry Meyrick, a gentleman settler who came to Port Phillip with his cousins, observed the power labourers could exert over their masters: 'The more poverty stricken they are in England, in exactly the same ratio, the more bounceable are they when they come out here. This Wiltshire scoundrel had precisely the same food as I eat myself', yet he had had the temerity to complain, 'There aint no pudding after dinner.'[13]

Relying on the evidence of Mr Cunninghame, a barrister from Port Phillip who had testified that 'the colony will absorb many more than we could count upon for future years', Shaftesbury argued that his plan to transport the children was practicable, for Mr Cunninghame had also said that the colony could 'employ any species of labour because shepherding is not an exhausting or fatiguing operation'. One of the criticisms brought against the Children's Friend Society had been the dead-end nature of the job of herding cattle, but this did not deter Shaftesbury. His arcadian idyll was the subject of a charming if somewhat unrealistic series of engravings in the *Ragged School Magazine*. The poor boy's home is shown; he is next depicted stealing a loaf of bread; he is then shown, rescued from a life of crime, on board ship *en route* for Australia; the final tableau shows him as a contented shepherd boy in his new country.

Unfortunately these touching scenes were not enough to persuade Parliament to renew the grant of £1,500 to the Ragged School Union. It would appear from the debate in the House of Commons in 1850 that the scheme had not turned out as well as hoped and in spite of Shaftesbury's strenuous denials in the House, some of the first party of 150 boys had, it was said, sustained themselves by petty pilfering.

Shaftesbury was not only interested in rescuing boys, he was

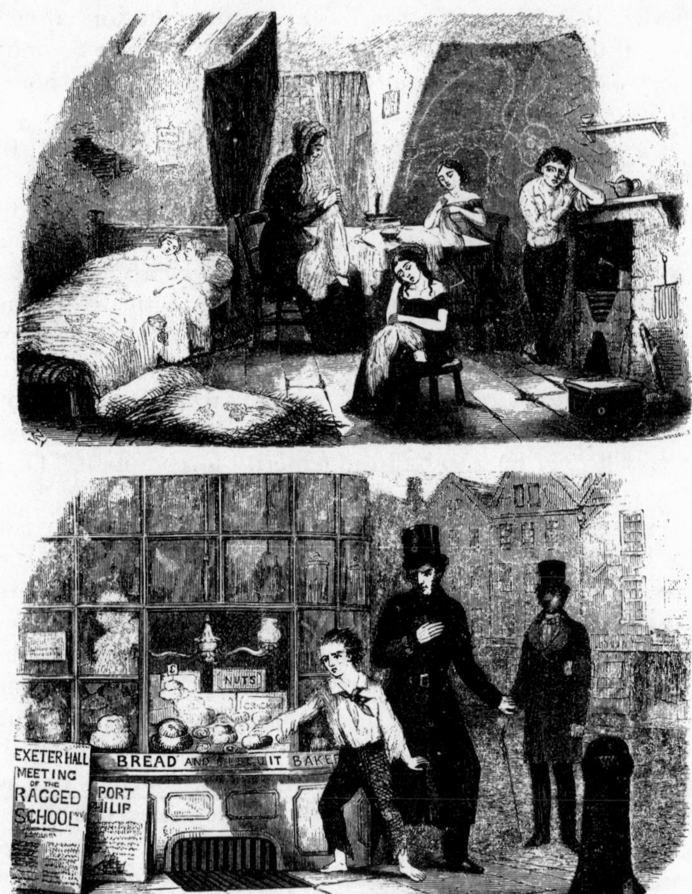

Four scenes from the 'History of a Ragged Boy' from the Ragged School Union Magazine, *1850*

very much aware of the imbalance of the sexes in the colony. He urged that girls should be sent out, citing the evidence of one gentleman who found a young girl who had just landed finding herself in such demand by 'gentlemen wanting to engage her as lady's maid for their wives, that she knowing how valuable her services were, refused to take less than £50'. This

was certainly true as the rapid absorption of the Irish orphans proved. But when the question of the emigration of orphan children was discussed in the House at the request of Mr Miles who presented a petition from the Board of Guardians of the Union of Berwick-upon-Tweed for a measure to promote the emigration of young females to act as domestic servants in the colonies, the House was even less interested than it had been when Shaftesbury made his case for the ragged school children and, there being less than forty members present, the House adjourned without voting on the question.[14]

The Ragged School Union, notwithstanding the withdrawal of the grant, continued to send small groups of children to Australia, relying on voluntary contributions to finance the journey. To keep public interest in the scheme alive, a series of letters from the children sent to Australia appeared in the magazine and these show that for some of the children life in the colonies had a great deal to offer.

Quite a number of the boys did, in fact, become shepherds.

> I write to let you know how I get on at my new home. I am keeping sheep, at one of Mr Austin's out stations. I am hired for twelve months (being the first move I could make in the country) at £12 per year, but I expect I shall soon get £15.
>
> I have got a very nice time of it. I have to get the breakfast and supper ready for the shepherds, and that is all I have to do; then I go out native cat hunting and make rugs of their skins. I am going to have a dog for the purpose of hunting kangaroos. It is very nice country for those who like to make their minds happy and comfortable, as very few do except us bushmen. Many new comers go cranky for the first week or so if they are sent shepherding. But when I go out with the sheep I go at sunrise, take a good lump of damper and beef, my jew's harp, pipe and tinder box and go and sit in some mimi and let my sheep feed out a head, and then I am as happy as a woodcock.[15]

Obviously it was important to have the right temperament for the job, but it certainly suited another boy who wrote:

> The country is a beautiful place, and I have got a good master. I get ten shillings per week and board and lodgings for the first six months; after that I shall get, I dare say double, as I am at present a shepherd. I have got a nice dog, so if any of the sheep should stray, I have no trouble, but just to say 'Fetch him back'. I go out of a morning at sunrise, and all I have to do is to see that my flock don't part. I lay down and read all day, then at sunset I come home, have my supper and go to bed. Coming from England to Australia is like coming from a dirty town to the garden of paradise. . . .[16]

Not all boys were quite so lucky, as one who wrote to say that he had got a place cattle minding for two and sixpence a week:

I had to mind of a Sunday and I did not like it; besides it was such a lazy way of life. I did not like it so I left it and they would not pay my wages which was £3 so I had no money. They were such bad people at the farm. I was up three hours before sunrise to sunset; and when I brought them home I had to milk them; when I had done that I had to clean out the stables, clean horses and fetch in hay and give them and clean shoes and when I had done that it was twelve o'clock at night, and besides they were never satisfied, the Irish are never satisfied.[17]

He eventually found a job as a brick-maker at three and six a week which was more to his liking.

Boys continued to be sent to Australia until 1853 but the altered state of the Australian colonies after the discovery of the gold fields gave the committee of the Ragged School Union pause and they decided to discontinue emigration to Australia because as they said, 'even if direct contamination of the Diggings were avoided yet that exposure to the social ferment and disorganisation of the great towns ... would be scarcely less injurious; many of the boys would be particularly susceptible of the contagion of those moral diseases which have broken out in the train of the Gold Fever'.[18] Canada, New Brunswick and Nova Scotia were seen as a good and safe substitute for Australia and in 1854 twelve boys were sent across the Atlantic.

No particular provision had been made in the 1834 Poor Law Act for the emigration of destitute children, although the advantages of emigrating such children had been clearly set out at the time. The Poor Law Commissioners had been deterred both by the expense involved in paying the passage of the children to the colonies and by the difficulty of selecting and approving colonial applicants for apprentices. The Irish Boards of Guardians had been troubled by no such qualms when they sent their orphan girls to Australia, nor, so it was discovered, had the Guardians of St Pancras who had sent three small parties of children to the Bermudas in 1849 and 1850.

The new legislation which was enshrined in the Poor Law Act of 1850 provided legal authority for guardians to send children under sixteen years of age overseas under two conditions. Every application for the emigration of each individual child had to be submitted to the Poor Law Board for approval and each child had to consent to emigration. Very strict rules were laid down as to the form this consent was to take. There was to be no emigration of any orphan or deserted child until such 'Child shall have consented thereto before the Justices assembled in Petty Sessions . . . and a Certificate of such Consent under the Hands of Two of the Justices present thereat shall have been transmitted to the Poor Law Board'. The workhouse child now had, in theory, far greater protection than the merely vagrant or destitute child who might be emigrated without having to go through any such formality.

The Poor Law Board only heard of the activities of the St Pancras Guardians because a report of their activities appeared in the *Morning Chronicle*.[19] Upon investigation it was discovered that the scheme appeared to be excellent in every way. Far from being coerced into going, some of the children had cried because they were not taken. No child went whose parent or guardian had refused consent, they travelled as 'cabin' passengers, they had been given a generous supply of clothing and were equipped with a pound of soap, a Bible, a Prayer Book and two shillings and sixpence in money. An independent Bermudan gentleman in England had vouched for all the masters who had offered jobs to the children, and letters written by the children showed that they were well content, many of them asking that relatives be allowed to join them. The Poor Law Board inspector ended his report by saying: 'It appears to me that in sending out these children to the Bermudas the directors did what was for the children's good; that their motive was a regard for their welfare; that the affair was transacted with deliberation; and the children so long as they depended on the directors were amply provided for; but the whole proceeding was illegal.' Under the new legislation it obviously was illegal: no permission had been asked of the Poor Law Board, nor had the children been brought before the petty sessions, and their verbal agreement had been accepted as sufficient.

While firmly checking the unauthorised emigration of workhouse children, the Poor Law Board did recognise that the St Pancras Guardians had acted in the best interests of the children. As this was to be the last attempt to send workhouse children overseas before the great Canadian emigration movement got under way at the end of the 1860s, the fact that it had been successful predisposed the Poor Law Board to recognisethe potential benefit emigration could provide for the workhouse child. During the remaining years before 1869 there was little further emigration of children, apart from those sent out by Shaftesbury through the Ragged School Union.

Three

'OUR WESTERN HOME'

Is this a holy thing to see
In a rich and fruitful land,
Babes reduced to misery,
Fed with cold and usurous hand? . . .

And their sun does never shine,
And their fields are bleak and bare,
And their ways are filled with thorns:
It is eternal winter there.

WILLIAM BLAKE, *Songs of Experience*

IN OCTOBER 1869 and May 1870 two parties, the first consisting of seventy-five little girls between the ages of four and twelve and the second of a hundred young boys, sailed across the Atlantic under the care of Miss Maria Rye and Miss Annie Macpherson respectively. Miss Rye brought her little charges to Niagara-on-the-Lake where she had recently converted the local jail and courthouse into a temporary home for the girls. The local newspaper, the *Niagara Mail*, was almost right when it reported, 'Miss Rye has inaugurated a novelty in emigration. For the first time we ever heard of has occurred the emigration of orphan children of tender age.' Young orphan children had been sent overseas before, but this group were the first of many thousands of children who were to cross the Atlantic in the next seventy-five years and their arrival marked the start of a new development in the history of juvenile emigration.

The story of how those two parties of children came to cross the Atlantic, and the stories of the thousands who were to follow them are full of fascination and drama. They are the prototypes of all the hundreds of other parties that were to travel to Canada in the following years, each child carrying within itself the trauma of a final parting, the grief, the excitement, the hope, and bewilderment that were inseparable from such an event.

The welcome given to Miss Rye and her party in the *Niagara Mail* was unqualified:

> The scheme of relieving destitute children is a most judicious movement. It enables the children to be trained here and begin life under better auspices than they would generally meet at home. They will grow up in this country, become easily assimilated to its ways – though in this respect they will have little to unlearn. The importance of Miss Rye's practical and extensive scheme for the emigration of girls and female children is beginning to be realised by benevolent people in England, and we are satisfied that as soon as they discover that it is a real and vital movement of practical benevolence, aid will flow in from all sides to assist her in carrying out on a still larger scale what, in its beginning even, is one of the most important emigration movements that has been made for many years.[1]

Initially Miss Macpherson's welcome was less warm. As she wrote to her sister it wasn't the first time Canadians had had to deal with boys from England and 'the reports which had gone before of London Arabs and the different batches of reformatory boys sent out in a kind of wholesale way, made our path no easy one'.[2] However, these difficulties seem to have been speedily overcome, for she continued,

> When we look back upon the work, all is wonderful – the very appearance of the lads, looking so clean in their white jackets and so intelligent, found us favour with the people. Emigration agents, *after* they had seen the lads were ready to dispose of the whole at each point of our journey, but we steadfastly adhered to our plan of distributing them as much as possible to form a wider basis for our future plans.

Unlike Miss Rye, Miss Macpherson had no base of her own from which to operate, but she clearly saw this as an advantage, writing that several gentlemen in Montreal had offered her two hundred dollars each if she would establish an Industrial Home in their town, but she said that she did not want to be bound by this first offer until she had visited a few more towns.

The ease with which the ladies had been able to place the children encouraged both of them to continue and enlarge their endeavours. Miss Rye wrote that not only had she placed all the seventy-five little ones whom she took over last October into good Christian homes, but that she had been enabled to open the doors of nearly two hundred more homes in Canada and the United States, while Annie Macpherson described how her boys were 'almost torn from me' at some of the stopping places as they got out of the railway cars.

For almost a decade Maria Rye and Annie Macpherson were to be the undisputed leaders of this new development in the history of juvenile emigration and although their names are in the history books, little enough is known about them. Both were exceptional women, both were natural leaders, both were determined and courageous and both devoted their lives to the cause of the destitute and homeless child, but despite all they had in common their relationship with each other remained distant and they made no attempt to co-operate.

Both had been to America and both had learnt much from the work being done in New York to help destitute and homeless children by people like Charles Loring Brace of the Children's Aid Society and Mr Van Meter, through the Howard League for Children. As a result of the civil war many children who had lost their parents in the fighting had been left destitute. The policy of sending these children out west to be fostered or boarded out on the farms and in the homesteads in the mid-West had been most successful. Both ladies met Van Meter and heard from him at first hand how the scheme worked. It was but a short step for both ladies to see that they could adapt the ideas of the Children's Aid Society of New York to the problems facing those trying to deal with destitute children in England where there was already an established tradition of emigrating unwanted children.

Maria Rye would probably have liked to concentrate solely on the emigration of girls, leaving the boys to Annie Macpherson, as she made clear in a letter stating, 'I have no hesitation in saying that Miss Macpherson could place a thousand little boys, the younger the better, and I and my workers could place a thousand little girls wisely and safely in Canada for the next ten years.'[3] Annie Macpherson, however, who gave help to girls as well as boys, never had any intention of altering her work to take into account Maria Rye's preferences.

There was a more basic difference between the two women which kept them apart. Maria Rye was more of an establishment figure, if one may use that word retrospectively.

She made her appeals through *The Times*; she sought the support of men like the Archbishop of Canterbury, Shaftesbury and Sir John A. Macdonald; she dealt directly with Boards of Guardians; and she was granted a Civil List pension for her work in 1871. When she died, obituary notices appeared in all the major newspapers and she has her place in the *Dictionary of National Biography*, though none of these publications make any mention of the controversial nature of her work. Annie Macpherson, whose work was to be more important and more influential, has no such memorials. Annie was a 'twice-born' Christian, a committed evangelical who shunned the secular world. She made no direct appeals for money, but the pages of *The Christian*, an influential weekly evangelical newspaper with a large circulation, printed her letters, extracts from her journal, reports and stories. Her niece wrote the only account of her work which exists. Her work was known to a much smaller constituency than that of the more extrovert Maria, and after her death the important contribution she made to the emigration movement was forgotten. Both ladies died within a year of each other, Miss Rye in 1903 and Miss Macpherson in 1904. Some years after their deaths their work was handed over to larger agencies. The Church of England's Society for Waifs and Strays, now The Children's Society, took over from Miss Rye, and Barnardo's assumed responsibility for Miss Macpherson's emigration work.

Maria Rye was born in London in 1829. Her family was professional and learned, her father and brothers being both solicitors and antiquaries. She herself was widely read and early came to appreciate the disadvantages of her sex. She soon discovered that teaching was the only profession open to a woman of her abilities and although much influenced by Charles Kingsley's father, who was then rector of St Lukes, Chelsea, she did not find parochial work satisfied her restless need to help women find wider opportunities for work. Fully aware of the risks involved, she decided to set up a private law stationer's business to give employment to middle-class girls. She was no doubt helped by her family's legal interests; nevertheless her success reflected her entrepreneurial ability. Encouraged by this success she next established the Victoria Printing Press and in 1860 she also set up a telegraph school, accurately anticipating the need to employ girls as telegraph clerks.

Even at this stage Maria's career, by any standards, was a remarkable one, but for a woman brought up in an age when women were not supposed to have careers, her success in providing new opportunities for women to work was all the more notable. She was, predictably, a founder member of the Women's Employment Society, but surprisingly disagreed with the women's franchise movement, which the Society supported, and she resigned for that reason. Her next move was to establish a registry office, but she soon found that there were not enough jobs available for all the girls who applied to her for work. It was at this point that she started to look overseas for opportunities for the employment of women. With her associate, Miss Jane Lewin, she began to raise funds to assist middle-class girls and domestic servants to emigrate. In 1861 she founded the Female Middle Class Emigration Society and for the next seven years travelled extensively, escorting parties of women and girls to Canada, Australia and New Zealand.

A powerfully built woman, Maria Rye's robust appearance was matched by a strong and forceful character. Enterprising and resourceful, she obviously revelled in the opportunities which her work gave her for travel. She wrote cheerfully in 1863 of the glorious passage to New Zealand she had had in *John Duncan* – which had taken all of ninety days.[4] Aged only thirty-four at the time, she was escorting a hundred women to New Zealand; her confidence in her own abilities is clearly demonstrated in her description of how when she had marched them off to the depot they went 'as quietly as they would have done in London, in spite of the influx of thousands of miners from Melbourne who had been enticed over by the discovery of gold fields at Lake Waikatip'.

She continued to travel in the following years, and in 1868 crossed the Atlantic twice with parties of women bound for Canada. Perhaps it was her inability to persuade the first Prime Minister of the new federal dominion of Canada, Macdonald, to give her more than a complimentary hundred pounds which, she declared, would scarcely do more than pay the fares of the women from Quebec to the west that made her turn her thoughts to the possibilities of emigrating children.

When asked how she had come to start the work she said that she remembered having a conversation with Lord Shaftesbury about the desirability of emigrating girls as well as boys, and that when she had met Mr Van Meter of New York and had heard from him how he had successfully boarded out children from New York around Chicago, the idea of extending the work and of getting children off the streets of London and other large cities in England and sending them out west had filled her mind.[5] She chose the pleasant quiet town of Niagara-on-the-Lake, conveniently near the border with the United States, as a base. There she purchased the old jail and courthouse, an agreeably roomy red-brick building and converted it to accommodate up to 120 children. How she acquired the money to make this purchase remains uncertain, for although it was thought to have been purchased by voluntary donations, it later was found to belong to Miss Rye personally.

Back in England she wrote a letter to *The Times* which was headed 'Our Gutter Children'.[6] Whether Maria chose the heading or not, the word guttersnipes came into general usage at this date to describe the children whose only home was the streets. In her letter Maria described how Van Meter had removed two thousand children from the slums of New York and given them a fair start in 'the mighty West'.

> Why not [she wrote] take the 'gutter children' of London, Manchester, Birmingham, Bristol and Liverpool and emigrate them to Canada and the Western States of America? . . . We are so over-taxed, overburdened, overpopulated, that people will scarcely credit me when I say I know a land where happy is the man with his quiver full of children . . . a land where corn is burnt for fuel and where a million men only occupy territories larger than the whole of Great Britain.

Maria tried to pre-empt the question of how these children were to be supervised; anticipating criticism that the children, so far away from home, would be open to exploitation, she made the remarkable statement that nothing could be worse than their present plight.

> What treatment will they receive from the cold, the starvation, the temptation they receive in our gutters; what justice will they receive from our hands when the police, the gaol, the hospital and the Magdalen receive them? Can anything I introduce them to in Canada or

America be worse than that to which they are doomed if we leave them where they are now?

At that time Maria had no refuge of her own in London, and in her letter she said she would need to acquire a sheltering home in or near London for the children and in all would need at least a thousand pounds to start the work properly. The money was rapidly subscribed and in spite of the controversial nature of Maria's proposed plans only one voice was raised in opposition, that of George Cruikshank, the illustrator and cartoonist. He wrote and published a bitter denunciation of Maria and illustrated the pamphlet with a savage cartoon showing hundreds of babies and little girls being swept out of the gutters into waiting rubbish carts.[7] Cruikshank was an active temperance worker and he wanted money and effort put into temperance work – seeing drunkenness as the cause of so much child destitution. His was a lone voice calling for reform at home rather than emigration schemes to relieve the tax-payers of their responsibilities.

Unlike Annie Macpherson, who was living in the East End and working among the children she was to send to Canada, Maria had never become actively involved in such activities. Realising that basic work with such children was not her *métier* and that she could hardly send to Canada children straight from the streets, she came to the conclusion that there must be many children in the workhouses up and down the country who would be suitable candidates for emigration. It would greatly simplify matters for her if she could take pauper children direct from the workhouse who could already be supposed to have been given a modicum of schooling and some training. She enlisted the support of William Rathbone, the philanthropically minded Member of Parliament for Liverpool and he introduced her to the Board of Guardians of Kirkdale Industrial School, who were only too pleased to equip and dispatch fifty little girls to join Maria's first emigration party.

Examined closely, everything about Maria's work was controversial, but she possessed that kind of plausible personality which inspired confidence and she certainly was able to attract influential and wealthy support. It was entirely in keeping with her character that the majority of children she took to Canada

OUR" GUTTER CHILDREN".

'Our "Gutter Children"' by George Cruikshank

The dialogue is as follows:

Bearded Gentleman with spectacles: There are many plans suggested for providing for the neglected children of Drunken parents, but none such a Sweeping measure as this, for by This plan we provide for them at once, we get rid of the dear little ones altogether.

Lady with chignon: This is a delightful task for we shall never want a supply of these neglected children, whilst the Pious & respectable Distillers and Brewers carry on their trade and we shall always find plenty of the little dears about the Gin Palaces and the Beer shops.

Clergyman: According to the teaching of Jesus, all these little Gutter girls are our sisters, and therefore I feel it my duty as a Christian Minister to assist in this good work.

Lady with Whip (Maria Rye): I am greatly obliged to you Christian ladies and gentlemen for your help and as soon as you have filled the cart I'll drive off to pitch the little dears aboard of a ship and take them thousands of miles away from their native land so that they may never see any of their relations again.

First Child: Mother! Mother! I want my mother! Oh! Mother! Mother!

Second Child: I want my Father!

were to come from the workhouse, paid for by Boards of Guardians who were responsible for them until they were eighteen years old, although her appeal had been for 'gutter' children whose fate, she had implied, could not be worse than it was already and for whom proper supervision was an unnecessary luxury.

Maria was a fast worker. Having successfully launched her appeal in *The Times* she went back to Canada to give the finishing touches to the jail and courthouse which she had christened 'Our Western Home' while at the same time placing out a further party of women. Less than a month later she gathered up the children who sailed with her on the *Hibernian*, one of the Allen Line's steamships to Quebec. From Quebec the children had a long train journey west to Toronto which they reached on 13 November. Crossing the lake by steamer, the party was met by a variety of carts and buggies belonging to

'Our Western Home'. The jail and courthouse in Niagara-on-the-Lake that became Maria Rye's distributing home

the local farmers who had turned out to convey the little girls to their new home.[8] The house was all but empty and even for the physically strong and resilient Maria the task of unpacking the two hundred odd bales and boxes they had brought with them and getting everyone settled into the practically empty home was an exhausting process.

The children had arrived two hours before Maria, who made her appearance accompanied by a reporter from the local paper who described the scene thus:

> The confidence and trust of these children in Miss Rye is unbounded. They regard her with the strongest affection, which they show in a thousand artless ways – fondling round her, kissing her hands and the like ... when that good lady arrived at the home, an hour or two after the children's arrival, the way they came clustering round her with exclamations of joy was a pleasing sight. Still more affecting to see them all kneeling round her in the attitude of perfect devotion while she read a portion of the Evening Service and put up a Prayer of Thankfulness to Almighty God for having brought them to the end of their long and toilsome journey.[9]

Maria stayed in Canada all that winter seeing to the placing out of the little girls, which took longer than she had anticipated, and preparing the ground for the next party she was planning to bring out in the spring. One of her first priorities upon her return was to go before the Liverpool Vestry to give an account of how she had dealt with the fifty children they had placed in her care. Maria told them that everyone who applied for a child had to fill up a form giving their names and addresses, stating how many children they had and what their profession or trade was; if they did not belong to the Episcopal Church they were asked to state with what body of Christians they worshipped and they were all asked to give the name of a reference. They were also asked to state what position the child would hold in the family and to state the age of the child they wished for.

If this procedure was completed satisfactorily the child, in Maria's words, was 'regularly and legally' placed out under the care of her foster parents until she was eighteen. Maria had devised forms of Indenture for Adoption and forms of Indenture of Service, both very impressive-looking documents, but which in reality had no binding force on the signatories. The children who were to be adopted were to be maintained, educated and instructed in the principles of the Protestant religion. The foster parents were in all respects to regard and treat the child as they would their own lawful child. The child who was not adopted was indentured and bound out as an apprentice until the age of eighteen as a good and faithful servant 'who shall well demean and conduct herself'. In return the foster parents were bound to educate, clothe and feed her and to see that she attended a place of worship on Sunday and Sunday School if possible. From fifteen to seventeen years, in lieu of clothes, the girls were to receive three dollars a month wages rising to four dollars a month in the last year of apprenticeship.

Over the matter of supervision Maria confidently laid the responsibility for the arrangements for providing this at the feet of the Canadian Government quoting an Act of Parliament passed in 1851, to amend the law relating to apprentices and minors, which had never been intended to cover any such cases as those of the emigrant children. For good measure she also stated in a casual sort of way that she relied on 'such personal supervision as good friends will give me'. Two of the more prominent citizens of Niagara-on-the-Lake, Henry Pafford, the Mayor and Robert Ball, a Justice of the Peace, had agreed to act jointly with Maria as guardians to the children. How these two gentlemen could be expected to make sure that the children were not over-worked or exploited was not spelt out, but Maria assured her audience that the children's duties would be suited to their age. Seeking to still any further anxieties she said that 'in many instances the duties amounted to little more than playing with another little girl and keeping her company'. She could even aver that her chief worry was that her little ones would be too kindly treated and get spoiled. The Liverpool Vestry were convinced by her arguments and promptly voted her funds to take out a further fifty of their girls.

Having so far succeeded, Maria now went for hard sell. She based her arguments on solid economic and financial facts which she felt would influence those in positions of authority and in this she was not disappointed. At a meeting of the National Association for the Promotion of Social Science, presided over by Lord Shaftesbury, she gave the facts as she saw them. In London alone, she said, there were more than 10,000 children in the workhouse and more than 46,000 children on outdoor relief. She had shown with the children from Liverpool that if she were allowed to take children in good health, provided with a small outfit by their union, she could take them to Niagara-on-the-Lake for ten pounds a head and find families who would be only too pleased to receive them. Not only would the position of the children be materially improved by their removal from poor homes, but the rates would be lessened.

Dr Hayward, addressing the Liverpool Literary and Philosophical Society reinforced this argument in a paper on the 'Emigration of Public Orphans' in which the role of the pauper child as a liability was still more forcefully underlined. The 2,000 Liverpool orphans cost the town thirteen pounds a head per annum, he said, and if interest on the cost of land and buildings were added to this it came to eighteen pounds per annum; this meant that Liverpool had to find £36,000 out of rates to maintain these children. Dr Hayward argued that that Miss Rye had already saved the ratepayers £5,000, the cost of maintaining fifty orphans from eight to eighteen. He ended with a forthright attack on the unions saying that keeping girls in the workhouse only contributed to their ruin; inducing parish orphans to emigrate at the age of eight would benefit both mother country and colonies. Arguments similar to these were to be used by those who supported juvenile emigration for the next fifty years.

In 1871 Maria published some of the letters she had received from supporters and some from the children themselves as a way of providing her friends with information about her work. Declaring that she had neither time nor inclination to write reports, and saying that she believed in them as little as she did in committees, the letters were intended to stimulate interest in her work and to still any doubts. One can well believe she had no time for committees. Thirty-six unions had now entrusted her with their children and Maria claimed that over a quarter of the four hundred little girls had been adopted or were being treated as members of the families who had taken them in. She had been invited to send children to New Brunswick by the provincial government and paid by them to do so.

Obviously Maria only printed the letters from children who

were contented with their situations, but beneath the surface the children's anxiety as to the whereabouts of friends and relations runs through their letters with striking regularity. A letter from Annie McMaster from Chichester workhouse shows vividly how painful these separations were.

Mrs Gourlay is a good mother, and Mr Gourlay is a good father, and they are all good and kind to me; this is the best house I have had for many a long day. I have learnt many things since I have been here. I am learning to cook and to bake and to iron ... and how many is there left that came out with me? I guess there is but a few who helps the cook now I am gone. Dear Miss Rye, I thank you for getting me such a good home.... Have all the boys got homes yet? I have heard that my brother as got a home, but I have not seen him or heard of him. Please Miss Rye would you tell me where he is gone; is he in St Catherine's? Would you please tell me the name of the place he is gone to, and the name of his master and the church and the minister and what work does he do? Did he cry much after I went away? I know I don't feel quite so happy as I should feel if I knew where he was and hear from him. Did you ever hear him speak of me while he was there? How long ago has he been at his home? I hope he has got as good home as I have.... I give my best love to you. Please don't forget to write and tell me about my brother.[10]

As it happened Annie had cause to be worried about her brother. His story was told by Andrew Doyle, the inspector sent by the Local Government Board to report on the children sent to Canada by Boards of Guardians. Doyle made his visit in 1874 and discovered that he was the first person who had ever visited the children or taken any interest in them. Doyle reported that George, Annie's brother, had been placed with a farmer in Port Hope where he was very unhappy and that Annie had received a 'pitiable letter' from him saying that the farmer 'had used him very badly'. Mrs Gourlay, whom Doyle described as being 'a very kind decent sort of woman', took pity on Annie who was greatly distressed at this news and sent her son to fetch him to St Catherine's. She got him a situation with a saw-maker who does not appear to have been a very satisfactory employer. The boy was twice turned out of doors.

Upon the last occasion he was found at the corner of the street sitting on his box crying. He was taken in by Mrs Gourlay, who kept him for some weeks, and got his present situation, assistant to a small market gardener, where he is in a very humble home, but is kindly treated.[11]

Although neither Annie nor George had been visited, reports seem to have been sent to Chichester workhouse for the Guardians were told with regard to George, 'Good accounts are received from this child, he is in St Catherine's in a "gentleman's family".'

Robert Ball, Maria's friend and one of the joint guardians of the children, must have been a little mortified at the publicity given to the McMaster children by Andrew Doyle in his Report, and shortly afterwards he visited Annie himself. The results of that visit were also published by Andrew Doyle in a further report he made to the Local Government Board.[12] Mr Ball had to report that Annie was 'one of the few we have to record on the list of men's wickedness and women's frailty'. Doyle wrote, scathingly, quoting Miss Ryes more homely English that she 'had a child by one of the young Gourlays'.

Doyle published the facts about the McMaster children to show what could happen to children who were not supervised. It was just chance that Annie's letter was one of those Maria Rye decided to publish in 1871, as it was chance that led Andrew Doyle to report on George McMaster in 1874. Of the other children who wrote, nothing more is known, but judging by Annie's experience their anxious queries seem unlikely to have been answered by Maria Rye.

Selina Newbold, one of the original party from Kirkdale wrote:

Dear Miss Rye,
I write these few lines to you to ask you would you please tell me were my sisters is, for if you would I would much a blaise to you [be much obliged to you] indeed. Dear Miss Rye, would you tell me were Jane Tatlock is, and how she his, for I like to know, and Mary E McCabe and Annie McMaster send there kind love to you, and I ham verry glad that you have got me such a good place, for I very happle inded, and I would like to see my sister if I could get to see her, but I don't think I could. Dear Miss Rye, are you quite well, for I like to know, becourd I heard that you was very sick indeed, and are you quite well now? I hope you are. Dear Miss Rye, have you brote any more out of our school, for if you have would you tell me, for I like to know very

much indeed, so I have no more times write any more, so this is all I write. So no more from,
Your afectanet Scoolar, Selina Newbold
So good night and god blest you.[13]

Sarah Harding had been picked up from the London streets. It seems she had been living with two others, one a baby of three months, all alone in a room in Whitechapel. She too came out with the original party and the baby came too.

Dear Miss Rye,
I write hopeing to find you better, as we heard in the paper that you were very sick, and how is the dear baby, and is she gone? Please would you send me my brother's address, so I may write to him? I am getting a little stronger, and I like my place well. How are all the girls? Would you write and tell me if the baby is gone; if she is will you tell me what place? Mrs Murray is very kind to me. I often wish I was back in England again; I wish I could go back. I have no more to say, so will you write and tell me all I ask you?[14]

There was no affectionate greeting from Sarah: she merely ended the letter S.E. Harding, and clearly her feelings about coming to Canada were ambivalent. Another child from Kirkdale wrote from New York:

I am sorry to hear Lizzie Taylor was not liked by her mistress for having such a bad temper. . . . I often think of the time I left you all and came to New York. I do not know whether you ever heard about my coming or not; when I got to N.Y. there must have been some mistake about the express, for I was out on the streeet walking along, when I was picked up by one policeman and put in a cab, taken out of that and put in another, and was driven to Mr Ward's office, waited there for a little while, when Mr Potter came, and we all went to Bloomfield.[15]

It would seem from this letter that Elisabeth Chesworth was one of those who either decided to change her place herself, or it was decided for her by her first employer, but that the change was made without Miss Rye's knowledge.

Miss Rye's somewhat free and easy management style laid her open to criticism and in 1874 rumours were already circulating in the press about her work when the Islington Board of Guardians received a letter from Allendale Grainger. Grainger had married a Miss Martin, a girl once in Maria Rye's service in Canada but who had been discharged by her, and Maria made it clear that there was no love lost between them. Grainger's letter asked the Guardians if they were satisfied that the children they had sent to Canada had really benefited; he asked if the ratepayers and general public were not paying too much for the service they received from Miss Rye; he pointed out that the work of a servant was almost treble that of a servant in England, that the children were scattered all over the country and were friendless; if cheap labour was needed so much why not import negroes and coolies instead of orphan girls?[16] He ended by suggesting that the Local Government Board should send out a proper person with knowledge of North America to report truthfully on the project.

This was the first time that Miss Rye had been challenged so openly, but doubts about her work had been voiced privately in 1868 before she turned her attention to children. William Dixon, the senior Canadian emigration agent in Britain, had made known his suspicions as to how the Female Middle Class Emigration Society was run in a letter in that year:

> She is not a philanthropist but she is a passenger agent of the sharpest description. She has removed her office from Adelfi to the Strand and she conducts the business thus. She appeals to the public through the press for contributions to aid her in assisting poor girls to emigrate – she signs her name as Hon. Secretary (as many others do) because it appears disinterested and funds freely come in as they always do in London for any object. She then applies to the registry offices for girls and asks them how much money they can raise towards the price of passage to a place where they can get high wages – she also applies to the unions of factory towns and in those cases the guardians pay all the expenses. If the girls have two pounds and Miss Rye's subscriptions come in freely she supplements what is required, retaining what she considers reasonable for her trouble, and as far as I can see it is a profitable business but it is a gross imposition to think that girls she obtains in this manner are good servants.[17]

Dixon added that 'where her interests are concerned it is impossible to control her or keep her in check'. She certainly always showed great flair in manipulating a situation to her own advantage and according to Dixon, managed by bringing pressure to bear on Mr Disraeli to get her name down on the good service list for an annual grant of £75 for her work in

Australia. Correspondence between Lord Kimberley, the Colonial Secretary and the Governor-General, Lord Dufferin, in 1873 on the subject of the emigration of pauper children, reveals that anxieties existed on that score even before Grainger wrote to the Islington Union.

Maria had all the answers. She supplied the Chairman of the Islington Board of Guardians with a list of all the people who had been designated the children's custodians. She pointed to the fact that there was a surplus of a million women over men in the country and said that as a nation we were guilty of wife desertion, wife beating, child selling and child neglect to an extent that had no parallel in any other civilised nation under the sun. She rejected the idea that Canada imported children, saying she had at first been refused entry by the Minister for Agriculture, who forbade her to bring the children into the country, and it was only after she had been able to persuade Sir John A. Macdonald, the Prime Minister, with the help of a letter from Shaftesbury, that the decision had been reversed. Meeting the challenge of an inspection she said she had nothing to fear and ending on a personal note with a burst of rhetoric she wrote,

> Do you think any woman would work as I work, would or could live the life I live, without some such glorious result – some harvest and some seed sowing? No! It would not be possible to continue such work unless the reaping and sowing were almost in due proportion. And I thank God this day, and say it without fear of contradiction, that my work is a glorious success and has in many ways exceeded my most sanguine expectations.[18]

She won her case! The Board passed a vote of confidence in her and her work, only one voice dissenting.

Four

TO THE LAND OF THE MAPLE LEAF

Behold, the Lord thy God hath set the land before thee: go up and possess it; fear not, neither be discouraged.... Moreover, your little ones and your children shall go in thither, and unto them will I give it, and they shall possess it.

Deut. 1:21, 39; Quoted in Lillian Birt, *The Children's Homefinder, the story of Annie Macpherson and Louisa Birt*

In 1866 a cholera epidemic had swept through the East End of London making conditions for the swarming population who had crowded into that area still more desperate; the epidemic, which killed over 3,000 people, was succeeded by a bad harvest, a hard winter and a cyclical depression in trade. It was during those two years that Annie Macpherson, Thomas Barnardo and William Booth, who was to found the Salvation Army, started to work among the poor and destitute in the East End. To all of them emigration seemed the one certain way for the unemployed and distressed inhabitants of the metropolis to extricate themselves from the hopeless poverty in which they otherwise seemed doomed to spend the rest of their lives.

The Cow Cross Emigrating Club was only one of many such clubs that came into being at this time to assist East End families to emigrate. Emigration funds were started by the charitably minded and the British and Colonial Emigration Society actively helped many thousands to go overseas to Canada and the United States. For those working specifically with children, juvenile emigration was a natural development of this movement. Annie Macpherson, who was to play such an important

Annie Macpherson

role in the inauguration and development of the movement to emigrate children, was living in London at the height of the distress in 1867. She had been involved with the emigration of whole families and had herself escorted a party of widows and children to Canada, returning from that journey completely exhausted: 'I confess I have suffered from my too great anxiety to bear the burdens of the widow and fatherless. My head is completely done from the pressures of sorrow I have had to enter into . . . Boys are comparatively easy to attend to compared with these.'[1] This experience doubtless helped to convince her of the wisdom of concentrating on work with children. Children were easier to handle, cheaper to outfit and more rewarding to deal with.

Annie Macpherson was born in 1833, the eldest of seven children. Two of those children, Rachel and Louisa, were to be closely associated with Annie's emigration work, and Louisa's work in Liverpool would complement Annie's in London. The Macphersons had originally been farmers and small landowners in Stirlingshire, but Annie's father, a member of the Society of Friends, was a teacher. He had studied the work of Pestalozzi and Froebel and at the invitation of Lady Lovelace had come to England to establish schools in the neighbourhood of her estate.[2] Annie sometimes accompanied her father to his classes and saw at first hand from an early age how to gain and keep a child's confidence. She herself was educated in Glasgow and was trained as a teacher in Froebel's methods at the Home and Colonial Training College in Gray's Inn Road. Annie's father died in 1851 when the youngest daughter, Louisa, was only eleven, leaving Annie and her widowed mother responsible for the care of the younger ones. An only brother had run away to sea; it was perhaps to compensate for his loss that Mrs Macpherson adopted two orphans, an experience which gave Annie and her sisters a practical demonstration of how a child's life could be altered by adoption into a family.

Rachel married a prosperous Cambridgeshire farmer the year after her father's death and Annie and her mother moved to Cambridgeshire to be near them in 1858 after Louisa had married a wealthy London merchant. Annie was always the serious one of the family: not only were responsibilities thrust on her at an early age, but it seems that she too had been engaged to be married but that just before the marriage was due to take place the young man was killed in particularly tragic circumstances. Whether this happened before or after a visit to a revival meeting in London, which was to change her life, is not known. What is certain is that after hearing two well-known evangelicals, Reginald Radcliffe and Richard Weaver, preaching at the Shoreditch Theatre she had a profound spiritual experience. Inspired by their preaching, she found at the end of the meeting that she had been given the power to speak and make known to others her own belief in the saving grace of salvation and redemption through Jesus Christ. Afterwards she wrote in her journal, 'from that good hour revival work has ever been my greatest joy'. She started to preach and teach among the rural population and one of her converts, Frank Smith, who was to work with Hudson Taylor in the

China Inland Mission wrote of her at that time, '. . . village life was transformed. Her personality was magnetic. How we all loved her. . . . There were many brought to the Lord.'

Annie came to London in 1862. Through her involvement with the revival movement she got to know two ladies, Clara Lowe and her cousin, Lady Rowley, two of a small band of women who were drawn by their discovery of the misery and squalor that existed in the East End to devote much of their time and energy to helping the poor. Clara Lowe, who was born on St Helena where her father had been responsible for guarding Napoleon, had been so stirred by Reginald Radcliffe's words,that she had left her home in Hyde Park Square. Taking only a little fold-up bed and a few possessions in a hired cab, she had gone to live in the East End to involve herself in revival work.[3] Lady Rowley had already established a home for girls in Spital Square under the auspices of the YWCA and was actively involved in running it. Annie's initiation into the appalling conditions in which many poor families lived was made in the company of Clara Lowe, whose quiet and gentle personality allowed her to visit where others dared not venture. It was with Miss Lowe that Annie first came across an example of what can only be called child slavery, the manufacture of match boxes by tiny children, 'the little matchbox makers' about whom Annie was to write so movingly.

Annie had just returned from a visit to New York with her family, where they had been to visit relatives, when she discovered these unhappy children. While in New York she had visited the different missions working in the city and had been much impressed by Mr Van Meter's work with the Howard League for Children, which was successfully placing out desti tute children in western rural districts, as had Maria Rye. Her subsequent decision to take destitute children to Canada and place them out in the west was taken under no misapprehensions as to the dangers and difficulties that were involved in the journey. A graphic description of the trials that beset the family on the outward voyage in the *Caroline* 'an overloaded, leaky vessel, short of sails, food and water' appeared in her journal.[4]

We had on board a hundred emigrants of all nations, not a few Whitechapel roughs, some recently out of prison, several of the vilest and lowest that can be imagined. The half-fed emigrants broke into the cargo, getting fearfully drunk with London porter, threatening a mutiny. Their pistols were locked up by the officers, and a band of them were hand-cuffed. Often in the midnight hour the sea would come rushing into our cabins, several of the boats were washed away, the bulwarks stove in, the sailors telling us that humanly speaking the vessel could not stand another gale. The last week our provisions had been chiefly salted meat and our last tank of water had shipped the sea, and even this we had on short allowance.

Annie's baby nephew caught typhus fever and, although he survived, several children died on the voyage. The description continued:

On Sunday December 23rd every trial reached its height; boils had broken out on officers and crew, diphtheria among the foreigners, many were disabled among the emigrants, robbing was going on in mysterious ways. A band of fierce Irishmen lay manacled over our heads. When light broke the sea went down, the wind calmed. Then a shout from stem to stern was heard: 'Land! Land!'

The wonder is that after such an experience Annie ever thought of crossing the Atlantic again. But her discoveries in the East End were to make the discomforts of that journey fade into insignificance.

The misery and distress that Annie encountered in the wake of the cholera epidemic caused her to believe that it was better for the children to die rather than grow up to face the grim future that awaited them. 'We can but be deeply thankful that in parts of the East End four out of every five infants die before they reach their fifth year, because the other side of the picture among the living ones is so black, so awful, so crushing in its dreadful realities.' The dreadful realities included drunkenness, for Annie reported that 'while yet in their mother's arms gin is poured down their infant throats . . . alas! no uncommon sight is it to see little girls of ten years old reeling drunk along the streets'. It was however the discovery that children could be hired to make a gross of match boxes for just three farthings and that hundreds of children were spending all their waking hours in small dark rooms, slaving to produce the boxes which the matchmaking industry needed to package their matches, that spurred her to action. 280 pieces of wood had to be bent, sanded and covered with paper to make a gross of boxes. Children became really fast workers by the time they were eight to ten years old, but to achieve this they had to start early, learning to paste sandpaper on to boxes when they were but three to four years old.

Annie wrote *The Little Matchbox Makers* to publicise the plight of these children. She described how she took on her knees a little girl of four whose mother told her that the child had earned her own living since she was three.

> The infant now makes several hundred boxes every day of her life and her earnings suffice to pay the rent of the miserable room which the family inhabits. The poor little woman is grave and sad beyond her years; she has none of a child's vivacity; she does not know what play means. All her thoughts are centred in the eternal round of lucifer-box making, in which her whole life is passed. She has never been beyond the dingy street in which she was born. She has never so much as seen a tree, or a daisy, or a blade of grass. A poor, sickly little thing, and yet a sweet obedient child; the deadly pallor of her face proclaiming unmistakably that she will soon be taken away to a better world where at last the weary little fingers shall be at rest.

As a result of this publicity money was sent to provide a treat for some of the little matchbox makers, and this was followed by further donations which enabled Annie to arrange classes in the evening for the children where they were given religious instruction and an evening meal was provided. Within a year sufficient money had been collected for Annie and her supporters to acquire the old cholera hospital in Commercial Road which she called the Home of Industry. She not only used the premises to teach the children, she invited their mothers to come and sew, and thus, while they earned a sixpence, Annie could offer them both practical help and talk to them of the Gospel.[5]

The Home of Industry was to become the main base for all Annie's subsequent work, and although she called herself the honorary secretary, it was her dynamic personality that made it into a flourishing centre for evangelical work. Annie was nothing if not thorough in her methods and soon after acquiring the building she felt she should spend the night there, to be able to enter into its needs and to understand what she was asking of her matrons. She wrote: 'No words can describe the sounds surrounding it at the midnight hour – yells of women, cries of "murder" then "police" – rushing to and fro of wild, drunken men and women into the street adjoining the building whence more criminals come than any other street in London . . .'

Annie was not only concerned about the little matchbox makers. She had been approached by the Society of Friends and asked to take classes for boys and youths at Peter Bedford's Institute in Bethnal Green. This she found a real challenge. The class of twenty she got together with difficulty deserted her lessons for gayer pastimes and night after night she sat alone. She tried to get them to come to tea, but they refused and one of them told her frankly, 'We chaps don't like religion licked down our throats'.[6] She finally succeeded in getting two hundred of them together at George Holland's ragged school. There she learnt, as Shaftesbury had learnt, that many had no homes and slept where they could; many were dressed in rags and covered with vermin. It seemed to her a mockery to try to teach the Bible to children whose lives were so wretched. Enlisting the support of the editor of the influential Christian weekly journal, then called *The Revival*, but soon to be known as *The Christian*, sufficient money was raised to make it possible to take not one but three houses, which became known as the Revival Homes where both boys and girls could be taken in. George Kirkham, who also worked among the poor in the East End, was a guest at the first anniversary of the opening of the Revival Homes which was held at the Home of Industry in May 1869. From him we have a vivid description of the bounding energy and faith Annie brought to her work.

I soon discovered the Refuge at the corner of Flower and Dean Street – a street where the unfortunate and the vicious may be found by the hundreds in the lodging houses. There was no difficulty in recognising the building, even at a distance, as texts of scripture, in large blue letters on white canvas were placed in each window. . . . This was my first visit and although I thought I had a tolerably accurate idea of what was being done, from the frequent reports in *The Revival*, I found I knew next to nothing. . . . Miss Macpherson was speaking when I entered; she seemed to know everything about the hundred and twenty-five children before her. First one group, then another, rose at her bidding while she told visitors about the particular Home to which they belonged and sketched the former history of some of them, aided by their own intelligent answers to her questions. Miss Macpherson knows the potency of *facts* and has sufficient in her possession, and such a striking way of telling them, that her appeals are irresistible. . . .

The appearance of the children proclaimed health, contentment, intelligence and industry – a striking contrast to what they were when admitted, as shown in a capital shilling photograph, containing twelve boys which may be obtained at the Refuge.[7]

George Kirkham's reference to the photograph is of particular interest, because among the names of the East End workers mentioned as present on that occasion was that of Thomas Barnardo, still a medical student at that time. Barnardo was later to become famous for the use he made of photographs for publicity and fund-raising purposes. He was to learn much else from Annie Macpherson besides the value of photography in promoting the cause of children, for he was again present at the Home of Industry when Annie gave a tea party to finalise her arrangements with the parents and friends of those boys she thought suitable for emigration. Barnardo was the first to arrive, 'enlivening the scene with boys from his wood-chopping brigade, boys well fitted to emigrate'. They were joined by Annie's own boys from the Revival Homes and after hymns and prayers a small printed form was read out by Mr Merry, Annie's brother-in-law, giving Miss Macpherson entire charge and responsibility for taking the children to Canada, which parents and friends were asked to sign. The forms had no legal validity, but Annie would not accept any child whose parent refused to sign the agreement.

Annie had sent nine of her boys to Canada under the care of Christian men earlier in 1869, before Miss Rye had sailed with her party of girls because, as she said in her appeal for further funds, 'Here there is nothing for them but a criminal's life; there fresh air, plenty of food and work; providing them with work seems to be the secret of their temporal well-being.' Funds had been forthcoming. Mr Dixon, the emigration agent for Canada, to whom she had written, had assured her that there would be immediate employment for the children saying it was 'impossible to overstock the country with them' and Annie had had no difficulty in collecting her first party of a hundred boys.

Miss Lowe accompanied this first party on the train as far as Liverpool and left a detailed description of the journey which also gives the feel of the highly charged religious atmosphere in which the whole operation was conducted.[8]

Now they stood in ranks ready to depart, their blue rough jackets, corduroy suits and strong boots, all made within the Refuge, the work of their own hands. All alike had scarlet comforters and Glengarry caps and a canvas bag across their shoulders containing a change of linen for the voyage, towels, tin can, bowl and mug, knife, fork and spoon, and one kind friend the last day before starting brought a hundred strong pocket knives. A Bible, a *Pilgrim's Progress* and a little case of stationery were provided for each, and while they stood thus, singing their last farewell, a dense crowd filled the street without, waiting for hours in the pouring rain. It was with difficulty that the police could keep the way clear for the lads to enter the vans, and as they came out most blessed was it to think that, altered as they were in outward appearance, that change in many of them was small compared to the change within – that with many old things had passed away; behold, *all* things had become new.

The train left St Pancras at 8.30 pm and at one station where the train stopped at midnight a friend was waiting to give money for the expenses on the journey. At Derby the lads had a run on the platform to warm themselves and then gathered round their beloved leader, and in the dead of night the arches rang with their songs of praise. The boys followed Miss Macpherson in prayer, and in the carriages prayer was still continued by many till sleep overcame them. There is reason to believe that with two souls the answer to these petitions was given before the train reached Liverpool.

The train arrived in Liverpool at 4 am and the boys immediately went on board the *Peruvian*. The poor lads had to wait several hours before they got any breakfast which was a trial of patience but restraining grace was so manifest throughout, one's heart was continually lifted up in praise and thanksgiving for this mercy as well as for countless others.

The boys were probably too exhausted by this time to cause much trouble, but doubtless Annie Macpherson would have been capable of dealing with any who might prove awkward. She did manage to hold a service with some of the boys and Miss Lowe reported that the last sounds to be heard from the boys as the ship cast off was the boys singing the hymn 'Yes, we part, but not for ever'.

Annie had her friend, Ellen Bilborough, with her on board, another remarkable woman who was to play an important role in Canada and about whom even the severest critics of the emigration movement had only good to say. The *Peruvian* belonged to the Allan Line, a shipping company started through the enterprise of a Glaswegian shipmaster Captain Alexander Allan. Most of the children who went to Canada travelled on ships belonging to his company. Captain Smith of the *Peruvian* evidently had a particular fondness for children. He had captained the ship in which Maria Rye had taken out her first party of little girls. Some of the lads gave Annie an anxious time, and she was especially worried by the 'evil examples shown my poor lads by the gentlemen of the cabin, with their smoking, drinking and ribaldry of song'. Captain Smith helped to keep the boys occupied by giving them responsibility for keeping the watch and pulling on the ropes, the sailors shouting 'Hey little Macpherson' to all and sundry. His final kind act was to give her a written testimonial saying that he felt it was his duty to say 'how well the boys conducted themselves on board the ship during the voyage', which encouraged Annie to write to her supporters asking them to prepare not only more boys, but girls also to make up another party for Canada.

Annie placed twenty boys from that first group as 'buttons' in some of the first families in Montreal, a shrewd move, for if they did well Annie would be able to count on the support of these influential families in the future. At the same time she was aware of the temptation to which the boys might well be exposed and asked for them to be remembered at the daily prayer meetings which continued to be held at the Home of Industry, now being supervised by Annie's two sisters, Rachel Merry and Louisa Birt. Annie's two sisters were by now completely involved with her in her work. Rachel Merry, whose warm and motherly personality provided a happy balance to Annie's more forthright and dominating character, was to cross the Atlantic many times with her husband, escorting children to Canada. Her son, William, would in due course take up farming in Canada and his experience in this field was to be useful to Annie. Had it not been for a series of personal tragedies the beautiful Lousia, who was the gay one of the family, with a gift for friendship and a talent for music, might never have become so personally involved in the work. Louisa's two elder children both died and shortly after that her husband was terribly injured in a railway accident which resulted in his becoming a nervous invalid for the rest his life. Louisa took her husband abroad in the vain hope that it might improve his chances of recovery; instead it almost killed Louisa who returned home, her heart affected by rheumatic fever and malaria and exhausted by the strain of travelling and nursing an invalid.

Although Annie refused to set up a distributing home in Montreal, she did gratefully accept an offer by the Mayor and Council of Belleville of a house, Marchmont. The rental was to be paid by the citizens of Belleville, a pleasant small town . The management of the home was to be left entirely to Annie Macpherson who put Ellen Bilborough in charge. Ellen was to remain at Marchmont for the next thirty years in the role of honorary superintendent. Leslie Thom, a Scottish school teacher who had also accompanied the party, remained behind as well to visit and supervise the children who had been placed out.

That first year Annie made two more journeys to Canada, her sister Louisa, finding the strength and courage to accompany her on one occasion. It was obviously a relief to have a home to go to in Canada after the strain of the first journey when Annie had travelled round the country with her group of boys, staying where opportunity offered, either with the help of a mayor or a well-disposed farmer. Annie writes of the 'intense joy of being met and welcomed home' by Miss Bilborough 'with a face beaming with joy'.[9] The exhausted children, girls and boys, slept in hammocks or on beds of clean straw. That first night Annie permitted herself a moment to enjoy the scene 'with the moon shining like glittering gold on the lovely bay of Quintie, with not a rustle on lake or leaf' before retiring after prayers and praise, to be ready to deal with the stream of applicants the morrow would bring.

Unlike Maria Rye, Annie never appealed directly for money, but her letters to *The Christian* were nicely calculated to arouse the sympathy of her readers in a practical manner. Writing of the Marchmont Home she went so far as to claim that as 'a home of love' it was 'a sweet foretaste to these unloved and uncared for children of the home in heaven'. Describing the scene she wrote:

> Oh, could you, beloved ones, who have given your substance, see them lying, basking under the lovely maple trees around the house,

pulling and eating the hickory nuts till their fingers and lips are dyed a deep brown colour, the neighbours throwing them over from their orchards quantities of apples! The very cow seems to love the little folk, permitting them to pat and pet her. . . .

Unfortunately for the children their sojourn at Marchmont was likely to be a short one. Like Maria Rye's children, they too would be sent under indentures to work in the homesteads and on the surrounding farms. Unlike Maria, however, Annie had sought to provide supervision on a more systematic basis and as the record books show, a real attempt was made to visit and keep in touch with the children.

There is no direct evidence from the children themselves as to how they viewed their changed circumstances. Annie gave the readers of *The Christian* her account:

It is very encouraging to be welcomed in Montreal by my first detachment of young lads. Canadian air and good food had already worked wonders for them; and to hear *them* give sound, wholesome advice to these now newly arriving was a quicker return than I had ever expected – such as entreating them to shun drink, keep to church and Sunday School, and have a money box for all small money, and to call it 'Miss Macpherson's Box so as to be fellow helpers of this great work'.[10]

The policy of encouraging the children to contribute to the emigration funds of the Home of Industry was heavily criticised by some; as Miss Macpherson doubtless realised, the example of children, theselves only recently rescued from destitution, contributing to the emigration fund was a hefty reminder to those wealthier supporters as to what might be expected from them.

Annie spent the winter of 1871 in Canada, obviously finding the cold winter weather immensely invigorating. She had always been fearful of driving, but she overcame this fear, travelling extensively to talk of her work and to prepare the ground for future parties of children. Little was said publicly of the difficulties Annie and her helpers had to overcome in those first years, apart from the occasional reference to a 'black lamb'. As for the Canadians their need for cheap labour was such that they gave no thought, in those early years, as to where the children came from or who they were.

In pre-industrial Canada nearly three-quarters of the population lived in rural areas. There were no machines to replace human labour and the more hands the farmer could secure to work the land the more prosperous he was likely to become. His wife needed help in the house, either with the young children or, later when she was older and no more able to manage on her own. Canadians put their own children to work at an early age, and in a developing land there was little sentiment about the nature of childhood or any understanding of the way a child developed. Children were perceived as the 'raw material' from which hard-working, God-fearing adults were fashioned. Good working habits had to be inculcated at an early age. Children played a very important role in the success or otherwise of a pioneering farming family.

Unless a farmer had a large family, with a constant succession of children able to fill the gaps left as the elder children moved on – either to work in the cities or to take up land further west on their own account – there would only be a few years when he did not require the extra labour that his own children had supplied. It was the more isolated frontier farmers who most wanted the children. They were too far from the towns to sell or buy much, so were well able to absorb a child into their households at small cost to themselves. The simple needs of a child for shelter and food were easily provided on farms where food was plentiful because there were few market outlets. With little understanding of the loneliness that such isolation would mean to a city-bred child, the child rescue societies dwelt on the moral and physical advantages of such a healthy rural life, far from the temptations of the big cities. They never mentioned the fact that child labour was cheaper than hired labour and saw the children taking on the lighter work, freeing the adults for the heavy work in the fields.

Both Maria Rye and Annie Macpherson made much of the fact that some of the children were adopted by the families that took them and brought them up as one of the family. This was true to a certain extent. Figures are difficult to come by, but infant mortality was high among the farming community and it has been estimated that as late as the turn of the century one out of every five to seven Canadian babies died in the first year of life.[11] It was not the long cold winters that caused the casualties, but death came during the hot summer months from a disease known as 'the summer complaint'. It seems to have been accepted with a sense of inevitability and resignation, but it brought grief and an aching sense of loss. Children as young as two or three, and sometimes even babies, were brought out from England; they may have been among the more fortunate, accepted with joy to fill a gap in the family rather than for their future labour potential.

Although 1872 started with a tragedy it was to be an extraordinarily productive year for Annie. Just after her return to England Annie received a letter from Ellen Bilborough dated January 1872 telling of the fire that burnt Marchmont to the ground.

> It is indeed difficult to begin a letter to you, when you always open our letters sure of good news. And yet this one brings you the best you ever had. Spared lives, I trust, saved to work more than ever for Him who has done such great things for us. . . . Our beautiful Home lies in ruins, only the walls standing, and there is one little grave dug by Benjamin Stanley containing the ashes of little Robbie Gray . . . I hardly know how to begin, it still seems so terrible and real. I awoke thinking it was daylight – I jumped up, and oh! the feeling when I saw the house full of dense white smoke, I knew well what it must be.[12]

Two boys, Phillips and Keen, who had remained to help in the home were sent to get the children out while Miss Bilborough roused the other members of the household. Her letter continues:

> The flames were coming on with frightful rapidity; it was blowing a perfect hurricane and the whole was enveloped in smoke and ashes. I ran back half way upstairs to see if I could get a dress, or my cash box, or watch, but I was too much suffocated and had to get back to the front door.
>
> Your Scotch cloak was hanging up and I put that round me and seized Mr Thom's great coat and ran out. I found poor Miss Moore in her thin cotton nightdress in the snow and threw the coat over her; the snow was up to the knees. I saw Mr Thom and called to him to search again with Phillips for the children. The intense cold in the snow seemed almost worse to bear than the fire. Poor Mrs Wade had got her hands frozen in even that short time. Mrs Baylis's nightdress was ice to the waist.

When the names of the children were called over little Robbie was found to be missing. The boy Phillips said that he had lifted him out and he had seen him running across the snow with the other children. It was thought that blinded by the smoke the child had run back into the house.

It was all over in a few minutes, all around fearfully bright and lurid. The engine came, but of course was too late, the fire spread with such fearful rapidity. We sat, almost stunned with fright and cold. Soon the Shearings and the Elliotts came bringing clothes, and we went to dear Mrs Elliott's house in a sleigh. It was not four am and the fire was almost out, burning round the verandah and the window sills.

As soon as it was daylight I went with Mr Thom to see the ruins. All around the melted snow had frozen like iron; the thermometer which hung on the verandah was found uninjured; nothing was sound, but a table and one stove; all gone – books, papers, clothes, everything, but there in the blackened ruin lay distinctly the charred frame of little Robbie. His history in our book is very touching: 'Robert Gray, aged six, a happy little man who can say little or nothing about himself.' The rest of the page is blank, as he had never been away from Marchmont.

Considering the severity of the fire and the narrowness of their escape it is slightly puzzling that the record books survived, but survive they did for they are now in the Barnardo archive.

The local inhabitants reacted with generosity and practical help. The children were taken in by different families and less than a month later Miss Bilborough was writing to let Annie know that the people of Belleville were determined that they should not move from the area and that another substantial house had been found on the Kingston Road with five or six sitting-rooms and twelve bedrooms.[13] The Council again agreed to pay the rent and taxes for three years and the people of Belleville insisted on paying all the bills for furnishing the new Marchmont. Ellen Bilborough was able to assure Annie that all would be ready in May for the first party of children.

James Palmer was one of the boys in that party. Described as an orphan, he was accepted by Annie Macpherson, following his father's death in the workhouse, and sent to Canada with a particularly glowing character reference. Described as 'a nice boy, good scholar, most obliging, grateful, affectionate and obedient boy, a treasure to anyone', no other details are given, not even his age. All that is known of his family is summed up in a brief note which says simply, 'James wrote again asking for his sister'. The date is 1887 and he probably enclosed a photograph of himself with the letter. For although there is little written evidence about James, a striking series of photographs, stuck across the page of the record book, provide ample evidence that he grew and flourished in Canada. From the forlorn abandoned child the photographs show him growing through boyhood and adolescence into a successful and confident young man.

The need for cheap labour apart, Miss Macpherson's evangelical approach to emigration with her insistence on the missionary nature of the work was sympathetically received by Canadians who were, on the whole, a God-fearing people who went to church on Sunday and who drank little other than tea. *The Christian* had reported on several occasions that a religious revival had been very successful among the people of Galt, a small town to the west of Belleville which had been settled mainly by emigrants from Scotland. Annie, with her Scottish background, was a particularly welcome visitor when she spoke there, and as a result of her visit the people of Galt gave her a farm at Blair Atholl with a hundred acres of land.[14] Annie threw herself into the work of transforming this bleak farm into a home. During the brief Canadian spring she bought a span of horses and a plough and with the help of neighbours corn and clover were soon sown. The ladies from the surrounding churches brought equipment for the house; the threshing floor was made into a dining-room and the barn turned into a dormitory; the chaff house was made into a lavatory; one farmer's wife set them up with poultry; the Minister welcomed Annie and thanked her for coming 'to give his people something more to do for Jesus'. The involvement of Annie's family in the work was one of her great strengths. Rachel and Joseph Merry took over the superintendence of Blair Atholl, which was an ideal arrangement as Joseph Merry had farming experience.

Another speaking engagement which Annie accepted that year, this time in Quebec, was to prove equally fruitful. Invited by a Miss Barber to speak at her Sunday School, Annie found she was to stay with Miss Barber and her half brother, Mr Justice Dunkin. Mr Dunkin was Dominion Minister for

Agriculture and he was interested in Annie's work not only from the philanthropic and religious point of view, but also because of its practical importance. Miss Barber accompanied Annie back to England, and after inspecting the work being done by the Home of Industry became so convinced of the value of the work of emigration that she and her brother determined to raise sufficient funds to enable a distributing home to be bought. Knowlton in the province of Quebec was acquired, half the purchase money being paid by the Province of Quebec and the other half contributed through the efforts of the Barber and Dunkin families.[15]

Knowlton cannot have been an easy house to manage. It was in a remote country village and it was an extremely lonely place to live in during the long winter evenings. It had no running water and was lit by paraffin lamps; the only heating was by French Canadian box-stoves which needed constant stoking all through the night otherwise the house would have been freezing in the morning. It was fortunate for Annie that Miss Barber herself offered to take over the superintendence of the house and to oversee its management. Annie now had three distributing homes in Canada, and back home in England she had acquired another home at Hampton in Middlesex where her children could be assembled and given some training in rural surroundings before going overseas. Knowlton was later given by Annie to her sister Louisa for use as a distributing home.

Maria Rye and Annie Macpherson did not have a monopoly of juvenile emigration for long. Others involved in the work of rescuing destitute children from the streets of the large cities, like Bowman Stephenson, the founder of the Children's Home in London and John Middlemore of Birmingham, were also soon to see the advantages of sending children overseas. A fellow Methodist minister, Dr Morley Punshon, then living in Canada, encouraged Dr Stephenson to send his children to that country and enabled him to do so by buying a home in Hamilton, near Galt, and giving it to be used as a distributing home. It was Bowman Stephenson who, while on a visit to inspect the new home, persuaded the Federal Canadian Government to make a grant of $2 a head for each child brought to Canada, a move which was taken as an expression of approval by the Federal

Dr Bowman Stephenson

Government of the migration of children. However, the Federal Government had no intention of taking over responsibility for the children and were content that such responsibility should remain with the people who were bringing the children to Canada, none of whom were bound by any rules or regulations.

The uncoordinated and haphazard way in which the juvenile emigration movement developed is clearly illustrated by John Middlemore's account of his first journey to Canada in 1873 to board out children from the Emigration Home he had founded in Birmingham. John Middlemore was the third son of William Middlemore, a wealthy and successful business man from Birmingham.[16] The family were nonconformist and John found the strict discipline of family life hard to take. According to a family memoir endless sermons on sin and hellfire had given the children a sense of guilt,[17] and it must have been with relief that John learnt that he was to go to the United States to stay

John Middlemore

with cousins in Boston where life was much more free and easy. During the three years he was there he studied medicine at the University of Brunswick in Maine where he took a medical degree. He also travelled widely in the United States and in Canada. He returned to England in 1868. He was appalled by the number of homeless and destitute children he saw in the streets of all the major cities. He set to work to raise money to found a home which he called simply the Emigration Home as its sole purpose was to board out children in Canada, to lift them out of conditions which he described as 'perilous to their future welfare'. Like Annie Macpherson and Maria Rye he had returned from America with a practical knowledge of the opportunities that existed for the placing out of children across the Atlantic. However, when he set off with his first party of boys he seems to have done even less preparatory work than either of them.

Middlemore's first Emigration Home, opened in Birmingham in 1872

I left for Canada with my twenty-nine children on the first of May 1873. The journey was entirely one of discovery and speculation. I had not a single friend in Canada and did not know what to do with the children when I arrived there. In the course of my enquiries I heard of the Hon. George Allen and Professor D. Wilson of Toronto and sent them telegrams soliciting help. Both these gentlemen interfered most generously and most cordially on my behalf. They procured temporary lodging for my children and treated me with much personal kindness. My arrival was made known by articles in the Toronto newspapers and by personal correspondence and in the course of three or four weeks I had found good homes for all my children.[18]

It seems amazing that John Middlemore could set off with these children with no idea as to how he was to dispose of them when Annie Macpherson and Maria Rye had been operating a more or less organised system of emigration for more than three years. Although he later wrote that his first boy became a landowner and his first girl married happily, one cannot help wondering if he realised how Canadians perceived their role as providers of homes for the children. The children's only protection was a written agreement which simply stated,[19] 'I promise to take and adopt —— —— and to treat him in all respects as if he were my own child; to attend to and supply, as far as I can, all his needs, to send him to school and to church or chapel: and finally to teach him or cause him to be taught, some trade or calling, by attention to which he may make himself an honourable and independent position.' Since Middlemore had no home in Canada, nor any kind of organisation, the children were entirely at the mercy of the family with whom they had been placed. There was no one to whom they could appeal if the family chose to ignore the terms of the agreement. Of all the children brought out in the early 1870s they would appear to be some of the most vulnerable. The account of the placing out of little Robbie is hardly reassuring in this respect, although it does reveal John Middlemore as a sensitive and caring man, whose understanding of the extremely painful emotions that were experienced by most of the children on being separated from everything that was familiar and everyone they had ever known was perhaps greater than most.

When Robbie, who came from Ilkley, first entered the Emigration Home in Birmingham he had become very attached to John Middlemore, invariably walking beside him or holding on to his coat or hand. About Christmas time he became ill and his former friendliness was replaced by a new reserve in his manner toward his benefactor which continued after he had recovered from his illness. Robbie went to Canada in a party of boys, and because he was small and therefore harder to place he was the last to be found a family. Middlemore describes driving over with him to see his friend Mr Wilson who lived toward the back country.

> Our way lay along narrow lanes which had been cut through forest and swamp, and which were made of the trunks of trees thinly covered with soil and gravel. When we reached Mr Wilson's he received us kindly as he always does. He told me of a home for my little companion and offered to drive me there after dinner. When this meal, which consisted of bacon, potatoes and green tea, was over, I lifted little Robbie into the buggy to which Mr Wilson was attaching two powerful farm horses.

The poor child now began to whimper and surely it was not hard to find the cause of his tears. His experience of the last few days summarised the experience of all of us in life. Companion after companion had left him, and I, his last remaining companion was about to leave him too.

Middlemore said that in his hour of loneliness and sorrow all his shyness and reserve forsook Robbie. Making much of the pity and interest shown by the farmer in Robbie, Middlemore saw nothing ominous in the totally disinterested way in which the wife received the child.

The drive to the poor child's new home was not a happy one for any of us, but an hour's jolting brought us there. The farmer who was to adopt him was in the fields at the further end of his land and while Mr Wilson went to seek him I talked to his wife.

When I entered I found her cleaning the floor with a patent American scrubber, and during our conversation she continued to do so, remarking that the old English method of scrubbing was 'very hard on the back'. When the floor was cleaned she let down her hair and combed and arranged it, talking to me with perfect nonchalance all the time, but never referring to the object of my visit.

At length her husband returned. He was a tall broad-chested Scotsman, with very direct and independent manners; his face was half concealed with great shocks of sandy hair and whiskers but amid them two kindly light blue eyes looked with much pity and tenderness at little Robbie. They filled with tears as we talked and as he heard his history.

At last he drew him between his knees and said that he was willing to take him as his own if his wife was willing too. She, on the other hand, wished to throw the responsibility of this step on her husband – she said, 'I leave you to decide; if you take the boy I will do my duty, if he does badly it won't be my fault.'

John Middlemore made the final parting as brief as possible, for, as he wrote, he knew it would be very painful. Many hundreds of applications were made to the Children's Emigration Home on behalf of destitute and neglected children. Middlemore would only accept the most extreme cases because, perhaps, the case of little Robbie had taught him that 'expatriation is too strong for cases of ordinary misfortune'.

While Maria Rye was successfully encouraging Boards of Guardians to entrust her with their children, Annie Macpherson found herself being asked by several Unions to take some of their children and place them out with families in Canada. It was not only the Unions who made use of her services in this way. Several evangelical children's organisations had a formal arrangement with her, whereby they sent her children and she undertook to find homes for them in Canada. Two Scottish organisations, William Quarrier's village home at Bridge of Weir and Mrs Blaikie's home in Edinburgh, both sent large numbers of children; Mrs Smylie's home in Dublin and Leonard Shaw's home in Manchester were both also associated with Annie Macpherson's work in this way.

Maggie May was only three when she found herself travelling on the train from Edinburgh with a small group of children on her way to the Home of Industry. Although she did not know it, she had been 'given up entirely' to Mrs Blaikie who, knowing she had no family or friend to care for her, thought that she could well fare better if she went to Canada where she might be adopted by a family as she was so young. So little Maggie found herself one of a party of children who crossed the Atlantic in 1874. She was the youngest of the party and consequently was made much of and 'a great pet'. She stayed only a few days at Marchmont before being adopted by a lady who lived nearby. A photograph taken of her at this time shows a solemn little girl in a pretty dress with a tartan sash perched on an ornate stool, her short little legs just crossed. She was frequently visited by her friends from Marchmont and was described as being 'old fashioned and sensible'. She was only just five when her adopted mother died and Maggie was sent back to Marchmont.

She was again adopted, this time by a family called McNaughton, who already had an adopted son. Mrs McNaughton reported that 'Maggie is well and thoroughly at home. She and the adopted little boy get on nicely together. Maggie gets her lessons every day except Saturday. She behaves nicely in church.' Mrs McNaughton was obviously delighted with Maggie and Maggie seemed happy. She was seven when Mrs McNaughton wrote, 'Maggie is quite well. She is a great pet; she reads nicely and is learning to write and make figures. She gets on very well with her music; she sits down and practises like a little old lady.' Poor Maggie, her happiness was not to last. That year Mr McNaughton died and Maggie was much upset.

Life was obviously difficult for Mrs McNaughton and when two maiden ladies, the Misses Spencer took a fancy to her, Mrs McNaughton let her go as they said they wanted to adopt her for company and that they would continue her piano lessons. Miss Bilborough must have agreed to this for when she was ten one of the Miss Spencers wrote saying that Maggie was in good spirits and had been going to school. They intended to send her to school for four months in the year, to give her good clothes and other necessary articles. But they also wanted to know what wages were necessary. Miss Bilborough then visited her and thought all was well. She sent her a nice blue dress for Christmas, but hearing nothing from Maggie she wrote to ask if the parcel had arrived and requesting Maggie's photograph. But all was not well. The record simply says that Maggie was ill used. She was probably overworked and exploited by the maiden ladies, but whatever the cause she left and went back to Mrs McNaughton.

But Mrs McNaughton couldn't keep her and Maggie returned for the second time to Marchmont. Maggie's fourth home was with a Presbyterian Minister and his wife who had two small boys of their own. They wrote that she had been attending school, but had met with some rough children who were spoiling her. Mrs Pearson, who was a teacher, said she had taken over Maggie's education herself and taught her at home and declared that she was doing 'better than at school'. It was perhaps more convenient for the Pearsons to have Maggie at home to keep an eye on their own two small sons. But Maggie was luckier than some, for her former foster mother seems to have been genuinely concerned about her welfare and wrote frequently asking for news of her. Miss Bilborough, visiting her when she was thirteen, reported that 'she was a strong fine looking girl in a good home where there are two small children of whom she is very fond'. A photograph taken at this time and one taken when she was eighteen show a good looking and quietly confident girl. The visitor from Marchmont did not see much of her on that last occasion because 'she was entertaining some young friends'. Two years later she married and the record in the Marchmont book ends. Was she one of the lucky ones, who, in spite of all the changes she had to face in her childhood, was able not only to survive, but to find happiness?

Throughout her record mention is made of a Miss Susan Jackson who sent Maggie presents through Miss Bilborough and to whom Miss Bilborough sent the photos and letters she received from Maggie. Was she Maggie's real mother, the one who gave her up entirely? It does not seem from the record that Maggie ever knew who sent her the nice blue dress for Christmas or that the photographs she had taken, at Miss Bilborough's request, were being sent on to someone else.

It was while Annie Macpherson was speaking at the Mildmay conference, an annual gathering of leading evangelicals, that she was approached by Alexander Balfour, a wealthy shipowner from Liverpool. He had helped found an orphanage for the children of seamen and had become greatly concerned at the plight of the homeless and destitute children of Liverpool. Ever since the Irish famine, when the population of Liverpool had been swollen by an influx of over 80,000 Irish families, there had been a steady flow of immigrants from across the sea, adding to the misery of those already there without money or work.

Annie's work had already grown so greatly in 1872 that she wisely said her hands were full and referred Mr Balfour to her sister Louisa. The challenge presented by Balfour was no easy one, but Louisa Birt agreed to go to Liverpool and explain to the Law Association the methods and objects of the work that she and her sister were carrying out in London. As a result of this talk a society was formed in Liverpool for the immediate admission of homeless children and children who had been cruelly treated, deserted and neglected. Mr Stephen Williamson, the Member of Parliament for Liverpool and a business colleague and friend of Alexander Balfour, became the first president; John Houghton gave premises in Byron Street; Louisa Birt agreed to become the home's first superintendent and it was opened on 1 May 1873. One cannot but feel the greatest admiration for Louisa. Annie's whole life had, in a sense, been a preparation for the work she was now doing. Determined, practical, her hair parted in the centre and pulled back in a bun, she looked the part, her formidable assurance softened by a certain kindliness of expression. Louisa on the other hand could have expected to have enjoyed a more leisured life. A photograph taken in 1870 shows her gently smiling, her beauty undimmed by tragedy and illness, her hair softly falling on her shoulders. Yet although the Liverpool Sheltering Home was in one of the worst areas of Liverpool, Louisa bravely took up residence.

Louisa was lucky with her committee, who were both wealthy, influential and committed. Mrs Williamson, wife of the president, was the daughter of the Rev. Thomas Guthrie, well known as the founder of the original Industrial Ragged School in Edinburgh. Many of Dr Guthrie's children had been sent to Annie for her to emigrate to Canada. Samuel Smith, another wealthy Liverpool merchant who, ten years later, when he was a Member of Parliament, was to press hard for the extension of juvenile emigration, was one of Louisa's staunch supporters and a member of the committee of the Sheltering Home.

Until now, although Canadians, both at official level and as private individuals, welcomed the arrival of the child emigrants, the initiative for finding the children and selecting those whom it was thought would benefit from the opportunities open to them in Canada, had been confined to individuals from the mother country interested in the problems of child destitution. Encouraged by the Canadian government, through grants and free travel facilities, to bring children to Canada, it was Annie Macpherson and Maria Rye who had to bring the children and find them homes. Louisa Birt doubtless thought that she would send her children to Canada under the auspices of the Home of Industry, and was probably surprised to receive a direct request from Colonel Wimburn Laurie asking if she would bring a party of children to Halifax. He offered to take full responsibility for placing them and supervising them afterwards.

John Wimburn Laurie had been newly appointed inspector of the militia in Nova Scotia and when every farmer was so desperately short of labour it was doubtless difficult for him to secure sufficient recruits. It therefore made good sense to encourage the emigration of children who could undertake some of the work on the farms, thus releasing men for other duties. Laurie himself had come from England but he now had a large estate about fifteen miles from Halifax and his own staff were mostly British emigrants. Laurie was also a member of the agriculture board of Nova Scotia and thus very much aware of the need for labour on the scattered farms, many of them small and desperately poor.

He was able to tell Louisa Birt that he had persuaded the provincial government to pay part of the cost and he himself guaranteed the rest. Louisa accepted his offer and sailed from Liverpool in August 1873 with a party of seventy-six children. Colonel Laurie had carefully advertised the arrival of the children all over the province so that the success or failure of the scheme could be better monitored. He was anxious that the children should be treated as individuals by the families that applied for them and was much annoyed to find that many of the families expected the children to be sent off as if they were pieces of luggage, labelled and addressed. He was determined to make the applicants realise that these were children in need of homes and families and that the transaction was a personal one. And to ensure that the children were properly treated he inaugurated a system of quarterly reporting, something which no other emigrating organisation could emulate. In three years Louisa was able to place nearly six hundred children on farms in Nova Scotia; then suddenly Laurie gave up the work leaving the children with no one to turn to and no home to come to if they were turned off for being too small or because they were considered inept by the farmer. They joined the band of unsupervised children Maria Rye had already placed out in the Maritime Provinces. Maria had left two friends vaguely in charge of their welfare, but they soon found themselves unable to cope with all the problems that inevitably arose, for there was nowhere for rejected children to go to, and the government of Nova Scotia firmly refused Maria's request to provide a home for those returned as unfit. The literature put out by the emigration societies extolling the virtues of 'Life in the Land of the Maple Leaf' must have seemed a cruel travesty of the truth to some of those children left to fend for themselves in that tough country.

The Sheltering Home itself lost track of many of the children, sometimes for good reason as in the case of a child called Kate Simpson, who was 'taken for adoption to fill the place of a lost daughter and has been loved accordingly. Her name has been changed. In the family there is no allusion to her not being always here therefore she does not like anything being said about it,' and there were no further visits or reports.[20]

The four Keen children were among an early party of children sent to Nova Scotia. Emily, who had been adopted, died of consumption, but her sister Ellen appears to have done well with her family, who wanted to take her with them to the United States. The entry in the record book reads: 'Wrote to say we could not allow Ellen to go to the States with her family. Another place engaged. They took her without our leave. Have written that she must be returned.' But Ellen was not returned as is made clear by letters from her two brothers, Henry and Edward Keen, who had both been sent to farms. Edward wrote to the Liverpool Sheltering Home some years later offering to pay up to $25 for information which would enable him to find his sister.

Mary Currin was seven when she was sent to Canada. Years later she wrote from Montreal:

> I do not know if this letter will find you after all these years and I do not know if you will remember me, but I think if you would kindly oblige me, Mary Currin, by looking in your record books you might be kind enough to tell me something about my people. What I mean is was I a Legal born child or please, who put me in the Home and why? Did they know the truth about myself. It is very hard to be as I am. . . .
>
> I am now going on thirty-nine years as I think, and I don't even know my birthday and I have had a pretty lonesome life. I was adopted on a farm when I was young and I left them years ago. I don't think they treated me right. In fact the woman who adopted me used to abuse me and that was why I left her.[21]

The report on this child, three years after she had been placed, reads 'Happy and loved in a good home'. But the letter continues:

> and each time you came to see me she was afraid I would tell on her and take me from her. I often wished afterwards that I had told you.

But there was no one who could tell Mary anything at the Liverpool Sheltering Home, and perhaps no one had ever known the answer to her question.

Five

A SETBACK FOR MISS RYE

I cannot believe that any Board of Guardians in the Kingdom, when informed of the condition and results of Miss Rye's present system, would ask you to sanction the emigration of another child under it.

ANDREW DOYLE to the President of the Local Government Board 1877

WITHIN four years the numbers of children being sent to Canada by Maria Rye and Annie Macpherson had grown to such a degree that it is hardly surprising that doubts began to be voiced in England as to the wisdom of placing out children on such a large scale so far from home. It was not only the Islington Board of Guardians who had been disturbed, other Boards of Guardians had had girls returned to them when they were discovered to be pregnant, and there were dark rumours that some of the children were being cruelly treated and exploited. By 1874 Maria had sent out over eight hundred pauper children and Annie about half as many. The Local Government Board was spurred into action when a question was asked in the House of Commons as to whether it was intended to follow up and inspect the children who had been placed out in Canada at the ratepayers' expense. No concern was expressed about the children who went to Canada solely under the aegis of the voluntary organisations.[1]

The Local Government Board chose one of their most senior officials, Andrew Doyle, to inquire into the system of emigration of pauper children to Canada under the supervision of Miss Macpherson and Miss Rye. It is hard to conceive of two characters more diametrically opposed than Doyle and Rye. Andrew

Doyle had been trained as a barrister and had spent twenty-seven years of his life in the civil service. He was sixty-five and had an orderly, disciplined approach to life based on a lifetime's work in government administration. He was a firm upholder of the virtues of the workhouse system and was known to favour workhouse education and training for the children rather than the boarding-out system. Even before he set foot in Canada it was not difficult to predict that there would be trouble between him and the imperious, mercurial Maria Rye who made a virtue out of her informal methods, telling her supporters that they should be grateful for even the most limited reports, so pressed was she for time and so exhausted by her responsibilities.

Doyle's brief was to investigate the work of Miss Rye and Miss Macpherson and to discover how pauper children came to be included in the emigration parties, how they were collected and sent to Canada, how they were received in Canada and how placed out. He was to investigate the homes the children were sent to and to evaluate the extent of the supervision exercised over the children. It was a tough assignment for a man of his age and habits, and he admitted to finding the task difficult and laborious. During the six months that he was in Canada, Doyle managed to visit about four hundred children. Unlike the inspection that was undertaken in South Africa, he had no assistants to help him and sometimes had to drive over forty or fifty miles a day through rough country to see half a dozen children. He said he thought it wise not to confine his visits to pauper children alone, and confessed that if he had done so he would have missed 'many striking examples of success'.[2]

He found that the great majority of Miss Macpherson's children were destitute and came from the streets and orphanages: of the eighteen hundred she had brought to Canada, only four hundred were from the workhouse. While Maria Rye advertised her scheme, sent circulars and spoke to Boards of Guardians, undertaking to look after the girls she had placed in service until they were eighteen years of age, Annie Macpherson only took workhouse children at the request of the Boards of Guardians.

As would be expected, the report was comprehensive and factual, but the greater part was taken up with an indictment of the system as it was operated. However, Doyle did not entirely damn the idea of juvenile emigration, and thought that the system could benefit the children if they were sent out at a much earlier age. It is perhaps typical of the official mind that Doyle's first and last complaint was that the children taken from the workhouse were not differentiated from the children taken from the streets. The workhouse child, he argued, had received some education and training, while many of the children taken from the streets had run wild all their lives and a few months in the care of Miss Rye or Miss Macpherson would not change their habits. Furthermore, he claimed, and with justification, that they were stigmatised by their benefactors, being referred to as 'guttersnipes', 'waifs and strays' and 'street arabs', ignoring the fact that the 'pauper taint' which clung to the workhouse child was every bit as damaging. The informality of the Canadian procedures clearly shocked Doyle: the child from the streets did not even have the protection of being taken before a magistrate to make a formal declaration agreeing to go to Canada and he noted that there appeared to be nothing in either the laws of England or Canada to prevent any person of philanthropic or speculative turn of mind raising money and shipping such children to Canada and through Canada to the United States.

Doyle had a quick ear for dialogue and his report is illustrated with some telling phrases from the children he questioned. Beginning at the start of the journey he thought the children were sent out in parties that were too large, as many as 150 of Miss Rye's girls being in the care of a single matron. They were packed into the restricted space reserved for emigrants and unable to get in or out of their bunks unaided in heavy seas. As one of them later reported 'we all sicked over each other'. It was no wonder they arrived in a filthy and neglected condition.

He next visited all three homes belonging to Annie Macpherson and 'Our Western Home'. Far from being the 'homes of love' claimed by Annie, he found they offered the children no training before placement; they could not provide an adequate refuge for children who were ill or unhappy in their situations; and he singled out Maria's home in Niagara as an example of the way in which children were occasionally ill-treated. Citing the case of a girl whose second mistress had said of her 'you couldn't hire that girl to tell a lie', he found she had been returned to Miss Rye for bad temper and recorded by Miss Rye as having a 'violent temper'.[3] As a result she was locked up in a room at the top of the house and kept in solitary confinement for eleven days 'upon bread and water, with no book or work to divert her thoughts. The only persons she saw during that time were the child who brought her her bread and water allowance, and Miss Martin, who used to ask her if she had received it.' If that child's statement was true, he said that there should be regulations to 'put it out of the power of any irresponsible person to do so grievous a wrong to a child for any offence whatever'.

Neither Miss Macpherson nor Miss Rye knew enough of the homes to which they were sending the children, and he thought the 'recommends' so much relied on by both ladies had little real value. One farmer's wife told Doyle that her minister 'may know that ours is a respectable family – but I guess he can know very little about my being fit to bring up a child'. As for there being adequate supervision he accepted that Miss Macpherson had intended to see that every child was visited but said the original intentions had been abandoned and that emigration had outgrown its capacity to cope with superintendence. As for Miss Rye, 'she trusts to the accident of being able to find persons in different districts who will relieve her from the responsibility, not only of finding suitable homes, but of looking after the children when they are placed in them'.[4] Doyle found that a few of the children who were adopted, especially the younger ones, were fortunate, but the idea that children were adopted out of 'religious feeling' was in general far from the truth. They were wanted on account of their services and their future usefulness, it being 'as easy to feed a child as a chicken' in Canada, as one of the farmers told Doyle. One shrewd girl told Doyle bluntly, ''doption Sir, is when folks get a girl without wages'. Doyle said he did not mean to imply that the 'adopted' child fared worse than the farmer's own child on the whole, but that the Canadian farmer is 'often an exacting and unthoughtful master. Bound to make the most of his short season, he works through the seed time and harvest from daylight to dark, and expects every hand that is capable of work to do the same.'[5]

As for the terms under which the children were indentured to service, Doyle wrote, 'the whole machinery of indentures, though it has a look of being businesslike, appears to me to be worthless or delusive. To the employer it affords no security for the service of the child; to the child it affords no protection so long as there is no efficient agency to see to the fulfilment of conditions'.[6] Finding one visit to Canada an exhausting business, Doyle marvelled at the energy of both ladies. He noted that in 1873 Maria Rye had sent over and placed 190 children in three parties, had travelled 6,000 miles by rail visiting children, crossed the Atlantic three times, returning to England on the last occasion 'to dive into your slums and the sins and sorrows of your great cities', as she graphically expressed it. Doyle followed this up by remarking drily, 'It is amazing how these ladies can undergo such extraordinary toil; still more amazing how they can express so much confidence in the immediate and ultimate results of a system of which they can personally know so little.'[7]

The final pages of Doyle's report were concerned with the delicate question of Miss Rye's and Miss Macpherson's pecuniary interest in the emigration of pauper children. Suspicions had been raised in the Canadian press on the subject. The emigration expenses of pauper children and children from the streets were so mixed up that it would be difficult to separate them, as Doyle acknowledged, but he would be prepared to undertake the strict audit that would be necessary to clear up the question, if the ladies desired it. As things stood, taking into account the assisted passages given by the Government, the free railway travel, the assistance given by the Government of the Dominion and the Province of Ontario, the cost of conveying a pauper child from Liverpool to its destination in Ontario could not exceed one-third of the sum paid on that account by the Guardians; in other words, there seemed to be a clear gain of five pounds per head on every pauper child taken to Canada by Annie Macpherson and Maria Rye. Annie Macpherson came in for additional reproof for asking her children to repay their passage money, allowing them to contribute six to seven pounds when the assisted passage money came to half.[8]

Doyle's final recommendations reflect his own personal prejudices. His belief in the positive value of the workhouse system for the training of pauper children was certainly a very proper one for the Chief Inspector of the Local Government Board, but it was not one shared by many who were increasingly concerning themselves with the welfare of the destitute child. Nor, can it be said, did his experience in that capacity equip him to appreciate the opportunities Canada had to offer, for he had shown no enthusiasm for boarding-out children even within their own parishes, so was almost bound not to favour a system which removed children so far from those who were legally responsible for their welfare. However, his training did enable him to pinpoint the very serious defects in the system as it had come to be operated.

What made Doyle's report such a powerful document, was his understanding of the children's predicament and his evident sympathy with them. If he had his way no pauper children would be sent overseas but if Boards of Guardians were determined to emigrate their children, then let them be sent as young as possible. Doyle recommended that they should not be older than seven or eight years so they would remember little of their former lives and adapt more easily to their new surroundings. Girls between nine and fifteen had no other option but to go into service, and Doyle was remarkably perceptive in realising how uninviting this could be when the work was hard and the child was friendless. He said he had 'often been painfully struck in speaking to children of that age with the sense of loneliness manifested by them' and he realised from talking to employers how long it took for the children to get over their feelings of homesickness. He did accept, though, that when they could be completely adopted into families there was no question as to the advantage of sending them to Canada.

Doyle also recommended that the children should have an extensive period of training in Canada before being placed out, an idea that was to be taken up more than thirty years later by a young idealist from Rhodesia, Kingsley Fairbridge. He thought that for the right type of boy Canada was a country of great opportunity, but for them, as much as for the girls, there must be much more careful placement and supervision. His final plea was that a distinction should be made between 'arab' and pauper children. Although admitting that workhouse children were sometimes referred to as 'the refuse of the workhouse', the 'arab' children were relentlessly portrayed as the offspring of thieves and vagabonds, just swept from the streets, which tended, he argued, to prejudice their position in service. And he quoted the story of one girl who had left her place because 'I was not going to be told that I was glad to come to Canada, for I was half starved, and was picked off the streets of London, and my parents were drunkards.'

Doyle's report was not a document that could be ignored – nor was it. Reaction on both sides of the Atlantic was strong. *The Times*, recognising the factual accuracy of Doyle's charges, called for the report to be accepted, while the Canadian response was almost uniformly hostile to Doyle. There was widespread newspaper comment throughout Ontario and in the Maritime Provinces.[9] Canadians realised the seriousness of the implications in the report for themselves as a nation. Thirty-five years earlier the governor of Cape Colony had expressed pained indignation at the need for an investigation into the conditions under which child apprentices from England were living, because such an investigation necessarily called into question the bona fides of the colonists who had taken on such children. Cape Colony didn't need child labour so Napier was able to recommend that no more children should be sent to South Africa. This was an option which the Canadians did not wish to take up. They needed the children. Doyle's implication that Canadian homes and Canadian family life were not necessarily superior, and that conditions were not always to the children's advantage, rankled.

In March 1875 the Local Government Board decided to suspend the emigration of pauper children. The Canadian Government also acted with speed and set up a Commons select committee on immigration which reported in June of the same year. Maria Rye and Annie Macpherson were both called to make statements as were numerous Canadians involved in the work. Miss Macpherson was the first to give evidence and she was listened to with approval. Maria Rye arrived in fighting mood saying she had come to protest against Mr Doyle's 'unjust, ungenerous and most inaccurate report'.[10] She admitted that she did not attempt to keep a detailed account of the work and freely stated that the accounts were the weakest part of her organisation, but that other and more important work kept her from keeping the books as they should be kept. Turning to Doyle's more specific allegations she gave detailed answers, stating in the case of the girl 'who could not be hired to tell a lie' that the girl had been returned to her a fortnight after Doyle had seen her for 'slapping her mistress's face'[11]. This was an unruly and intractable child and she had put her on bread and water for two or three days, not eleven as Doyle had stated. 'Anyone who knew anything of the training of children of this class would admit that punishment of some kind was necessary in certain cases.' Besides answering questions Maria put in a large number of letters of support from friends expressing astonishment and dismay at the way 'her good works' had been 'evil spoken of' by Mr Doyle. She also put in several pages of notes rebutting charges Doyle had made.

It is scarcely surprising that the select committee reported favourably on the work of emigration, saying that the information that had been gathered was:

> . . . sufficient to establish that the work which has been done by Miss Macpherson and Miss Rye is, on the whole, of a satisfactory character; and that it results, with very little exception, in the permanent advantage to the children who are brought out, and to the country which receives them.

It did, however, agree that the provincial governments should be given the responsibility of investigating the condition of the children. Doyle's report would thus be superseded by later Canadian reports. Nor was the committee later disappointed in its expectation that these reports would be favourable: the great majority of the children were judged to be doing well, and the few children who failed were deemed unimportant exceptions to the general success of the scheme.

Doyle, whose voice was to be the only one raised in protest at a system which sent young children overseas without proper regard to their welfare, was vigorously attacked by the Canadian press. The most vicious attack was made by the editor of the *Ottawa Free Press* who called Doyle 'an itinerant dead beat' and accused him of seeking to create a lucrative job for himself, writing that, 'he paid a visit to Canada, we have no doubt, with the express intention of reaping to himself pecuniary profit out of an agitation which he had initiated in the old country against the benevolent work of Miss RYE and others ... we do know that the report which he made to the British Government is not only false in fact, but, as we have proven before a Committee of our own Parliament, utterly without the slightest foundation.'[12]

Doyle's work for the Local Government Board was another weapon used against him. In the same editorial in the *Free Press* Doyle was not only accused of aiming to secure for himself a 'fat salary'; he was accused of wanting 'the privilege of inspecting the homes of Canadians, who are generous enough to welcome the waifs and strays of the motherland, and who do not wish, and who will not permit any taint of the old country poor law taint to make bitter the sweetness of their generosity'. The newspaper articles reflected a rejection of anything approaching the British workhouse system and wanted little if any government intervention. *The Globe* said Doyle had no faith in the good instincts of the human heart, and 'if he had his way, Canada would be pock pitted with beadles looking after immigrated children'.[13] In another article the dangers of introducing such a system were spelled out. The *Montreal Gazette* thought that if government inspectors took over responsibility for the children no one would want to become involved with them. 'The whole system would be reduced to a system of espionage, and no one would be bothered with the children when having them involved the inspection of their homes and household management on the part of government officials.'[14]

It is remarkable that there seems to have been absolute acceptance of the fact that thousands of children were destitute in the mother country; there was no questioning of the workhouse system or protest at the conditions in which the 'arab' children lived. The Canadian press reflected the same attitude as the upper classes in Britain: such children ought simply to be grateful for the chance of coming to Canada, regardless of what happened to them once they had arrived. There was no criticism of Canadians who hired children for work, and the importation of young children for their labour was seen as perfectly normal and reasonable. A long article in *The Globe* reflects this view:

Almost any change would be for the better, and the change which has been effected through the efforts of Miss Rye and others in the case of the vast majority of their little protégés has been as life from the dead. Of the seventeen hundred girls who Miss Rye has brought to this continent, not more than twenty or thirty have, as far as is known, turned out what could be said to be badly, while a very great number, indeed, are in circumstances of the greatest comfort and happiness.[15]

This sanguine assessment of the emigrated children's lives led the paper to campaign for a continuation of the system.

At a very moderate expense, these children are taken from positions the most unpropitious to those in which they can have a fair chance. The cost of their keep for a few months in the workhouses of England will defray all the expense of placing them in western homes, where they are needed, welcomed, and in the vast majority of cases well cared for. Why then should the work not go on? If the workhouse authorities or the British Government wish official superintendence, by all means let there be anything of the kind that will satisfy them. But, in the meantime, while they are debating what the supervision shall be, and how it is to be instituted there surely ought to be no suspension of a work in connection with which there has been no case of proved abuse, but very many of undoubted success and unalloyed blessing.

Maria Rye had been overwhelmingly successful in persuading Canadian public opinion as to the the virtues of her work, but she was, in a sense, pushing against an open door: Canadians wanted to be persuaded. But back in England Doyle was proving to be a much more formidable opponent. Without pauper children to make up her parties Maria Rye was forced to suspend work, and she sent no children to Canada for two years. Annie Macpherson, on the other hand, simply refused to take any workhouse children to Canada, and although this somewhat diminished the size of her parties, her work continued without interruption. Apart from her statements to the Canadian Commission, Annie made no public reply to Doyle's criticisms and continued serenely with her work of rescue. Many of her friends regretted that her work had not been considered separately from that done by Maria, and the accusations of pecuniary benefit were particularly resented. Many of her workers, like Miss Bilborough, gave their services free and Annie's accounts were published regularly. With the exclusion of the workhouse children her accountability to anyone other than her own supporters disappeared, and the suspicions raised by Doyle appear to have reinforced her decision at that time not to accept money from Boards of Guardians to emigrate their children.

Maria Rye was not going to allow Doyle's report to stand unchallenged in the history books. She, too, wrote officially to the president of the Local Government Board and her letter was published in 1877.[16] The letter was written in Maria's usual vein; she pointed to the immensity and rightness of the work she was doing; a lone woman struggling to carry on such a mammoth task could not be expected to keep records at the same time. Her letter was defensive and at times sanctimonious: 'The great glory of all true work is in the keeping of His Commands; there is the reward, and a thousand Mr Doyles could not touch me on that point.'

She did not see why children needed to be inspected when the class of Canadian men and women with whom the children were placed was 'substantial, orderly, comfortable and well established'. She admitted she had no 'set plans, no sharply defined policy about overlooking the children in Canada' and asked plaintively, 'Am I to be condemned and my work derided on that account?'[17] Believing attack to be the best method of defence she went on to quote the figures relating to the reformatory and industrial schools to show that, according to *The Times*, in 1876 hundreds of children had absconded and died. She continued, 'yet on paper these schools are perfect, their rules faultless, their expenses monstrous, their inspectors and officers numberless, their results – well their results are nil! and that I believe owing to the great multiplication and to the elaboration of the rules that govern them'.

Having disposed of the question of supervision to her own satisfaction she turned her attention to other matters Doyle had raised. She found it a little more difficult to explain away the fact that some twenty-eight children under fifteen had been lost sight of and that sixteen workhouse girls at least had had illegitimate babies. In seeking to account for these facts she identified what she called 'Freedom Fever' in children of fifteen and sixteen and in a very feminine way wrote that the children were 'just as foolish as you and I were at their age and just as unreasonable'.

She claimed that her scheme had already found imitators and mentioned 'Messrs Macpherson and Bilborough' among others, but she did admit that she was under-officered and that her accounts were badly kept. However, far from being put down by Doyle's criticisms as to the apparent discrepancy in income and expenses, she boldly stated that if she was to continue, as she very much wished to continue and devote herself only to girls, then Boards of Guardians should give her twelve pounds instead of eight to enable her to build another home for those girls who proved refractory.

As for the children being homesick, Maria Rye would have none of that. To prove her point she described how on one occasion when the ship was leaving the Mersey and slowly steaming away, 'while all the other passengers were waving their handkerchiefs and raising a true English cheer for the dear old land they were leaving, my large crowd of workhouse children took up the strain from the other passengers almost before it had ceased, and burst out into a long, loud and terrible groan, and three groans for England were raised before I had power to gain silence'.

Doyle's answer was published six months later.[18] Maria with her vague generalisations and sweeping statements had laid herself open to attack. Doyle, now retired and living at his home in North Wales and no longer bound by the terms of his previous assignment, was free to comment as he pleased and he took full advantage of the fact. Doyle, in his original report, had been almost as critical of Annie Macpherson as he had of Maria Rye. All this was changed now. While stating, 'I am still of the opinion that no pauper children ought to be sent to Canada under Miss Rye's present system'[19] he said that Annie Macpherson 'appears to have placed her system of juvenile emigration on such a footing as to entitle it to the support of all persons who take an interest in the welfare of the most helpless poor; the destitute and neglected children, girls as well as boys, who swarm in such localities as her "Whitechapel Home"'.[20] Why Doyle changed his mind about Annie Macpherson is not known, but he was full of praise for her work and wrote approvingly that her wide and varied experience in Canada had led her to the conclusion that the strictest personal supervision is absolutely indispensable. To underline yet again the difference between the work of the two ladies he wrote that under Miss Rye's scheme, 'there is a total lack of supervision and that consequently children are exposed to suffering and wrong for which they get neither relief nor redress'.[21]

His desire to make amends to Annie led him to upbraid Maria for what might be seen as a trivial matter, her use of the term 'Messrs Macpherson and Bilborough', when referring to Annie and her friend Ellen. 'This style of reference', wrote Doyle severely, 'might lead you to think it was a mere trading firm ... Miss Macpherson and Miss Bilborough are ladies, engaged, and very earnestly engaged in missionary and emigration work ... the senior partner being Annie Macpherson, the familiar name that is as much and as deservedly respected as it is widely known in the Dominion to which she is so true and disinterested a benefactor; the other (Ellen Bilborough) a patient, unostentatious labourer in a work of charity, to which she gives not merely her private means, but the most zealous personal services, guided by good feeling, intelligence and admirable judgement.'[22]

Maria never pretended to supervise her children methodically, but she did claim to keep track of them through correspondence. Doyle must have felt a certain satisfaction in being able to demonstrate how very misleading her written reports could be. Elizabeth Lynes had been taken from the Wolverhampton workhouse and placed with a Mr W. McKeel of Greenwich in New Brunswick. The report read, 'Remained with the same family until 1873 when returned to England. Did well while there.' On his return from Canada Doyle looked up the girl and found that Elizabeth, now aged fifteen, was in the able-bodied women's ward of the Wolverhampton workhouse awaiting the confinement of an illegitimate child. In the presence of the master of the workhouse, Elizabeth told her story to Andrew Doyle. She was taken from the workhouse with other women and children by Maria Rye in 1870 and landed at St John's. After a week at some institution she was sent up country to service with a farmer named McKeel. While she was there she was often and severely beaten by her mistress's children. When she wrote to her brother complaining of this her mistress took possession of the letter and told her she was not allowed to write to anyone without first submitting the letter to her. When she was fifteen she was seduced by her master's son and when her pregnancy was discovered she was taken by her master and put on board a steamer, her passage having been paid. She was sent back to Liverpool, with a few dollars in her pocket, to find her way back to the workhouse from which she had been taken 'to be looked after until she was eighteen'.

Maria knew well enough how to portray herself in the role of guardian angel to small children. An engraving in the *Canadian Illustrated News* depicts her in a shell-like boat, surrounded by little girls, approaching the Canadian shore. But Doyle well knew there was also a hard mean streak in Maria's nature. He published her letter to Mr Barclay ostensibly to show how little she cared for the welfare of her girls when they got into difficulties. The letter also revealed Maria to be petty and vindictive.

Charlotte Williams had been placed in service with a farmer, a friend of Miss Rye's, where she remained for three years. When it was discovered that she was pregnant she was turned adrift and was found by a Mrs Barclay in the poorhouse in Buffalo. Mrs Barclay took it upon herself to write to Maria expressing regret 'that although rightfully dismissed, some shelter had not been found for the orphan girl other than an American poorhouse'. Her husband received a stinging rebuke from Maria who did not like being told how to look after her children. It was obviously not the first time Mrs Barclay had had cause to write to Maria.

Sir,
Are you aware that your wife is constantly interfering and annoying me with absurd letters concerning matters about which she really knows nothing? Will you kindly tell me how long I am to bear this nonsense, and why I am subjected to this interference? The last letter I have received is about a girl named Charlotte Williams aged nearly eighteen. If Mrs Barclay thinks I am to turn my Home into a bad house for the reception of such girls during their confinements, all I can say is, she must think so, for I certainly shall never do it; and if Mrs Barclay instead of writing insulting letters to me, repeating village gossip, would open a Home for the 'Orphan' and the 'fatherless' about whom she so pathetically writes, I think it would be much more to the purpose and probably you will let me send her the next such case that I hear of. At any rate, I am thoroughly ashamed of anyone,

who like your wife, can make a profession of Christianity and yet be so wickedly spiteful and malicious as she is to . . .

Yours truly, Maria S. Rye.

P.S. I just remember that we have in the Home an incorrigible 'orphan and fatherless' girl, for whom we have found ten good homes. On my return to Niagara I shall send her express to Mrs Barclay, and no doubt she will be delighted to welcome her.[23]

The incorrigible orphan and fatherless girl whom Maria Rye threatened to send to Mrs Barclay was one of the girls from the Birmingham workhouse, which Maria visited in 1871, when she spoke to the girls collectively. E.M.'s record at the workhouse showed both her conduct and her intelligence to be indifferent. None the less Maria accepted her and took her to Canada where she was 'bound for service'. She was swiftly returned as 'too young, dirty and obstinate'. Her record shows that she was sent to nine more places, in one of which she was kept just twenty-four hours. She had been in hospital in Toronto and examined 'as to the state of her brain and not considered bad enough for confinement'. The girl was at the home in Niagara and Maria wrote of her, 'either an incorrigibly naughty girl or else a semi-lunatic; such a girl should never have been allowed to emigrate'.

Doyle used E.M.'s story to demonstrate that Maria Rye was more interested in getting hold of workhouse children to make up the numbers of her emigration parties than in their welfare. It may well have been also that the Boards of Guardians were only too happy to be rid of troublesome children, likely to remain a burden on the rates for years to come. What does come through strongly from this story is Maria's total lack of understanding or sympathy for the suffering that she undoubtedly caused this simple-minded child who was quite unsuited to, and unable to cope with, the demands of life in Canada as a household servant.

It is evident from Maria's letter and Doyle's reply that the argument between them had developed into something of a personal vendetta. The story of the manner in which Maria is said to have disposed of fifty of her children in London, Ontario, is an example of the way in which they tried to score off each other, Maria usually coming out the loser. In his first report Doyle had accused Maria of simply lining the children up round the walls of the town hall and giving them over to whichever farmer showed interest in them. Maria got together evidence and presented affidavits to show she had never taken children to London and that Doyle was wrong to have made such an accusation.

Alas for Maria. Doyle was able to show that the incident had taken place, although not in London. He proved that fifty to sixty children had been taken to Chatham where 'they were ranged round the Public Hall, on view, with their backs to the walls, while persons seeking them came in one by one and selected the child which he or she might happen to fancy'. As he said, 'it mattered little where such an objectionable way of disposing of the children took place, but that it should take place at all'. He accused Maria of intending to mislead by parading her affidavit hoping to give the impression that, as the transaction had not occurred in London, it had not occurred anywhere.

Doyle was also far from satisfied as to the state of Maria's financial affairs. With regard to the purchase of 'Our Western Home' he pointed out that Maria, in a letter to the Local Government Board in 1872, had stated that the monies 'which purchased and furnished "Our Western Home" came by public subscription' but since his report in 1874 Miss Rye had publicly stated that the house was not purchased for her; it was bought 'by money which I earned by writing for the press in England'. On the face of it it seems highly unlikely that in the space of two years Maria could possibly have earned over $4,000, the cost of the home, writing for the press. A more likely explanation is that the money, subscribed as a result of her letters to the press, had been appropriated by Maria as hers to use as she thought fit, and that she had bought the property in Niagara in her own name. In fairness to her it must be said that, whatever Doyle's suspicions, when she handed over her work to the Church of England's Children's Society she handed over 'Our Western Home', only keeping a smaller property nearby for her own use.

She also said, in reply to Doyle's allegations about the lack of financial information, that while he was in Canada he had refused to work on her accounts and since his departure she had accounted to the Dominion Government for all items of expenditure. It was ever Maria's way to try to play off one body against another. Unfortunately for her she had written to Doyle, 'I blush when I look at the date of your last letter, but soon after you left Canada I was sick, very sick, the reaction I suppose from over-exertion and worry of the past summer . . . since I am well again, I have been trying to make time to copy out my accounts. . . . I have not succeeded in doing so yet. . . .'

Whether Maria did fraudulently appropriate money for her own use which had been paid to her for emigrating children will probably never be known. What Doyle, through his reports, did reveal was the unsatisfactory way in which she worked. She claimed to care for the children, she took money from the Boards of Guardians, yet she brought over far larger parties than she could hope to manage, placing them out without adequate safeguards and leaving them to fend for themselves when they were ill or in trouble.

Since Andrew Doyle was to be the only person to question the whole system of child emigration in those early years, and little primary evidence in the form of letters from the children themselves has been found, his reports, with their careful factual statements, provide important documentary evidence on the effects of emigration on the lives of the children. However, it is only fair to say that he never gave any examples to show how some children benefited from their changed circumstances, although he admitted that this could be so. It is also evident, from the praise he subsequently bestowed on Annie Macpherson's work, that he believed in the positive value of emigration for some children, and went so far as to say he was sorry that Annie would no longer take workhouse children in her parties. He was, however, obviously determined, in so far as it lay within his power to prevent it, that Maria Rye should not be given any further opportunity of taking children from the workhouses to Canada.

In the same year that Doyle was reporting so adversely on the emigration movement, a delegation from Stephenson's Children's Home, led by the Rev. John Burgess, was presenting a memorial to Mr Letellier de St Just, the Minister for Immigration, asking for financial help.[24] On the advice of the Prime Minister, Sir John A. Macdonald, Burgess was given an interview with Lord Dufferin, the Governor-General, who gave his unqualified blessing to the emigration scheme, saying 'nothing could be more excellent'. The reasons that prompted the Children's Home to seek financial assistance were ones which Doyle would certainly have approved of. They wanted to train their children in farm work or some other trade before sending them to Canada; they also wanted to provide a superintendent at the home in Hamilton to visit the children. The committee of the home ended by saying that they were 'exceedingly gratified to find that, with scarcely any exception, the boys and girls already sent out are doing well, and giving great satisfaction to their employers'. As a result of this request the Canadian Government agreed to pay a bonus of $2 per head for children, other than workhouse children, brought to Canada by voluntary organisations, which gave a further fillip to the emigration of destitute children.

While Maria was temporarily silenced, Annie went on quietly with her work. At this time the voluntary organisations were taking about five hundred children between them across the Atlantic annually. Not even the accident to the Allan Line ship *Sardinian* at Lough Foyle in 1878, when an explosion in the coal bunker caused fire to break out, affected the rhythm of Annie's emigration parties. The *Sardinian* had to be towed into shallow water and the sluices opened to bring the flames under control. *The Times* noted that, 'Miss Macpherson and her little band of Canadian emigrants showed no small amount of true fortitude and heroism. Most of the children behaved nobly under the trying circumstances and exhibited much of the fruit of their careful training. They kept repeating to one another many of the sayings they had heard from Miss Macpherson about being patient, good and brave.'[25] As for Annie, she wrote making light of the disaster, describing how the sailors helped to open all the wetted boxes which had been submerged for two days and how the ship looked like Petticoat Lane on one of its busiest days with all the children's clothing strung out to dry.[26]

The following year Annie found herself crossing the Atlantic in the company of several members of the Canadian Government. From them she learnt about the great possibilities that would open up when the railway to the North-West was completed. Sir Samuel Tilley, Lieutenant-Governor of New

Brunswick and Minister of Customs at that time, gave her an optimistic picture of future prospects and how emigrants could benefit from the development of the railway. She wrote enthusiastically to the readers of *The Christian* of the 'hundred million acres of virgin soil ready to produce wheat for countless multitudes of people'.[27] Those who entered first would have eighty acres given to them and 'with a yoke of oxen and a plough between two families they can plough in a fortnight fourteen acres, which will raise four hundred bushels of wheat and forty acres brought into cultivation will produce twelve hundred bushels of wheat worth $1,000. These acres cultivated for five or six years will probably increase in value to about $20 per acre.' Waxing still more enthusiastic she continued, 'by that time the railways will have opened up new and still newer lands for pioneers'.

In the coming years many more were to share her view that there were unlimited benefits for the hundreds of young men who had passed through her hands and were growing up in Canada, and they would support her work to 'get the young away from our foetid, closely packed dens, where drink is ruining thousands and parents, from want of room, have to turn out their boys and girls to cater for themselves'.

Six

THE SOVEREIGN REMEDY

The Departure of the Innocents

Take them away! Take them away!
Out of the gutter, the ooze, the slime,
Where the little vermin paddle and crawl,
Till they grow and ripen into crime.

Take them away from the jaws of death,
And the coils of evil that swaddle them round,
And stifle their souls in every breath
They draw on the foul and fetid ground.

Take them away! Away! Away!
The bountiful earth is wide and free,
The New shall repair the wrongs of the Old
Take them away o'er the rolling sea.

Verses in *Our Waifs and Strays*,
August 1887 – probably by Horsley

HAD THE 1880s not brought with it such a dramatic increase in the number of the chronic poor, particularly in London, the centre of the Empire and hub of the financial world, juvenile emigration might have continued gently as it was, with a number of voluntary agencies sending no more than five hundred children a year between them to Canada and occasionally further afield to South Africa and Australia, when suitable escorts could be found. Doyle's report had temporarily nullified Maria Rye's efforts and the Local Government Board had not responded to pressure from Maria or from interested Canadians to change its policy.

All was to change in the next decade, and by 1880 the number of children sent overseas had already doubled. Various factors contributed to the crisis of the 1880s, but in so far as the East End of London was concerned the acute shortage of housing combined with the seasonal fluctuations in the casual labour market made life for the poorest one long struggle for existence. Ever since the 1840s more people had been crowding into fewer houses. The demolition of houses that had taken place to make way for the railways in the 1860s had been followed by clearance for street improvement. Further demolition had taken place for the erection of school board buildings and for the Peabody and Industrial dwellings whose rents were out of reach of the poorest. The Artisans' Dwelling Act of 1875 had totally failed to provide housing for those most in need; rents had risen and slum owners had been the only ones to benefit. The Metropolitan Board and the City Corporation treated the Act as a continuation and extension of street clearance, and while new buildings could be expected to increase in rateable value they became out of reach not only of the casual poor, who were forced to crowd into ever increasingly sub-divided slum tenements, but also of the respectable artisans who found themselves forced to cohabit with the casual poor and criminal classes. Efforts were made to encourage the working class to move to the suburbs by imposing a duty to provide workmen's trains on more railway companies through the Cheap Trains Act of 1883, but the deepening economic depression made the working class fearful of moving out of reach of possible employment and the railway companies averse to committing further capital to such an economic venture.

Overcrowding was forcing the honest poor to associate with the criminal classes and the middle class began to feel threatened by what was seen as a general spreading of lawlessness and crime. Although London's problems were special, parallel problems existed in other cities like Liverpool and Glasgow, where the continual flow of Irish migrants exacerbated the situation.

Middle-class fears were further stimulated by Andrew Mearns, a Congregational minister whose inquiry into the condition of the abject poor in 1883 caused widespread alarm. In *The Bitter Cry of Outcast London* he wrote:

The Churches are making the discovery that seething in the very centres of our great cities, concealed by the thinnest crust of civilisation and decency, is a vast mass of moral corruption, of heartbreaking misery and absolute godlessness, and that scarcely anything has been done to take into this awful slough the only influences that can purify and remove it. . . .

Often is the family of an honest working man compelled to take refuge in a thieves' kitchen . . . where there is no question that numbers of habitual criminals would never have become such, had not they by force of circumstances been packed together in these slums with those who are hardened in crime.

If overcrowding aroused fears about the spread of criminal tendencies among the hitherto respectable poor, those who were working among the children in the East End were more than ever convinced that only by removing the children completely from such conditions could they save them from growing up to swell the ranks of what came to be called 'the dangerous classes'. Thomas Barnardo, whose work for children had grown from small beginnings in 1870 to become the foremost children's charity in the country in ten short years, answered Mearns' cry with one of his own for outcast children.

To behold young men and women crowded together in pestilential rookeries without the least provision for decency and in such conditions of abominable filth, atmospheric impurity and immoral associationship as to make the maintenance of virtue impossible, is almost enough to fill the bravest reformer with despair . . . but to know that thousands of unfortunate boys and girls commence life thus and grow up to a degraded manhood and a dishonoured womanhood . . . to know this and to witness the process being repeated from day to day – to be quite certain as what it must all grow to and yet to be quite helpless to deal thoroughly with the evil, is absolutely maddening.[1]

As is clear from this, it was not only the danger of children growing up to swell the ranks of beggars and thieves and joining the criminal fraternity that alarmed the social reformers. They were equally dismayed by the moral dangers to which the children were exposed, crowded together in rooms and lodging houses. Shaftesbury, giving evidence before the Royal Commission on the housing of the working classes, made no bones about it, describing how a friend of his, going down one of the back courts 'saw on the pavement two children of tender years, of ten or eleven years old, endeavouring to have sexual connection on the pathway. He ran and seized the lad and pulled him off, and the only remark of the lad was "why do you take hold of me? There are dozens of them at it down here." '[2] As Shaftesbury said, the child was imitating what he saw others doing every day.

Shaftesbury founded the National Refuge for Homeless and Destitute Children in 1856, but apart from George Muller's well-known orphanage in Bristol, it was not until the 1870s that most of the other large children's homes were founded. Then, Barnardo, J.W.C. Fegan, Bowman Stephenson and Charles Spurgeon started homes for children in London; Leonard Shaw opened the Manchester and Salford Refuge for boys; Mrs Birt's Sheltering Home in Liverpool was founded; in Scotland William Quarrier opened a home at Bridge of Weir. Spurred on by the activities of the non-conformists, both the Roman Catholic Church and the Church of England became involved in the work of child rescue. All the big children's organisations had one characteristic in common, their desire to remove the children completely from their former surroundings, and this meant in many cases, separating them from their parents or from friends. Although nearly all the rescue societies kept their children behind high walls to prevent them being got at by undesirable parents or friends, and restricted visiting to a minimum, the danger of outside interference was a constant source of worry. Emigration removed that worry at a stroke. It was the most thorough and effective way of cutting off the past and removing the child from the evils of city life, and was correspondingly popular for that reason.

When Barnardo wrote that he was maddened at being helpless to deal thoroughly with the situation he had described, he had, in fact, taken the first steps toward so doing. He had just sent his second party of fifty boys to Canada and was to cross the Atlantic himself to lay the foundations of the biggest emigration organisation of them all. Of the hundred thousand children who were to cross the Atlantic in the next decades, a third would be sent by the Barnardo organisation. The number of Barnardo children who went to Canada in the 1880s was modest compared to the numbers who sailed at the turn of the century. At that time more than a thousand children a year were sent by Barnardo's to Canada.

Barnardo was not the only one to feel that he should enter the field of emigration on his own account; both William Quarrier and James Fegan, who, like Barnardo, had been using Annie Macpherson's emigration facilities for their children, also set up their own organisations and distributing homes in Canada at this time. Although Quarrier was the owner of a successful boot business in Glasgow, he knew from personal experience what poverty meant. His mother had been left a widow when he was a boy and his first job, aged seven, was in a pin factory, where he worked ten hours a day for a shilling a week. In 1870 he turned his attention to the needs of children and by 1879 he had moved his original orphan home from the city to a farm with about forty acres of ground near the Bridge of Weir. Quarrier had not been religious as a young man and was converted to Christianity when he was sixteen, unlike his contemporary James Fegan who was brought up as a Plymouth Brother by his parents. Schooled by his mother until he was ten, the religious influence of Fegan's early years coloured all his life. It was through his experiences as a ragged school teacher that he came to know of the plight of the destitute boys who lived round Deptford. From small beginnings he built up an organisation to shelter and train boys, many of whom subsequently went to Canada. It was Lord Blantyre who encouraged him to look at the opportunities available to boys in Canada. Fegan had the good fortune to meet William Gooderham, a wealthy citizen of Toronto, who was anxious to help him and who gave him a distributing home in George Street, Toronto.

It is not surprising that Barnardo, Quarrier and Fegan should have wanted to set up their own emigration facilities. The number of children for whom admission to the homes was sought was increasing rapidly, and unless those already accepted could be moved on fairly speedily, the rescue societies, with their limited financial resources, had no option but to refuse to take in any more children. This for Barnardo, who had announced at the start of his work that 'no destitute child would be refused admission', was an impossible situation, and one may wonder why, with his great organising ability, he had hesitated so long before setting up his own emigration scheme. He

Dr Barnardo, from a photograph taken in Toronto in 1887

had always been in favour of emigration and had sent children to Canada since the very start of his work, when he marched the lads of his shoe-cleaning brigade into Annie Macpherson's Home of Industry to join her party of emigrants. He himself said that it was because he did not want to compete in fields already so well tilled. But his work for children had involved him in controversies in the 1870s and it may well have been that he did not feel able to undertake any new developments until public confidence in his work was completely restored.

It is time to look at the work of this dynamic, dedicated, difficult and forceful man, whose work was to change the lives of so many children. By the time he died, in 1905, more than 18,000 children would have been trained, equipped, sent overseas and placed in Canada by the organisation he had founded and directed. Thomas John Barnardo was born in Dublin in 1845, the son of a Prussian father and an Irish mother. He lived with his parents over the furrier's shop in Dame Street with his brothers and sister. Both his brothers and his mother had been strongly affected by the religious revival which had swept through Ireland, and Thomas Barnardo himself experienced a deep religious conversion when he was seventeen which changed his life. Although he remained in Dublin for four years afterwards and was closely associated with the Plymouth Brethren, he found opportunities too limited in Dublin and came to London hoping to be accepted by the China Inland Mission, having been inspired by a talk given by Hudson Taylor on the work there was to be done in China.

He arrived in April 1866 and hoped that he would be sailing to China in the *Lammermuir* that summer. He was not accepted: his youthful assertiveness and somewhat overbearing manner caused Hudson Taylor to recommend that he should study at the London Hospital so as to gain valuable medical experience. He was in London during the cholera epidemic that raged through the East End all that summer and he said in later life that it was during those months that he first learnt how the poor lived. Unable to serve the Lord in China he started preaching in the streets and took over as superintendent of a small ragged school in Ernest Street. Wanting to expand his activities, impatient of authority, Barnardo quarrelled with the committee over the way in which he used the name of the school to raise funds for further work with children. Leaving the school he started his own mission which he called the East End Juvenile Mission. It was housed in two cottages in Hope Place and he had soon collected round him a band of helpers, so that when George Holland of the George Yard Ragged School Mission visited him in 1868 he wrote:

> To give some idea of the work going on, there are held weekly special services for children; Bible classes for men, women and children, mother's meetings, girls sewing classes, a special service attended every evening of the week by an average of 130 lads. A little church has been formed, numbering to this date nearly 90 souls (adults). A day school is in formation and also a Refuge, to be nearly self supporting, in which orphan lads in work will be boarded and lodged at a charge of three shillings weekly. The total weekly expenses are about £4. 10s[3].

Because Barnardo refused to get into debt the Refuge mentioned by George Holland was not opened until 1870, but the time he opened his home for boys in Stepney Causeway he had come to realise that there was so much needing to be done for children in the East End of London that he gave up the idea of joining the China Island Mission. He had been helped to make the decision by a letter from Samuel Smith, the Liverpool philanthropist, who had sent him money for his work on condition he did not hand it over and gave up any idea of going to China. At the same time Barnardo abandoned his studies at the London Hospital and left before qualifying as a doctor.

Having made the decision to stay in the East End of London and to concentrate on working with children, Barnardo's work grew rapidly. Like Peter Bedford and Shaftesbury before him, Barnardo, too, discovered that children were sleeping in the streets, a discovery which gave new urgency to his work. Although when he arrived in London Barnardo was unknown, he soon gained the confidence of the evangelical philanthropic movement and, in particular, the friendship of Richard Morgan, the editor of the influential weekly paper *The Christian*. Morgan printed Barnardo's stories of children, (as he did for Annie Macpherson). Barnardo, however, directly appealed for money to help them. As a result of the money and support he received, Barnardo was able to set up large day and Sunday schools, to enlarge the home for boys at Stepney and, most ambitious of all, to purchase the Edinburgh Castle, a gin palace in Limehouse and transform it into a coffee palace and mission church. It was this dramatic purchase of what was called the Citadel of Satan that brought Barnardo's name to the attention of those engaged in temperance reform, and when Shaftesbury agreed to perform the opening ceremony, Barnardo's position among the evangelical social reformers seemed assured. He was just twenty-seven. Not unnaturally elated by his success he let it be known that in future he wished to be known as Dr Barnardo.

Barnardo was a complex man: fired with a very real desire to serve the Lord and do His Will, he was also ambitious, relished success and had a natural gift for publicity somewhat out of keeping with the evangelical tradition of the times. Annie Macpherson, like many other mission leaders, was a follower of George Muller, the founder of the orphan homes at Ashley Down in Bristol, whose proud boast it was that his work was done in answer to prayer and that he never appealed directly for money. Barnardo recognised from the start that such methods were not for him: he was too impatient, too eager for results. Barnardo didn't hesitate to appeal directly for funds for his work. Annie Macpherson had been photographing her children and privately selling the photographs to her supporters to make known her work. Barnardo went a step further: he took pictures of his children as they entered his home dressed in rags, had them photographed again soon afterwards neatly dressed, scrubbed and clean, busily at work learning some trade, and sold them in packs of twenty for five shillings or singly for sixpence each. He appealed widely for money to support his work and the results of his appeals showed that he was not mistaken in thinking direct action was effective. By 1876 Barnardo was disposing of sums in excess of £25,000 for work which now included work to care for girls at the Village Home in Ilford. The Village had been declared open by none other than the Lord Chancellor of England, Lord Cairns, the most influential evangelical politician in England.

The support given to Barnardo by the evangelical movement was to be of crucial importance to him during the difficult period ahead. It is not difficult to see why he obtained and deserved that support. Evangelical philanthropists were a tightly knit fellowship. They had been quick to realise that it was useless to preach salvation and redemption to people who were more preoccupied with keeping body and soul together than with the question of their spiritual welfare, so they had set about relieving distress by supporting and helping a multitude of missions. It has been said that more than three-quarters of the agencies involved in voluntary charitable work in the second half of the nineteenth century were evangelical in outlook. Barnardo's brand of zealous, practical, efficient Christian work exactly fitted the need of the time as identified by the evangelical leadership. He also had the inestimable advantage that he was able to relate to the working class without seeming either patronising or remote, yet with authority.

Barnardo's success in those early years was truly dramatic. Like Maria Rye he saw no need to encumber himself with committees and a treasurer and proudly boasted of the fact that he had neither. But his confidence in his ability to manage unaided such a huge enterprise was shaken when ugly rumours started to circulate about his financial integrity, his management of the homes, his personal life, his right to the title of doctor and the way in which he used photographs of the children to gain sympathy for the homes. The rumours originated with another mission leader, Frederick Charrington, who was working in the same area of the East End as Barnardo and who resented Barnardo's greater success. Charrington, whose family owned the great brewery in the Mile End Road, had become a temperance worker as a result of seeing a drunken man beat his wife outside a public house on which the family name was emblazoned. When Barnardo put in train plans to build a second coffee palace in the Mile End Road Charrington was incensed. He regarded that area of the East End as his special preserve and he was not long in finding an ally in the shape of a disgruntled Baptist minister, George Reynolds. Reynolds depended on the subscriptions of his small congregation and when they began to leave his church to attend services at the Edinburgh Castle, he was only too willing to work with Charrington in an effort to discredit and destroy Barnardo.[4]

Barnardo was vulnerable. In his attempt to stem the mounting criticism he became involved in a newspaper controversy which only succeeded in making matters worse. Anxious that the great work Barnardo was doing should not be damaged, a powerful group of young evangelicals rallied to his defence. Led by Lord Aberdeen, who was to become Governor-General of Canada in the 1890s, they formed a committee, took over responsibility for Barnardo's work and appointed him their Hon. Director. Their first action was to investigate his financial position, and, unlike Maria Rye, his books were found to be in meticulous order with every penny accounted for, and the only complaint was over the delay in publishing the accounts.

Charrington and Reynolds were not the only people to have been disturbed by Barnardo's rapid rise. Members of the Charity Organisation Society were also uneasy at the way in which Barnardo operated. The COs, as the Society was generally known, had been founded in 1869 by people who were worried by the growth of so many charitable missions and organisations, fearing that too much indiscriminate charitable giving would undermine the smooth working of the poor-law system. They felt the proliferation of charitable work would encourage the poor to lead a thriftless way of life and would attract an increasing number of itinerant beggars to the cities where they would hope to escape the rigours of the workhouse by living off charitable relief. The COs was founded with the object of organising and controlling charities, repressing mendicity and ensuring that the poor law worked efficiently. What many of its members failed to appreciate was the simple fact that the poor-law system was unable to cope with the rising tide of destitute and homeless children. The COs particularly disliked the way in which the children's charities admitted destitute and neglected children, with no regard to the question as to whether the parents were 'deserving' or 'undeserving', and that children of 'undeserving' parents were being admitted to the homes when they should properly have been sent to the workhouse. When Reynolds, encouraged by Charrington, finally came into the open with the publication of a stridently titled document called 'Dr Barnardo's Homes: Startling Revelations', the COs, seeing their opportunity, immediately called on the Committee of Barnardo's Trustees to allow the COs to conduct an investigation.

This request was unceremoniously turned down and under the guidance of Cairns a court of arbitration was set up in June 1877 to investigate all the allegations that had been made in Reynolds' document. After four months of detailed investigation into every aspect of Barnardo's work the arbitrators finally pronounced the various Barnardo institutions to be 'real and valuable charities and worthy of public confidence and support'. The charges Barnardo had had to face had been serious. The arbitrators were lenient about his medical misdemeanours, for Barnardo had managed to become qualified as a surgeon just before the arbitration case had started. The allegations of financial dishonesty, cruelty to children and personal immorality were all shown to be untrue.

Apart from Barnardo's refusal to answer questions as to the authorship of certain letters which had appeared in the newspapers and which nearly wrecked the whole arbitration case, the one matter on which the arbitrators ruled against Barnardo was the question of the production and sale of deceptive photographs. The arbitrators ruled that 'this use of artistic fiction to represent facts is, in our opinion, not only morally wrong as thus employed, but might in the absence of a very strict control, grow into a system of deception to the cause on behalf of which it is practised'. Although Barnardo was careful to heed the warning given, fortunately he did not give up the habit of photographing his children both when they entered the home and often just before they left for Canada. The children were no longer re-dressed in their rags for the first photograph or specially posed against a suitably depressing background; the photographs were never again sold, but as a collection they remain one of the most moving and compelling of social documents.

The arbitration case marks a turning-point in the history of the evangelical philanthropic movement. Had Reynolds, who had the powerful though covert backing of the COs, been able to destroy Barnardo's work, the confidence of the public in Christian charitable work might well have been undermined. This was clearly seen by the editor of the *Daily Chronicle* who wrote:

> The publication of the Arbitrator's Award will interest a considerable number of persons. But it will interest indirectly a much larger number to whom the particular persons and institutions concerned are but names and scarcely even names. The amount of money annually entrusted to individuals for charitable distribution is so enormous, and the direct supervision exercised by the contributors is so exceedingly small, that any suspicion as to its use cannot fail to have a very disagreeable effect.
>
> On the other hand the range of these charities is so large, the good, which if properly administered, they do is so important to society, and the gap which would be left by their failure is so serious, that no one who has the social welfare of the country at heart can contemplate their restriction or enfeeblement with equanimity.[5]

Apart from undermining public confidence, it would also have given the COs much greater power. To win their case the evangelicals had had to deploy a lot of legal muscle on Barnardo's behalf. He was defended by a brilliant young Queen's Counsel, Alfred Thesiger, and the legal costs of the case came to over four thousand pounds. No struggling charity could possibly have withstood such an attack, and Barnardo only survived it because the evangelical leadership recognised the threat to Christian work and were determined to defend their right to work according to their principles.

The arbitration was a traumatic experience for Barnardo and also marked a turning-point in his life. Before it took place he had been a relatively unknown mission leader; by the time it ended he was a public personality, but no longer free to direct his work as he alone thought fit. The trustees had appointed a committee to whom Barnardo was responsible and to demonstrate his faith in Barnardo's work the austere and influential Lord Chancellor, Cairns, became the first president of the newly named Dr Barnardo's Homes. Before and during the arbitration case there had been a disastrous falling off in funds, and although the number of children admitted continued to increase, it took several years for the income of the homes to reach previous levels.

Although by the 1880s receipts had begun to improve, the increased income could not provide for the increasing numbers of children forced on to the streets by the housing crisis of the eighties. Barnardo, his shattered confidence restored, threw himself with renewed vigour into the work. He embarked on a furious campaign to raise money, completely abandoning any lingering inhibitions about the way in which he appealed for funds, arguing against those who condemned his methods as 'unworthy' or 'paltry expedients', that it was his duty to make people feel responsible, to stir them up.[6] He said his appeals were helpful to Christian life and that they were both moral and necessary. He was always quick to take advantage of the popular mood and seizing on the fears that were current about the social dangers presented by the 'casual residuum' he wrote, 'if they were ever to be drawn together by some common cry against the rich we should be in measurable distance of revolution'. He went on,

> Every boy from the gutter is one dangerous man the less. It costs only £16 to keep a child in a home and train him to become a useful citizen while the criminal in prison costs the country £80 a year. What shall it be, eighty pounds and a life lost and society's laws irretrievably violated, or sixteen pounds and a life saved, law reverenced and the deepest wounds which society bleeds from staunched.[7]

Barnardo was aware that it cost only £10 to send a child to Canada and that he would be able to fill the gap left by an emigrant child many times over. Samuel Smith, who had already intervened in Barnardo's life once, became the Member of Parliament for Liverpool in 1882. His close connection with Louisa Birt's work in Liverpool had made him more than ever convinced of the merits of juvenile emigration. He added his voice to those who were urging the Local Government Board to change their policy and allow workhouse children to be sent to Canada. The Board reversed their decision the following year and unions were once again allowed to let their children go to Canada. Smith made Barnardo a conditional offer: he gave Barnardo a handsome donation, but the money could only be used to emigrate children. Barnardo was unable to resist. With more and more destitute children clamouring for admittance, unable to seek out children as he had done in the early days, he was scarcely able to carry out his policy of unrestricted admission of the destitute. Vacancies left by the children who went to Canada would allow him to receive, at no extra cost, others still homeless and destitute.

Samuel Smith offered the same inducement to J. W. C. Fegan, who had started his work among destitute boys at the same time as Barnardo. Fegan's work followed much the same pattern as Barnardo's, only his work was with boys only and unlike Barnardo he never abandoned his strict Plymouth Brethren principles. Fegan, like Barnardo, accepted Samuel Smith's offer and parties of boys from the Fegan Homes went to swell the numbers of children now crossing the Atlantic. Samuel Smith remained deeply worried by the social tensions that existed within society. Writing in the *Contemporary Review* in 1885 he made clear his anxieties: 'I am deeply convinced that the time is approaching when this seething mass of human misery will shake the social fabric unless we grapple more earnestly with it than we have yet done,' and he recommended an extension of the system of industrial training together with emigration as the sovereign remedy. Those who thought like Smith saw juvenile emigration as a 'safety valve'. It was a means of reducing the dangerously high level of juvenile unemployment. By relieving the country of its surplus children, who if left to eke out a miserable existence in the cities would only swell the numbers of the physically and morally degenerate poor, emigration would help to reduce the size and strength of the residuum whose very existence gave rise to exaggerated fears.

Barnardo's first party, numbering about fifty boys, sailed in the spring of 1882 under the care of Frederick Fielder, the governor of the Boys' Home at Stepney, and they went to Hamilton where Bowman Stephenson had lent them his distributing home. As expected, Fielder had no difficulty in placing the boys and the following year two more parties of boys sailed as well as a party of girls under the care of Miss Emily Morcroft. Several members of Barnardo's committee had business interests in Canada and the evangelical fellowship was world wide. It was not surprising to find Samuel Blake, a former judge and a leading member of the Anglican Church, offering to set up a committee to watch over the interests of the Barnardo emigrants. A more unexpected offer came from George Cox, then president of the Midland Railway Company, later to become a liberal senator, to place his home in Peterborough, rent free, at Barnardo's disposal. Hazelbrae, a spacious timber-framed house on the outskirts of Peterborough, was ideally situated and Barnardo regarded the gift of this home as a sign that he was meant to continue the work in Canada.

Not content to let matters rest, Barnardo decided to come to Canada himself, not merely to inspect Hazelbrae, which he had decided to use as a distributing home for girls, but to finalise arrangements between himself and a group of sympathisers in Toronto who were prepared to put at his disposal a house, 214 Farley Avenue, which was to remain his Canadian headquarters and boys' distributing home until the First World War. He had other more ambitious plans: he wanted his own training farm in the Dominion and he wanted to establish such a farm in Manitoba. Doyle in his report had recommended that if children were trained amongst Canadians on Canadian soil, in a Canadian climate and gradually accustomed to Canadian ways they would constitute one of the most valuable additions that could be made, by means of emigration, to the future available labour of the Dominion. Barnardo had certainly learnt of the new opportunities that the recently opened railroad terminal in Winnipeg opened up to emigrants, about which Annie Macpherson had already written so enthusiastically.

Barnardo opened his plan of campaign by writing to Sir Charles Tupper, the recently appointed Canadian High

Barnardo boys *en route* for Canada

Commissioner in London to ask for a grant of land on which to start such an industrial farm. Tupper, the son of a Baptist minister, had been a Member of Parliament since 1867 and was on terms of close personal friendship with Macdonald. Among other ministerial appointments he had been in charge of railways and canals and responsible for the management of the Canadian Pacific Railway, so was in a position to be particularly helpful. Barnardo's letter to Tupper marked the beginning of a new initiative in the history of emigration. In asking for a grant of land Barnardo said it would be used to establish an industrial farm, where under the supervision of a suitable bailiff, with his wife working as matron, forty or fifty lads would be trained every year. On leaving the farm they would be bound to accept any situation that was found for them. He also asked that in due course his boys might be given the same promises of grants of land which were made to all emigrants under certain conditions.

The idea of the outcast and unemployed lad from the streets of the big cities thus being given the opportunity of becoming a proud and independent farmer would command tremendous support in Britain. Barnardo was already aware, though, that unrestricted emigration had created problems for Canadians, and that the earlier unquestioning welcome given to emigrant children was no longer to be relied on. In his letter to Tupper he tried to answer the possible objections to his scheme.

> I need hardly point out the great advantages of a society like ours undertaking such work. First our lads would not be deserted and allowed to fight each one the battle for himself. In a new country like Manitoba where the weather is so very severe and where even a small amount of capital seems absolutely necessary in order to a Colonist becoming independent, it must be of the greatest possible advantage to immigrants of the class I refer to, that they should have a powerful institution as their friend who would be disposed under certain conditions, afterwards to be developed, to advance them a small capital as a loan as to enable those who are able to avail themselves of any allotment of land that would come to them as emigrants, to attempt work in the future on their own behalf.[8]

He makes the point that only the most suitable lads would be sent, 'of thoroughly approved character, without vicious habits or indeed any habits likely to be detrimental to their future'.

Barnardo ended with a typically grandiose flourish saying that 'in time our institution in Manitoba would, like those we have planted in other parts of the world, become noted for the character of its inmates and the thorough quality of the work done by them'. He was indeed anxious to include Australia and South Africa in his emigration schemes, but at the time of writing the only other institutions he had planted were in England. Barnardo wanted the best land for his enterprise and said his committee wanted the option of choice, land of first-rate quality and situated in a most favourable position. He would need between three and five thousand acres, and unless they were granted free transport by the railways from the port of embarkation he thought that any hope of establishing such a farm would be 'unlikely to materialise'. The promptness with which Tupper replied[9] to these not inconsiderable demands, saying he would be glad to co-operate, is a further indication of the desire of the Dominion Government to encourage juvenile emigration. Tupper wrote that although the Dominion Government would not be able to make available the full allocation of land, he thought, with the co-operation of the Canadian Pacific Railway, such a grant might be possible. Tupper sent Barnardo letters of introduction to John Pope, then minister of agriculture in Macdonald's government and also to the president of the Canadian Pacific Railway, who were both to be very helpful. By the time the negotiations for the industrial farm were concluded in 1887 Barnardo had secured a grant of seven thousand acres, which would in time be increased to ten thousand acres. The farm was beautifully situated on the banks of the Assiniboine River about three miles from the little town of Russell. It was partly in the valley of the river and partly on the upland prairie above so was ideal for the kind of training in mixed farming that Barnardo had in mind for his lads.

Barnardo found much to encourage him in his belief that his children in Canada would prosper. He liked the climate and he found the people hospitable. He was particularly impressed by their sobriety, and wrote, 'one great cause of the prosperity and permanent success of Canada is the widespread observance of total abstinence principles. It is a rare thing to see people in the streets under the influence of drink.' He was also favourably impressed by the active religious life and noted that, 'the kindly religious feeling of the great body of working people must be a powerful factor in the wellbeing of the whole country and should make one long that yet more of the children who have been so carefully trained in our Homes should find their future home in Canadian families'.

During his stay in Ontario he tried to see as many of his children as possible and commented afterwards,

> As may be imagined all employers were not equally pleased with the children, nor are all our children equally satisfactory in their demeanour and conduct. Sometimes a change of situation is absolutely necessary: but not infrequently, a girl, placed out at first in a situation where nothing has seemed to go well for her, has given the greatest satisfaction when removed and sent elsewhere.[10]

This was an early optimistic assessment. Although the children, who were bound under indentures, could not leave their masters and mistresses, those same masters and mistresses frequently returned the child to the home as being 'too small' or 'not strong enough' or unsatisfactory in some other way. Most girls had at least four placements with all the stress and uncertainty that constant change involved.

Barnardo had immediately realised that it was absolutely necessary for him to have an agent in Canada to oversee the work. The year after his first party of children had arrived he appointed Alfred de Brissac Owen, the son of an English Methodist minister, to superintend his work in Canada. Owen quickly became aware that juvenile immigration was no longer seen by Canadians as the unmixed blessing it had seemed in the 1870s. Adverse economic conditions in Britain had induced many people to emigrate in the hope of improving their condition. Emigration was encouraged as it was seen as one of the most effective ways of reducing the numbers of paupers and unemployed, with little or no thought given as to how the emigrants would fare in Canada: many proved to be totally unsuited to Canadian life. Canadians, not unnaturally, began to resent the idea that their country was being used as a dumping ground for the diseased, pauperised and vicious classes and this resentment spilled over and affected their attitude to the emigrant children.

The early enthusiasm for child migrants was now tinged with

a degree of anxiety. The wisdom of allowing large numbers of children to be brought into the country began to be questioned. However, the need for cheap child labour was so great that these fears had little effect on the work of the child emigration agencies. It was only after a series of scandals and tragedies in the next decade that opposition to the juvenile emigration movement was to become more widespread and more vocal.

Seven

THE SOVEREIGN REMEDY IN PRACTICE

> An empire such as ours requires as its first condition an imperial race – a race vigorous and industrious and intrepid ... remember that where you promote health and arrest disease, where you convert an unhealthy citizen into a healthy one ... you, in doing your duty, are also working for the empire.
>
> LORD ROSEBERY, 1847–1929

EVEN a random selection from the records and letters of some of the children who sailed to Canada in 1884 reveals the constant pattern of misfortune, adversity and poverty that lay behind their transformation from so-called 'waifs and strays' or 'arab children' of juvenile emigrants. Their stories also show the infinitely various ways in which they reacted to their sudden transplantation. The boys arrived in Canada in March, the girls in July while Barnardo was still in the country. I have slightly altered the names of the children, but the stories are as revealed by the records themselves.

The records of the boys are much more detailed than those of the girls. They have been carefully bound in handsome red leather volumes and contain the boys' admission stories and their photographs together with comments on their subsequent careers. Alfred Owen did a follow-up survey of this particular party of boys in 1900 to see what had become of them sixteen years later. The girls' records, giving the reasons for their admission only, are simply kept together in packets and there is little information about what befell them after they arrived in Canada, unless they themselves wrote to the homes, generally to ask for information about a relative. The later records are much more fully documented, but these, because they relate to the very beginning of Barnardo's emigration work, have a special interest. The themes that emerge would be repeated over the years.

Success and failure are to be found side by side. From the brief written record it is difficult to guess why one boy should have been able to rise above his troubles and become a promising business man, while on the following page his fellow companion is shown as having been an inmate of the Central Prison of Toronto. All had in common a background of poverty and suffering; none had escaped the trauma of a sudden parting from friends, family and familiar surroundings and the equally traumatic experience of being parted from their remaining companions in an alien land and expected to understand and adapt to a way of life which lay outside their experience.

The families who applied to take the children had their own preconceived expectations. The child was to work, to provide the farmer and his wife with an extra pair of hands at little cost. They had no understanding of how much a child might have suffered from having been suddenly uprooted from all that was familiar, nor, even if they had understood, the time to spend in helping the child to adapt to unfamiliar surroundings and strange working conditions. Living on an isolated farm where the child was neither treated as a full member of the family nor had the definite status of the hired help, was often lonely, confusing and, to a homesick friendless child, it could be a deeply depressing experience. Some children surmounted these obstacles and flourished, but many others gave vent to their feelings of frustration and despair by retreating into themselves; by what was seen as a rebellious refusal to work which caused so many to be returned to the distributing home as unsatisfactory; and some acted out their anger by ill-treating farm animals or destroying household furniture.[1] Among the boys, absconding was an immediate form of protest, an option not so readily available to girls, who showed their dissatisfaction and unhappiness by the frequency with which they had to be moved from place to place.

William Carter was described as a dark-eyed, intelligent but somewhat diminutive child when he was admitted to the Stepney Home at the request of a Mr Robinson when he was eleven and a half. Both his parents were still alive at the time, but his father, who had been a boilermaker, had become an imbecile through shock, despair and depression at losing his job. He was allowed two shillings and sixpence a week by his club. William's mother, who was described as a frail woman, tried to support the family by selling whelks in the streets. As well as her own scanty earnings from this source the union allowed her two shillings and two loaves of bread a week.

William seems to have been an unusually determined child with a great desire to get on in life. After his admission he spent two years at the Stepney Boys' Home before being chosen to join the 1884 Canada party. He was apprenticed to a Mr Duff and during his first year in Canada he offered to forfeit his wages during the winter if his employer would allow him to go to school. By the summer he had taken the second-class teacher's certificate, in spite of the papers being unusually stiff that year. It would seem that Barnardo took a personal interest in William because the record shows that he became and remained a teacher in school until he had earned enough both to repay the money Dr Barnardo had lent him and to go to the University of Toronto. By 1900 he is reported as being second-in-command at the Chatham National Bank in New York and receiving a high salary. Owen wrote of him, 'He is regarded as a promising business man. His career has been very remarkable throughout and he will probably reach a high position in the future.'

James Carver's story on the next page could hardly be more different. James was admitted to the Stepney Home following the death of his father who had been a bee-keeper. James had been employed by his father and was said to be very knowledgeable about all aspects of the business. During his father's illness he had easily managed to keep himself selling lights in the streets, and was reported as being 'a boy of nice disposition, and of more than usual intelligence'. After a year at Stepney he sailed with William to Canada where he had a very chequered career. He apparently did not even try to give Mr Ventress, his first employer, satisfaction and was returned to the home. It seems that Owen recognised that he had many good points and sent him to a Presbyterian minister on trial with a view to adoption, but James absconded. He was placed with another farmer in Peterborough, but while there was convicted of having stolen a watch and sent to the reformatory at Penetanguishere, the only reformatory for boys in the Province. From there James wrote that he was getting on well with his books and that the warden had promised him $25 on discharge if he behaved himself. But the record says that even the reformatory found him difficult to manage and 'in consequence of his refractory disposition and ungovernable temper' he was transferred to the Central Prison in Toronto before being released in 1889. James was only sixteen when he was discharged from prison. Owen probably lost sight of him after that for the 1900 report simply notes that he was last heard of as 'being on the tramp'. James seems to have been unable or unwilling to adapt to life in Canada and for him the New did little to repair the wrongs of the Old.

The difference Doyle had wished to establish between the workhouse child and the child from the streets was often more apparent than real. George Lister, another of the 1884 party, had been in the Stepney workhouse with his mother for nine years following his father's death. His mother, Susannah, had tried to find work outside the workhouse, but she was unable to keep any job because of George, a situation in which many widows with children found themselves. Susannah applied to Barnardo and asked him to admit George, because unless he did, both she and the boy had no alternative but to remain in the workhouse. George was ten years old when he was admitted to the Stepney Home and two years later he and his mother were parted more permanently when it was decided that he should go to Canada. Three-quarters of his young life had been spent in the workhouse, yet technically he was a 'street child' and Barnardo received the capitation fee of $2 for bringing him to Canada.

George remained on the farm to which he was sent for five years, then, when he was seventeen and a year before his indentures expired, he simply disappeared. A note on the record sheet shows that Owen had no further information about him as he explained, 'the boy wanted to escape from control'. Three years later Owen heard that he had left the land and was employed in a firm of commission agents in Toronto. George had made contact with the organisation again because he wanted infor mation about his mother and a married sister. By 1925 George had become a widower with two boys aged fifteen and seventeen and a daughter of twenty-two. He wrote to the homes with his own assessment of his time in Canada. He thought his life had been very successful; he had never drunk much; he owned a house of his own and had some land in Toronto.

Two boys, William Ellis and John Masters, simply couldn't settle in Canada. Within eighteen months William had saved up enough money to pay for his return ticket to England and no more is known of him after his return. On the other hand John, who had been admitted to the homes in 1883, had done so well in Canada that by 1886, when he returned to England, he brought with him a considerable sum of money. However, he is next reported as being destitute in London, and one wonders if he wanted or was offered a second chance to make good in Canada.

It is hardly surprising that children whose entry in the records reads 'no known history' or 'this lad has no known relative' should attempt to provide themselves with a background. Some had hazy memories on which to build fantasies and there was one such in the 1884 party. When Walter James was admitted to the homes in 1879 he was said to be the illegitimate child of Sarah James by a man whose name could not be ascertained. His mother had paid a Mr Harvey three shillings a week to look after Walter from the time he was sixteen months old until she died in 1877. Mr Harvey continued to look after Walter for two more years, although he had three of his own children dependent upon him and never earned more than twenty-two shillings a week as a servant to a marble merchant. But when his wife died he applied to have Walter admitted to the Stepney Home. Four years later Walter, then aged fifteen, sailed the Atlantic. He must have been one of the children that Barnardo managed to visit during his first stay in Canada because twenty years later Walter had not forgotten the occasion. He wrote a personal letter to Barnardo about a matter over which he must have brooded for many a long year.[2]

Dear Dr Barnardo,
It is with great pleasure to me to set down to write you a few lines to you to let you know how I am getting along. I suppose you can remember me well that you sent from your home in 1884. I was sent to John A. Smith across the grand river from Onondago in the Indian

reserve. I suppose you remember the Sunday that you met me at the Onondago School.

There is something touching in the expectation that so many years later Barnardo would be able to recall the details of that one placement among all the fifteen and a half thousand that had taken place since then. In 1904 Barnardo was a sick man, he had only a year to live, and as the records make clear, he never saw the letter himself.

Walter's letter is also a plea for information: he wants the key that would unlock his mysterious past.

I can remember the gentleman that took me to your home shortly after my mother died, about a month or so afterwards. It seems to me I used to stay at Mr Harvey's place a great deal part of my time. My mother used to come back for me and used to ask me if I wanted to go back home with her so I would go back with her and used to stay with her a while and then I would want to go back and stay with Mr Harvey's people for a while.

As far as I can remember my mother was well to do, for I certainly remember a part of the time she had two hired servant girls or one servant girl all the time to do her work. As far as I can remember she never layed hands over to do any kind of work, not even to wash a dish. She was always dressed very stylish and she had lovely furniture, everything I suppose her heart could wish for.

An besides I can remember about an old gentleman who used to come once and a while to see me when I used to be at Mr Harvey's place and he used to nurse me on his knee. But he would never stay all night, but before he would leave he would always put his hand in his pocket and fetch a big handfull of gold and silver out and give me one pound gold piece. He would give me that amount of money every time before he would go away. I used to call him Uncle for he said he was my uncle. He must have been very well to do for he was always dressed up as well as any gentleman that lives in the City of London.

There could hardly be a more classic description of the mother's life as the kept mistress of a rich man and one wonders how much 'Uncle' paid Mr Harvey to keep quiet about his relationship to Walter when the boy was taken to the Stepney Home. Walter obviously does not have the least idea as to the relationship between the rich city gentleman and his stylish mother, but the feeling that he has somehow been done out of his rights appears to have affected his life:

I cannot remember his name at all. I think if this matter of question can be traced up I would not be everybody's hired servant in America, but as I do not know any more about it I shall certainly get along the best I can for a while. I cannot express myself anymore into consideration to you because I was very young into my childhood, but I have a great memory about what I do know. I have never made anything since I have been to this country for I have been so much discouraged and worried very much for to think that I may have been cheated out of my mother's rights by someone. For I do not see into it any other way; for I think if it was only traced up right that I may be in good comfortable circumstances that I would be able to live happy now my friend.... so please give me all the information about it for I will pay big for all your trouble. There must be a big sum of money for me over there in England if only it can be traced, for I was the only child of the family.

A final entry in 1916 records that Walter, the mystery of his past unsolved, was ready to be called up and was prepared to go to the front, although he was already forty-eight years old, because, as he put it, he had 'the old country's blood in his veins'. He was just one of the thousands of erstwhile emigrants who joined the Canadian army in the First World War. For those who returned, their time in the army often enabled them to make a break with their old life and gave them the opportunity of embarking on a new career more to their liking.

There is no way of knowing what criteria were used to assess careers that were deemed 'eminently unsatisfactory'. Poor John Regan escaped that categorisation, but his conduct, which had been said to be 'doubtful' in 1888 was noted as being 'far from steady' in 1900. John was obviously one of those who did not do well in Canada, but the reason is perhaps not far to seek. His unhappy history and his sad and anxious admission photograph, taken when he was thirteen, might explain much.

One day in August in 1876 William Whitford was awakened at five o'clock in the morning by the distressed cries of a child. Getting out of bed he went to the window and heard thuds as though a child's head was being struck on the pavement and saw John's father kick him twice. John, with his brothers and young sister, lived with their father in a top garret in London Street, Ratcliff. When Inspector Rowse of K Division entered the garret, having being summoned by William Whitford, he found the children lying on a perfectly black mattress with nothing to cover them except a few rags. The smallest infant was in such a condition that he could hardly tell whether it was a child or not. John bore unmistakable marks of the ill usage he had received and his father was given a severe sentence of four months in jail.

When Barnardo heard of the case he sought permission to admit the children to the homes, but they had already been taken to the workhouse and the Guardians had no right, by law, to give them to anyone other than their father when he came out of prison. Mrs Regan had, by all accounts, been a 'clean decent person who had kept the children respectable'. Since her death, when John was ten, the children had been admitted to the workhouse at least twenty times in a most deplorable condition, sometimes covered with vermin and at other times suffering from seabus: twice through their father being sent to prison, once for neglecting to send them to school, and once for deserting them. Mr Regan was an Irish Roman Catholic who had been in the army, but since his discharge had spent most of the money he earned on drink. When he came out of prison this time, the relieving officer, Mr Jones, persuaded him to ask that all his children be admitted to the homes. John was photographed before he left for Canada. He was smartly dressed and held the regulation bowler hat in his hand. Only his dull and mournful expression mutely testified to childhood scars unhealed. A child with such a background would have needed to be placed with an exceptionally understanding family to flourish. His subsequent history indicates clearly that he was unable to respond to the demands made on him in Canada. He was one of the many children who simply disappeared. Although last heard of in Buffalo, in the United States in 1888, Owen's final words, written in 1900,were that his conduct was doubtful and that he was far from steady.

In the case of girls there is a notable addition to the pattern of poverty and destitution which caused so many boys to be sent overseas. Many of the girls sent to Canada were sent to save them from the moral dangers inherent in their situation. Mary Jane Parker and Sarah Burge are typical of thousands more who were removed from towns in England and sent to live on isolated Canadian farms, far from the temptations of city life.

Mary Jane's mother had died in 1877 and Mary Jane lived with her father and sisters in Colchester, a garrison town. The chief reason for her admission to the Girls' Village Home at Ilford was to remove her from 'the imminent peril to which she was exposed among the soldiery of the town'. She was ten at the time. She had an older brother who had been sent to sea and a sister already in another children's home, presumably for the same reason. The receiving officer of the Colchester union wrote in support of her admission that although her father did all he could to support the family, 'if the child could be taken from him I think it would be well for the temptations in a military town, especially for girls, are very great'. Four years later Mary Jane sailed with the second party of Barnardo girls to Canada and there her story ends.

Sarah Burge was eight when she was admitted to the Village Home. Her admission photograph shows an unsmiling face and questioning eyes framed by untidy shoulder-length hair and a windswept fringe. The photograph taken a year later, just before she sailed to Canada, shows her with her hair parted in the middle and tidily swept back. Her face has lost its hard scared look and there is the hint of a smile about her mouth. Her old worn frock is replaced by a neat cotton dress and she wears a cloak demurely fastened at the neck with a bow; in her hand she holds a pretty hat. Her whole demeanour looks as though she had found the world a less frightening place viewed from the safety of the Girls' Village Home. Her record does not say what happened to her when she first arrived in Canada. We only know that she herself later became a dressmaker in Toronto, because the homes gave that information to her brother when he wrote inquiring about her. However, she achieved fame of a different kind for an unusual reason. In 1974 Laurence Lerner, a poet, visited the photographic exhibition, *The Camera and Dr Barnardo*, which was being shown at the National Portrait Gallery in London. Sarah's photograph was one of the many thousands on view and her face with its half-frightened expression captured his attention. To her he dedicated a poem, entitled simply 'To Sarah Burge' which was subsequently published in the magazine *Encounter*.

You are wondering why
The man has disappeared under a black hood.
What will he do to my face you are asking.
Will he tear out my eyes,
Will he lock up my lips,
Will he tangle my hair?
What will he squirt at me,
Why was I chosen?
You were asking it then, you look out at us
Asking it now.

Well, I will tell you.
When your lips tighten with growing
He will plump them out.
When your eyes go hard and adult
He will keep them dewy.
When your hair turns grey
He will paint it black.
He will wipe off rouge and years,
Push your teeth back in,
Erase your wrinkles.

Sixty years from now you will bless him,
He dead and you dying.
He gave you the kiss of life.[3]

'Why was I chosen? You were asking it then, you look out at us asking it now.' Sarah Burge was chosen because her mother was left a widow with eight children to bring up. Her husband had been a cutler and a knife grinder and his wife took over the business. The small sum of four shillings, all the family were granted by the parish, was withheld because the children were not sent to school. They seem to have been a wild and wilful family, particularly the girls. Her record tells us that she was taken in by the Bournemouth Association for Friendless Girls, not because she did not have family, but to 'save her from the evil influence of both mother and sister'. From there she was 'forwarded' to the Village Home and a year later was on her way to Canada.

Twenty years later her brother William, who had been described as 'an incorrigible little vagrant', wrote to the homes asking for news of her. He had apparently gone to sea and found on his return that his mother had died and his sister had gone to Canada. He himself went to Canada under the auspices of the Salvation Army in 1902. In spite of exhaustive inquiries no trace of Sarah could be found, but there is some suggestion in the correspondence between the Salvation Army and Barnardo Homes that Sarah had deliberately changed her name, something that was done by a fair number of the children who wished to sever all connection with the homes.

The mystery surrounding little Margaret Trouvee's birth and parentage is reflected in her name. Found with her twin sister under a furze bush on Bostal Common near Plumstead in Kent, she was taken to the local workhouse. Her sister died, but she responded to careful nursing and became a thriving, healthy child. A local lady, Mrs Wood, became interested in her, doubtless partly because of the dramatic circumstances surrounding her birth, and had her removed to the care of a respectable woman where Margaret remained until she was five. Then, in a sentence which tellingly illustrates the ambivalence and limitations of middle-class benevolence, Mrs Wood is recorded as 'feeling anxious about the child's future and deeming it inexpedient to receive her into her own family', sought for her admission into the Village Home. Margaret, who had become a pretty child with a pleasing disposition, was placed in Cambridge Cottage. A year later, aged six, she sailed to Canada. She had no relatives to inquire about and so wrote no letters. We do not know if she was one of the lucky ones who found a family who truly wanted to adopt a child or if she was one of the many who simply spent her young life doing chores for other people. While she was under ten she would at least have had her board and lodging paid for, because Barnardo was one of the few who gave this protection to the younger children who were boarded out.

Ellen Mackenzie, described by her mother 'as the very sprite of mischief' was eight when she was admitted to Cambridge Cottage where she would be joined a year later by Margaret Trouvee. Ellen had been born in the workhouse and had spent the rest of her young life in a 'house of ill fame'. Her mother was said to be a prostitute who lived with six other 'fallen women'; the child, in the words of the report, 'being thus the spectator of every form of vice'.

Ellen's mother, who was said to be 'advanced in years' and

to bear 'the marks of her evil life' had herself been but a child of eleven when she had come to England. She told the homes that she had no known relatives and when she handed Ellen over and signed the Canada clause permitting Ellen to be sent overseas she doubtless hoped that her daughter's life might be less hard than her own. Two years later Ellen went to Canada and from Hazelbrae was sent to live with a Mrs William Thompson as a nurse girl to look after Mrs Thompson's two sons. Mrs Thompson apparently wanted to adopt her: perhaps she felt that was a more certain way of retaining her services, but the Barnardo Homes had made an agreement with Mrs Thompson whereby Ellen was to be paid and the money banked, so that when she was eighteen she would receive $100.

Ellen stayed with the Thompson family until she was twenty-one, and, when she left, the family refused to pay her the money she was owed. She wrote later of 'those terrible years under the Thompsons' roof' and described them as 'very sad to me, nothing but cruelty'. She might well have tried to forget, but was reminded of her unhappy childhood by a strange quirk of fate. Thirty-four years after she had left the Thompsons', Mrs Thompson died and left Ellen $100 in her will for 'all her loving kindness to us in those eleven years'.

Ellen had married and was living in San Francisco when the news of this bequest reached her, stirring memories of her unhappy past. She had already tried to discover who she was and how she came to be adopted once before, but the news from the Thompsons' lawyer brought old resentments to the surface. She wrote again to the homes asking for details of her adoption, saying that as she had been called an 'adopted' daughter, while she had been with them, she had a right to a share in Mrs Thompson's estate and, as she put it, 'I am going to stand up for my rights if I have any. There is still a strong English determinaton for the life they made me lead.'

Her letter also contained some very telling criticisms of the system that had allowed and indeed encouraged young children to be sent overseas:

> I don't think the English Government should send little girls all that distance and at such tender ages for nurse girls.... I think there should be some way provided for children who are taken by people in

this manner that they have some protection by people who have them for years here.

Few were to be as literate as Ellen. But from the stories and recollections of many of the children, which have been collected and published by Phyllis Harrison[4] and Kenneth Bagnall[5] in their recent books, it is clear that for a significant number those early years in Canada were so unbearably hard that even to remember that time is painful. But how do their lives compare with those of the Hancock children, Ethel, Louisa and Mary Ann, before they were admitted? The record shows that Ethel at twelve was tall, well grown and rather sharp; Louisa, five years younger, was a bright intelligent child; and the youngest, Mary Ann, who was only three, was pleasant looking with pretty features. Their mother made application for their admittance in person, and as the children were half starved, filthy and wretched, without home or friends they were admitted at once. Their mother, a woman of about thirty-four, strong and talkative, but exceedingly dirty, had gained her living by dragging the children about the streets begging and singing. When they were admitted the filthy condition of the children and the disgusting odour from all was very offensive. They had never had a home, but had tramped about, sometimes only earning threepence halfpenny in a day, and sleeping in lodging houses or casual wards. They had all been in and out of the Chelsea workhouse, sometimes three or four times a month for three or four days at a time. Their mother signed the Canada clause and they were all three admitted to Woodbine Cottage. A year later they joined the 1884 party to Canada, where the sisters were doubtless split up. Knowing nothing of home life, their ability to perform household chores must have been limited and the likelihood is that they had many changes of placement. Bewildered and lonely, one can but hope that the improvement in their physical condition made up for the trauma of family separation.

Eight

'ONLY THE FLOWER OF THE FLOCK'

C hrist
A lways
N ear
A lthough
D ear ones
A bsent

Acronym used by Barnardo

WITH the rapid growth of juvenile emigration in the 1880s and 1890s and the development of the system into an organised movement, the relationships between the Canadian Government, Canadian public opinion and the different agencies involved in the work became more complex. The simple objectives of Maria Rye and Annie Macpherson were subsumed within the wider considerations of the rescue homes' own needs and policies. If Barnardo's and the other major child-saving agencies were to be able to continue their work they needed the opportunities afforded them in Canada for the placement of their children. From their point of view the more children they were able to send overseas the better.

Since the rescue homes were dependent on public approval for their funding the fact that juvenile emigration began to be seen in Britain as more than an exercise in mere philanthropy, that it was supported by men like Samuel Smith, who spoke of the emigration movement as beneficial both to the nation and to the whole concept of empire, was an important element in encouraging the further growth of the movement. With Doyle's warnings forgotten, only financial constraints prevented even greater numbers of children being sent overseas

Allan Line S.S. "Tunisian."

than the 40,000 who had made the journey by the end of the century.

At the same time the uncritical acceptance by the Canadian people of the immigration of British children, controlled and directed from Britain by private agencies, was no longer to remain unquestioned. It was not concern for the welfare of the children that sparked off the criticism, but rather a generalised feeling that the unrestricted importation of children, whose background and upbringing were markedly different from that of the native-born Canadian child, was not in the best interests of the nation, and could even be injurious to the future healthy growth of the young country. As the numbers of immigrant children in Canada increased, so inevitably did the number of newspaper reports giving details of crimes committed by some of the children. Accounts of the unsatisfactory conduct of a few of the young immigrants, together with the renewed suspicion that so-called philanthropists were making a good thing out of juvenile emigration, was enough to tip the balance away from the previous unqualified approval to a more hostile questioning of the whole concept of child migration to Canada.

By the time Barnardo arrived in Canada the campaign against child emigration had already begun. The *Toronto News*, edited and owned by Edmund Sheppard, noted for the outspoken and extravagant language in which he expressed his strongly held opinions, launched an attack on the child emigration movement.

> We have enough orphan and abandoned children in our own streets to look after. The impudence of a large class of pseudo-philanthropists who make a trade of shipping outcast children from England to Canada and elsewhere, was well exemplified in the remarks of one engaged in the business, who had the cheek to contend that more immigration was desirable.[1]

A few months later the influential *Toronto Globe* ran an article warning against the indiscriminate importation of waifs. It was to be the forerunner of many such warnings. The enthusiasm of the British press in advocating emigration as a means of relieving the poor rates was beginning to be counter-productive in so far as Canada was concerned. 'Street waifs and inmates of reformatories, refuges and lodging houses ... are not the classes with which to build up a strong nationality,' the newspaper declared. It went on to voice a fear which was to spread and do much to damage the way in which the children were seen by the public. 'It is a terribly difficult process to get quit of the pauper or criminal spirit after it has taken full possession.'[2]

These editorials and others like them were to generate widespread prejudice against the children for the next two decades. It was a prejudice that members of the Dominion Trades and Labour Council were only too anxious to use as a weapon to oppose the whole child migration movement. Formed during the 1880s to protect the interests of the skilled working man, the Council had little effective power, but lost no opportunity to make its views known. Organised labour was particularly opposed to child migration for the very reason that made it so popular with the farmers: they feared that cheap child labour would drive down the wages of the ordinary agricultural worker. This fear was probably more apparent than real, for the farmers who employed the children employed them because they were unable to afford to hire adult labour. The need for the kind of work which could be done by children was so great that the danger of the children being exploited was far greater than the threat to the wages of the agricultural labourer.

None the less, D.J. O'Donoghue, a member of the Trades

and Labour Council, missed no opportunity of denouncing child emigration. He complained not only about the effect of competition from the children, but about the expense incurred by the Dominion in bringing the children to Canada and in supervising them once there. At a conference on Child Saving Work called by J.J. Kelso, the newly appointed Secretary of Neglected and Dependent Children in Ontario in 1897, O'Donoghue added a further point to the two he had been making continuously throughout the period. Many erstwhile child emigrants were now grown men and many of them, he said, had now joined the ranks of organised labour. He claimed that as children they had had to endure treatment 'of a character to make an ordinary Christian's blood curdle'.[3] This was a matter on which both the Canadian Government and the rescue societies were sensitive. Kelso, in his *Special Report on the Immigration of British Children*, specifically answered the charge he admitted was often made, 'that this species of immigration is child slavery pure and simple'.[4] 'There is no legitimate reason why it should be so,' he declared. 'Farm work should be healthful and enjoyable employment for young people, if the employers were reasonable and kindly disposed.'

Although there was opposition from the Trade and Labour Council, the power of organised labour in Canada was limited at this period. The suspicions and doubts voiced by the press were largely generalised fears which carried little weight when balanced against the great and continuing demand among the rural population for child labour. The Canadian Government saw child emigration as the cheapest way of gaining new immigrants and the reports made by the Canadian immigration officials did nothing to disturb their view that children brought to Canada by the child rescue societies were an asset to the country. Economic conditions in Britain enabled the voluntary organisations to present their work of child rescue to the public as a work of national importance.

Sending a child overseas involved a large number of people, and as the century wore on the numbers of people involved became greater as more rescue agencies took part in the scheme, and the number of children in Canada needing supervision became larger. Rescue societies, Boards of Guardians, immigration officials, the medical profession, government departments, all were to become involved in the decision-making required before a child could be brought to Canada, yet only the children themselves and their families had little or no voice in the matter. True, workhouse children could not be sent overseas without making a sworn declaration before two Justices of the Peace that they were willing to go, but they were in the minority and often of an age when such a decision was meaningless. For the majority of children there was no such protection. If those in authority in the rescue homes decreed that they were to go to Canada there was little the child or its family could do to reverse the decision. The system of juvenile emigration, as it developed in the nineteenth century, gave the rescue societies enormous power over the lives of the children in their care, power which they were not afraid to exercise.

Less than a third of the children admitted to the homes were total orphans or completely destitute. Of these some were children who had been sought out by the homes themselves and rescued from the streets and lodging houses, from the custody of thieves or, as the reports put it, from the custody of persons of abandoned life. Some children referred themselves, and others were referred by third parties such as city missionaries, charitable ladies who visited the poor, ministers of religion and, after its foundation in 1884, by the National Society for the Prevention of Cruelty to Children. Most of the parents, mainly widows or widowers, who brought their children to the homes, did so for economic reasons. For them it was often a choice of evils, but admission of their children to the homes, though painful and sad, did at least avoid the odium of having to make application to the hated workhouse. The majority of applicants in these cases were widows, and their children were sometimes lent clothes for their admission in a brave attempt to conceal the abject poverty which had forced them to surrender their children.

There is a notable lack of any reference to the children having parents or family in the publicity put out by the homes. The very names used to describe the children – 'waifs and strays' and 'street arabs' – almost presuppose that such children have no families, yet such was not the case. The records show that the ties of family affection were strong and this is further demonstrated by the many letters in the files from parents and children seeking information about each other. Yet if parents were mentioned they were often described in terms of opprobrium as degenerate, drunken, abandoned or dissolute, so that the children could be portrayed as being saved from moral ruin. It is certain that the homes mostly saw the parents as a threat to the children. All the homes were surrounded by high walls to keep intruders out and the children in. Visiting rights were restricted, in most cases to four times a year. Pressure was put on all parents or guardians to sign the Canada clause and most parents had little option but to sign.

From the first, Annie Macpherson had refused to take any child whose parent would not agree to the child being sent to Canada, and Louisa Birt and William Quarrier followed her example. In so far as the Middlemore Homes were concerned, they were only interested in taking in children for emigration. Barnardo, certainly the most autocratic and forceful of the leaders in the field of child rescue, did not apply such a rigid admission policy. Children were not turned away from the homes if parental consent to the clause could not be obtained, but if Barnardo deemed it expedient for the child to be sent to Canada, then that child was simply sent, without even the flimsy pretext of legality which the signed Canada clause conferred. Barnardo made no attempt to hide his attitude toward parents: he stated openly that 'parents are my chief difficulty everywhere; so are relatives generally'.[5] He had little doubt as to the reason: it was, he said, 'because I take from a very low class'.

Barnardo was more ruthless than any of the other mission leaders in the way in which he made use of emigration to remove children from surroundings he considered unsatisfactory. He openly proclaimed the fact that he practised what he was pleased to call 'philanthropic abduction'. In a provocative article entitled 'Is Philanthropic Abduction ever Justifiable?',[6] Barnardo sought to challenge the law which as yet did not allow for the removal of children from parents who were leading infamous and immoral lives or who were ill-treating their children. 'Are we as Christian men, always, under all circumstances to be governed by English Law?' he asked. 'Is *judicial* law always to be co-extensive with *moral* law? Does a period never arise when a higher law may compel a man to take a step which the law of the land would possibly condemn?' Barnardo then went on to confess that there were forty-seven cases on his registers where children had been abducted 'in order to save them ... in defiance of the law of the land and by modes which [were] legally indefensible'. For such children the obvious next step was to send them overseas where there was little or no danger that they could be traced or returned to their former way of life.

Barnardo might not have confessed so openly to this disregard for the law of the land had he not been encouraged by the success of William Stead's shock tactics in getting the Criminal Law Amendment Act passed which raised the age of consent from thirteen to sixteen. Stead, who edited the *Pall Mall Gazette*, in a series of articles designed to shock, had drawn attention to the way in which young children could be sexually exploited, abducted and sold to brothels overseas, by arranging to buy a child himself and publishing the fact.[7] His sensational approach was successful and although Stead himself was sentenced to six months' jail for his pains, the new act was passed within weeks of his articles appearing, having previously been defeated in the House of Lords.

Barnardo was not alone in believing the law needed altering and that more effective powers were needed to deal with parents who neglected or ill-used their children. Until such time as the law was changed, he found, as did others, that emigration provided a very effective means of separating a child from an unsatisfactory parent. Samuel Smith used the term 'preventive emigration' implying that in certain circumstances the emigration agencies were justified in sending a child overseas with no legal right other than their belief that their action was in the child's best interest. Bowman Stephenson, of the National Children's Home, thought emigration the best solution for those youngsters whose 'parents showed only a sort of unintelligent and almost animal affection which thinks nothing and is prepared to sacrifice nothing for the permanent welfare of the child'.[8] The danger was, that in seeking to promote the welfare of the child, the rescue homes were led by excessive zeal to disregard the normal ties of family affection. The records abound with instances of families being parted, brothers and sisters separated, with no understanding of the emotional distress that these partings caused.

The history of the two little sisters, Margaret and Victoria Smith, exemplifies the judgemental reasoning which made emigration such a favourite solution for girls thought to be in moral danger. The report in the Marchmont record book reads:

> These two sisters (then aged eleven and eight and a half) have been in the Home for three and a half years. They are illegitimate and their mother is living a bad life. She is a woman who has a great affection for her children to which they respond, but this forms a great danger and I am in consequence extremely anxious to get them beyond her influence.

The sisters sailed for Canada in 1897. Agnes Milne's story provides another example of the same kind. She was admitted to the Saltcoats Home in Glasgow after her father died. Her mother was said to be living a disreputable life in Glasgow. In spite of the fact that Agnes had two respectable brothers who were extremely anxious to keep her in this country, the record states, 'As I had no guarantee that they would be able to bring her up properly and was afraid of her coming under the influence of her mother, I determined to send her to Canada in order to put her beyond her mother's influence.' Agnes duly found herself one of a party of children from the Saltcoats Home who were sent to Marchmont in the spring of 1900. It was not the girls alone who were treated in this high-handed manner, and although figures are only known in respect of Barnardo emigrants between 1882 and 1908, these show that 6 per cent of boys and 8 per cent of girls were shipped to Canada without their parents' consent.[9]

The general public knew little of this aspect of the emigration operation and the rescue homes kept quiet about it. They preferred to emphasise the more positive aspects of the movement. Barnardo took his camera with him when he went to Canada in 1893 for this very purpose. He met and photographed Lavinia Tours, 'a true sensible girl who has evidently flourished in Canada'. Moreover she had money in the savings bank. He published her photograph alongside the one taken when she was admitted, aged three, 'desolate enough in all conscience'. She had been sent to Canada when she was twelve. William Jacobs was photographed at the same time. He was one of those boys who had actually asked to be admitted. His

Miss Rye in her office

Kingsley Fairbridge pruning peach trees at the first Fairbridge Farm School at Pinjarra

Annie Macpherson, depicted as the protector of little children

Thomas Barnardo, photographed in Toronto on his second visit to Canada in 1887

Eva Scott, *left*, and Lillie Loveland were shipped to Canada in the same party as Marion and Amy Holder – a party containing an unusually large number of small children

The photograph Marion Holder sent with her letter asking for news of her sister, and, *inset*, Marion as a baby

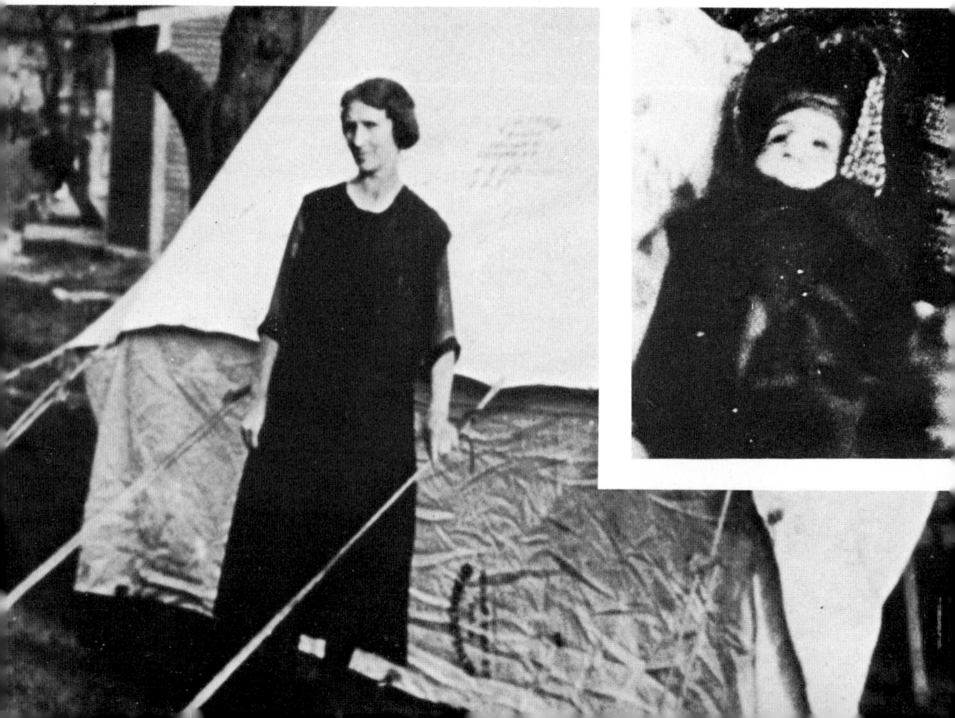

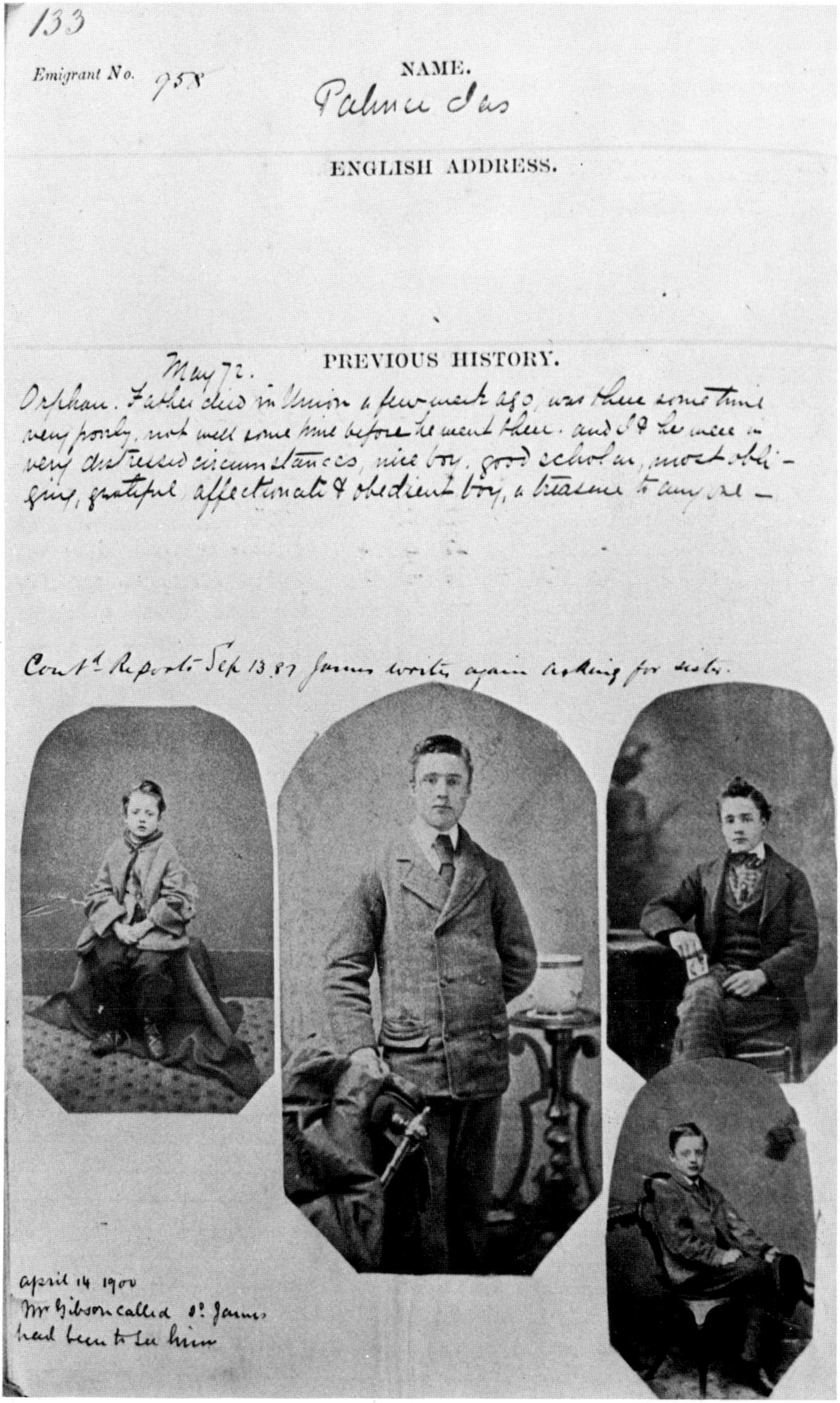

133

Emigrant No. 958

NAME.

Palmer Jas

ENGLISH ADDRESS.

PREVIOUS HISTORY.

May 72.

Orphan. Father died in Union a few weeks ago, was there some time very poorly, not well some time before he went there. and S & he were in very distressed circumstances, nice boy, good scholar, most obliging, grateful affectionate & obedient boy, a treasure to any re–

Cont^d Report Sep 13 87 James writes again asking for sister.

april 14 1900
Mr Gibson called & James
had been to see him

James Palmer's record sheet from the Marchmont Homes history book

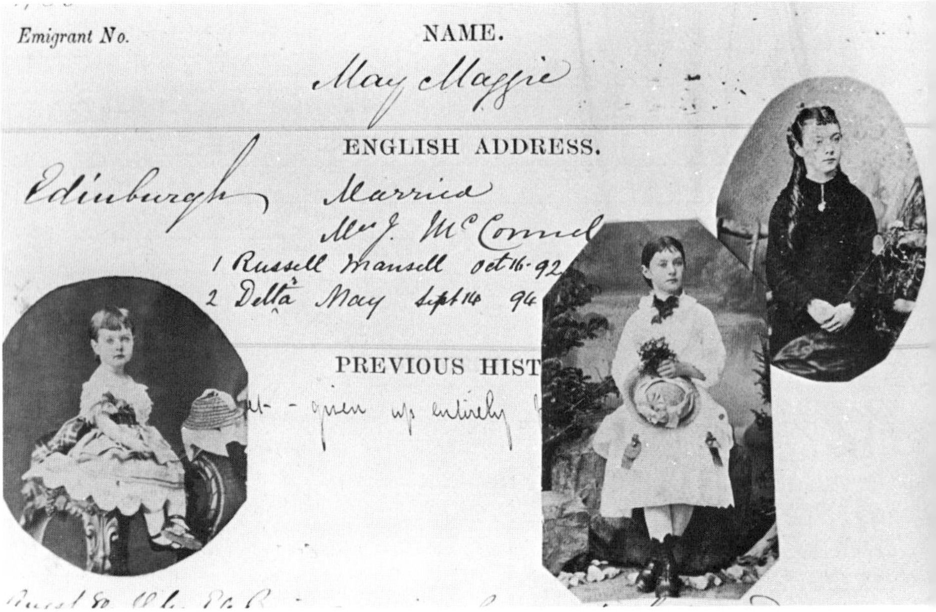

Emigrant No. NAME.

May Maggie

ENGLISH ADDRESS.

Edinburgh Married

Mrs J. McConnel

1 Russell Mansell Oct 16-92

2 Delta May Sept 14 94

PREVIOUS HIST

– given up entirely

Maggie May's record sheet from the Marchmont Homes history book

John Regan, on his admission to the Barnardo Home, and before emigration to Canada

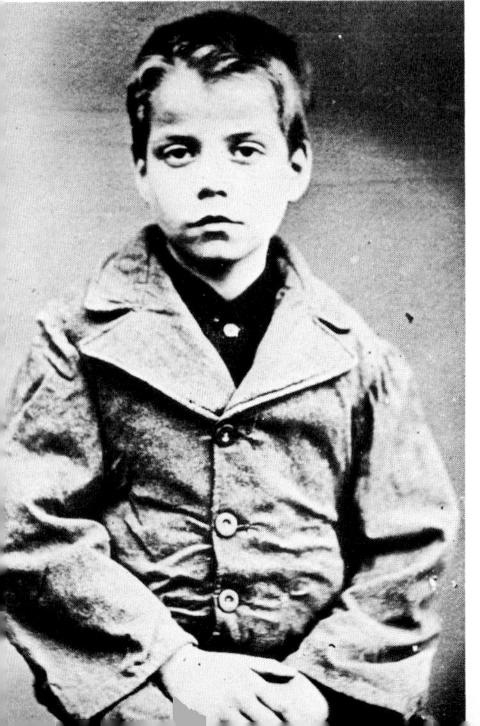

Charles Zakharov, aged fourteen, in the uniform of the British Army, as shown on the travel documents issued in 1919, and as an 'Onglisky solder' with his friend Freddy Felks

Charles Zakharov arriving in Sydney on his way to the Barnardo Home and as he is today

Group of children from the Bristol Emigration Home, including 'Dickie', aged four, who were sent to Marchmont in 1892

Sunday morning at Miss Rye's

Group of Barnardo boys who came to Fremantle, Western Australia, in 1883 on board the *Charlotte Padbury*

Postcard showing Rev. Mayers and the musical boys, 1909; Jo Wade is the third boy down on the right

Group of Barnardo boys and girls arriving in Nova Scotia in 1921 and, *below*, the reality of life on a Canadian farm

Party of Barnardo children *en route* for the Fairbridge Farm in Pinjarra, Western Australia, 1928 and, *below*, boys at work on the Prince of Wales Fairbridge Farm School in British Columbia, 1936

Group of girls outside the Marchmont Home, 1913

Party of children on board the ss *Ormonde* on their way to the Fairbridge Farm at Pinjarra, 1949

Medical inspection

The Prince of Wales with a group of Fairbridge children in the 1930s

One of the last parties of Barnardo children who flew to Australia in the 1950s

HOW SHE REACHED ME.

WHAT CANADA HAS MADE OF HER.

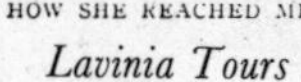

Lavinia Tours

mother had died of starvation and after wandering the streets he was taken in, aged fifteen, and sent to Canada where he was not only able to save money, but became a Sunday School teacher.[10]

Few children came to Canada as young as Marion Holder and her sister Amy who were two and three years old respectively. They came to the Wallaces (Ellen Bilborough had married the Rev Robert Wallace) in a party which contained an unusually large number of very young children. It was often argued by the rescue societies that the younger a child was sent to Canada the easier it was for the child to adapt to its surroundings. Letters written by Marion thirty years later, when she was married and living in Rochester, show that this was not always so, that even such early partings leave an enduring sense of loss.

I am writing to see if there is any way I could get in touch with my sister. She came out to the Marchmont Home with me in 1893. I think it was in the spring from Bristol. My adopted mother, dear Miss Ramsey, just before she died told me that her record was still in the books and she would try and find her for me, for I have nobody now, only friends I make over here and I sometimes feel I would like to know if she is dead or alive. We might be a lot of comfort to each other yet in this world.... You will pardon me for troubling you, in this, but I am not so young now and I would like to feel as I had some one of my very own.

"OLD THINGS HAVE PASSED AWAY; ALL THINGS HAVE BECOME NEW."

WILLIAM JACOBS ON THE STREETS.

WILLIAM IN CANADA, THE CHRISTIAN WORKER.

What makes this letter so unexpected is that not only had Mrs Richardson been in Canada since she was two; she was now married and had six children of her own. Her sense of isolation and loneliness is very evident, in spite of the fact that her placement was a happy one as is shown in her next letter.

You will know doubt be surprised when I tell you that my home town is Belleville and there isn't a corner of the Marchmont I don't know for many a happy day I spent there. Our private home was over on the corner of Dunbar and Holloway Street, where Mr Woodley the furrier lives, across from the Church. All the old residents will remember my adopted mother for she was loved by everyone she came in contact with. Her memory will never be forgotten in Belleville. . . .

The record shows that Mrs Richardson's sister, Amy, was three years old when she had come out to Canada. She had been less lucky than her younger sister and had been placed with several different families during her childhood. When she was finally traced by Mrs Richardson she, too, was found to be living in the United States.

I have been intending to write to you, but wanted to be able to tell you some good news. For my dear little sister came last Sunday from Detroit with her family and I was just so delighted to see her. She is such a lovely girl and her husband is very nice, and she has three lovely little children. I don't think I shall ever be able to thank you enough for your kindness in helping me to find her.... It really seems terrible to think back how long we have been separated when we might have spent the best part of our lives together when she was so near me. Why is it the Lord allows those things. It must be for our good but we cannot see it that way.... I am sending you a very short letter this time, but it is late and sis and I have so much to talk about, we haven't time for anything else it seems.

What makes this letter so particularly poignant is that when Amy and Marion were sent as babies to Canada both their parents were living.[11] Their father is described as a very respectable man, well to do and fond of society. Unfortunately, after borrowing £500 from his mother-in-law, he left his wife who then went back to live with her own mother, taking her eldest child with her. Her second child was adopted by an uncle and Amy and Marion were emigrated. In spite of the fact that the report stated that there was no reason why the mother should not write to her children, no inquiry seems to have been made for six years and by that time Amy had been adopted and the report simply noted, 'there was no need of inquiries'.

If the records of these children reveal how easy it was for families to be split up, the story of Harry Gossage and Martha Tye, sent overseas in 1888, shows how simple it was for the homes to 'lose' a child, so that even when the courts ordered that the children be returned, Barnardo, whose wards they were, could plead ignorance of their whereabouts in Canada and thus defy the court's ruling. Both children had been ill-treated and neglected by their mothers. Harry's mother had sold him to an organ grinder who had abandoned him and the boy was found wandering, hungry and wretched, in the streets of Folkestone by a clergyman who asked Barnardo to admit him. Martha's life had been made so intolerable by the cruelty of her stepfather and her mother that she had referred herself to Muller's Ashley Down orphanage in Bristol. Because the orphanage did not take in illegitimate children she was sent to Barnardo who immediately admitted her.

Both mothers were informed that their children had been admitted to Barnardo's. Harry's mother was only too willing to agree that he should remain in the homes because his father was dead, his two brothers were already in Canada and she was unable to keep him. She did not, however, sign the Canada clause. Mrs Tye also agreed that Martha should remain with Barnardo, but only for two years and she, too, did not sign the Canada clause.

In November of that year one of Barnardo's many visitors was a certain William Norton, a gentleman unknown to Barnardo, but bearing letters of introduction and recommendation. Almost nothing is known about William Norton except that he wanted to 'adopt' a boy of ten or eleven and take him to Canada. Barnardo sent for five of his boys and William Norton, liking Harry's bright intelligent expression, chose him. Norton had asked that the child he chose should not have parents or relatives who might cause difficulties later on, and Barnardo, knowing Harry's past history, felt there was little likelihood of any such danger. However, to guard against the possibility of subsequent interference Barnardo agreed that Norton should take the boy without leaving any address, and the cryptic note 'disposed of by the Director' is all the information that is given concerning Harry after he left for Canada.

Martha Tye's disappearance took place in rather more mysterious circumstances. She is said to have gone out of the country in the care of a certain Madame Romand who lived mainly abroad. Madame Romand was said to have offered to take abroad any two or three little girls about whom Barnardo felt anxious, and Barnardo did indeed feel anxious about Martha for her mother and stepfather had written to him asking for her return. It is almost certain that Martha was sent to Canada after having been kept at a secret address in the country and that the whole story of Madame Romand was invented by Barnardo to conceal her actual whereabouts.[12]

Neither Mrs Gossage nor Mrs Tye would have been able to take any effective action against Barnardo for the recovery of their children on their own account. But unknown to Barnardo at the time, a more powerful organisation was not only willing, but anxious to help them. It seems unlikely, on the face of it, that Mrs Gossage would even have thought of asking for Harry's return had her cause not been taken up by the Roman Catholic hierarchy. The unprecedented growth of the evangelical children's rescue societies had alarmed the Roman Catholic authorities who saw an increasing number of their children being swept into Protestant homes and thus lost to the Faith. Not only were the Protestant homes more numerous, owing to the growth in emigration figures, but the number of children they could take in had also greatly increased. There simply were not enough Catholic institutions for all the children who needed caring for because of lack of finance. Emigration was a cheaper form of care and the main reason for Catholic societies going to the expense of emigrating children at all was 'to save their faith'. Their Canadian agent was expected to recognise 'that the highest object of his work is to place his children so that they will have every influence to draw them into the closest possible union with the Catholic Church'.[13]

Both Mrs Gossage and Mrs Tye were Roman Catholics and when Mrs Gossage learnt that Harry had been sent out of the country, prompted by her Catholic priest, she took out a summons against Barnardo for the return of Harry so that he could be placed in a Roman Catholic Home. The judge refused to issue a writ of habeas corpus because Harry was out of the country and no longer in Barnardo's custody. When, however, Mrs Tye also made application for a writ of habeas corpus for the return of Martha, on the advice of a well-known firm of Roman Catholic solicitors, the same solicitors who had acted for Mrs Gossage, the judge, Mr Justice Mathew, who had dealt with the Gossage case, was no longer prepared to accept Barnardo's assertion that he could not produce Martha. He declared Barnardo to be in contempt of court and liable for the consequences.

As a direct result of this ruling a fresh application for the issue of a writ for the return of Harry Gossage was made to the Divisional Court in November 1889. Barnardo was supported by his committee and they approved his decision to go before the Court of Appeal. However, before the appeal could be heard Barnardo found himself involved in yet a third case.

When John Roddy was admitted to the homes, also in the year 1888, he was said to be neglected, half starved and his mother given to drinking. It was not long afterwards that Mrs Roddy became incensed at being refused permission to see her son. She complained to her niece, a practising Roman Catholic, who advised her to get in touch with a priest. He put her in touch with the same firm of solicitors who were handling the Gossage and Tye cases. A writ of habeas corpus was duly obtained for the mother in respect of John Roddy. The stage was thus set for another court battle, the third in a series where the soul of the child rather than the body was the cause of the fight.

There was no question, in this case, of Barnardo sending John Roddy out of the country, although, had he not been fighting the Gossage and the Tye cases, it is not impossible that he might have been tempted to solve the problem of the boy's restoration to his mother by sending him to Canada. For Barnardo lost the Roddy case and was forced to hand the child back to his mother, the judge deciding that there was nothing to interfere with the mother's rights and ruled that, 'Dr Barnardo is bound to hand over the child as directed by the Divisional Court.'

However, the Gossage case went to the Court of Appeal, and Lord Herschell's judgement – that to use a writ of habeas corpus as a means of compelling one who has unlawfully parted with the custody of another person as a means to regain that custody, or of punishing him for having parted with it, struck him as being a use of the writ unknown to law – pleased Barnardo. But it was not the end of the matter. Lord Herschell went on to say that where the court entertained a doubt as to whether this was the fact, it was unquestionably entitled to use the pressure of a writ to test the truth of the allegation that the defendant was no longer in possession or control and to require a return to be made. Though by this time Barnardo had certainly handed over custody of Harry Gossage and Martha Tye, when both writs were first served there is no doubt that the children were in his custody. Barnardo was ordered to make a return in three months and pay costs. There was no way the court could force Barnardo to produce Harry or Martha in the face of his assertion that he did not know where they were. Emigration had put them beyond the reach of their parents, the Catholic Church and the courts.

These three cases highlighted the anomalies that existed over the question of parental rights and it was during the Roddy case that the act to amend the law relating to the custody of children was finally passed in 1891. Of the three main clauses of the act, it was the third, setting out the criteria the court must employ to decide whether or not a child should be restored to a parent or guardian who had neglected or abandoned it, that was the most important to Barnardo's and the other rescue homes. A parent who had been deduced unfit to have custody in the past had now to prove to the court that he was fit to have the custody of the child. For the first time parental rights were subordinated to the overriding consideration of the welfare of the child.

After the Prevention of Cruelty to Children Act of 1894 emigration could sometimes be deemed to be in the child's best interests. Where custody had been transferred by magistrate's order, a youngster could be sent abroad with permission from the Home Secretary. For the homes wanting to separate children from undesirable parents, there were now legal procedures available, but 'philanthropic abduction' was certainly a quicker, easier method of achieving the same result. While Barnardo fought over eighty attempts by parents to reclaim their children through the courts, he also adopted a whole variety of procedures to ensure that children destined for Canada did leave. Parents deemed 'respectable' were given notice that their children would be leaving for Canada, while those described as 'not moral' or 'not respectable' were only notified after the ship had left the quayside, so there could be no question of their postponing or preventing emigration.

So while the number of children crossing the Atlantic grew more numerous, averaging over two thousand a year, and the distributing homes were still receiving far more applications for children than they could supply, public opinion in Canada became increasingly uneasy about the whole concept of juvenile emigration. Every reported case of lawlessness, be it burglary or assault, committed by an emigrant child was seized on as evidence that they were somehow inherently different from Canadian children. Fiction reflects fact, and when the author of *Anne of Green Gables* described the reaction of Marilla Cuthbert, Anne's adoptive mother, to the suggestion made by her brother, that they should adopt a Barnardo boy to work on the farm, she was accurately reflecting an attitude which did nothing to ease the lot of the young emigrants or to foster their integration into Canadian society.[14] Marilla's reply, 'They may be alright – I'm not saying they're not – but no London Street Arabs for me.... Give me native born at least. There'll be a risk, no matter who we get. But I'll feel easier in my mind and sleep sounder at nights if we get a born Canadian ... he can't be much different from ourselves', exemplified an indefinable feeling that the emigrant child was somehow different, different even from a Canadian orphan. If these children were the offspring of paupers, depraved or criminal parents, then sooner or later, it was felt, these evil tendencies would manifest themselves in the child's behaviour. The published stories of some of the children reveal how this attitude affected them.[15] They were often made to eat apart, excluded from family occasions, expected to work longer and harder than other children in the family and denied the affection, not to mention love, that any child needs. The ambivalence that was felt about their status was often reflected in the non-payment of their small wage by their employers, and unless the organisation that brought them out was aware of the situation and able to bring pressure to bear, some children left, when their indentures expired, with nothing to show for their years of toil.

It needed only one well-publicised incident to fan the grumbling opposition into a more positive attack on child emigration. Although numbers of children had been in trouble with the law, most of the cases reported had received little more than local press coverage. It was an apprentice from the Barnardo farm in Manitoba who was charged with indecent assault that caused the storm in 1894. The lad came before the grand jury at Brandon but because the jury disagreed over the charge he was sentenced to only one month's imprisonment. It was not the offence nor the sentence that caused the uproar, but the remarks made by the foreman of the jury, James Smart, who referred to the number of serious crimes committed by youths brought to the Barnardo Home from the old country and categorised them as 'emigrants of an undesirable sort, being lawless and criminal in tendency'. He went on to express the view that legislation should be enacted as would prevent the further importation of the class of children now being brought from the slums of the cities of the old country. Smart's remarks were taken up by all the leading Canadian newspapers and reproduced by the press all over the English-speaking world, showing just how sensitive and emotive the subject had become.

That Barnardo was well aware of how damaging such comment could be is amply demonstrated by the long and careful letter he wrote to the Minister of the Interior protesting vigorously at the injustice of the accusation.[16] It is an important letter, not only because it sets out the principles on which Barnardo worked, but because it was the first time that anyone had tried to analyse the success or failure of the young emigrants. That Barnardo was also aware of how the publicity could adversely affect the children already in Canada is shown by his statement that the Brandon grand jury's presentment had 'inflicted an undeserved and almost irreparable injury upon a section of the Canadian community, who have proved by the very small number of their offences against the law, to be among the most law-abiding portion of the whole population of the Dominion'.

Very soon after starting his emigration scheme Barnardo had drawn up a set of conditions which governed the choice of children sent to Canada. These conditions, repeated in his letter to the minister, including the phrase, much used in all publicity concerning the children, that 'only the flower of our flock shall at any time be emigrated to Canada', were re-stated:

> Only the flower of our flock shall at any time be emigrated to Canada – that is, those (1) who are in robust physical and mental health; (2) who are thoroughly upright, honest and virtuous; and (3) who, being boys, have been industrially trained in our workshops; or who, being girls, have had careful instruction in domestic pursuits.
>
> That continued supervision shall be exercised over these children after they have been placed out in Canadian homesteads; first, by systematic visitation; second, by regular correspondence. Emigration in the case of young children without continuous supervision is in our opinion presumptuous folly and simply courts disaster.
>
> That in the case of total failure of any emigrants, the Colonies shall be safeguarded by their RETURN at our expense, wherever possible, to England.

Under these conditions 6,128 children had already been sent to Canada. Barnardo now set out to prove that since 1884 the total number of convictions had been no more than fifty-two and that many of the offences thus recorded were of a very trivial nature. Giving case No. 37 as an example Barnardo wrote:

E.E.B. Convicted of the theft of an old saddle, said to be worth 50 cents, was sentenced to a term of three months imprisonment. A clergyman of the town made strong endeavours to get the sentence reduced as he knew the boy took the saddle supposing it to be worthless, and his whole previous record had been thoroughly satisfactory.

Claiming that the total number of convictions represented less than 1 per cent of the whole number emigrated, he demonstrated, through the use of comparative tables, which he included in his letter, that only 0.136 per cent of his children had been convicted as opposed to a conviction rate of 0.775 per cent among the general population. He admitted that another sixty-six were known to have done more or less badly, but even that, he argued, represented less than 2 per cent of the total number sent to Canada. There is no way of knowing how accurate these figures were, and J.J. Kelso thought that Barnardo's claim was 'altogether too favourable an estimate' because a number could be vagrant and worthless without breaking the law. But as there were no other statistics the figures quoted by Barnardo provided a useful and positive defence against the widespread prejudice against child immigration. In his fight to clear the names of his children from unfair aspersions Barnardo found himself supported by Mr Justice Street who said he had been looking into the history of the young men convicted of serious crimes at the present assize, and had found that as a rule, with only one exception, they were all young fellows who had been brought up in the city of Hamilton and who had been educated at the public schools. Addressing the jurors of Brandon he said, 'If these are a fair specimen of the criminals who were causing the outburst of crime in Hamilton, the remedy you suggest of prohibiting the importation of people from other countries is not going to help it.'[17] He went on to say that as far as he understood matters these young fellows, born in Canada, had never been taught any principles of morality at all: 'They are simply taught reading, writing, arithmetic and a smattering of other things, but they are not taught the difference between right and wrong.'

Two years later the cruel death of the lad George Green was to throw into vivid relief the strength of feeling on the subject of the immigrant children. Although his death was a sad and terrible one, it was used, not to protest about conditions under which the children worked, but to demonstrate that boys like George Green, from the slums of England, constituted a menace to Canada. During his short career in Canada George had had two placements. The first was with a farmer named Cranston who had kept him for a month on trial and returned him because he had defective vision and was unable to perform the work required. It is obvious from his photograph that he had a very severe squint and this, coupled with his total lack of any experience of life on a farm, would make him a liability rather than an asset to begin with. However, three days later George Green was placed with a Miss Helen Findlay. Alfred Owen had placed boys on the Findlay farm before, but none since Helen Findlay's brother George, for whom she had kept house, had died.

> Helen Findlay was dour and tough as might be expected of a woman wresting her living from a farm single-handed. She needed help but couldn't afford a hired man. Whatever humanitarian instincts she may have had were overcome by her irritation with George Green's inability to do the work she required of him. He was not only physically unfitted for the job, the fact that he was simple minded and a 'Home' child militated against him. Six months later George was found dead in a filthy upstairs room at the farm, his body, caked in excrement, was covered in welts, scabs and abrasions and severely emaciated. The stamped post card he had been provided with by the Barnardo organisation to be used in case of need was never sent.[18]

When Dr Cameron, who had been the first to see him, gave his evidence to the court he said that the boy had died of neglect, starvation and violence. Helen Findlay's lawyers had asked for permission to exhume the body, and this they did five days later. Their evidence gave a very different impression to the jury. A boy with defective vision, limited strength and mental ability, said to be suffering from a scrofulous condition had, it was implied, a constitutional defect, and might well have come to Canada with some disease inherent in his system which had caused his death.

Several of Helen Findlay's neighbours gave evidence to the effect that they had seen her abusing George Green, kicking him, striking him and prodding him with a pitchfork. This she denied, describing him as puny, defective from head to toe, cross-eyed, left-handed, and hump-backed; his right hip was always drawn in and he walked sidling along with his right side forward. His mouth was at the side of the head and his lower jaw stuck out a quarter of an inch beyond the upper so that his teeth did not meet. His intellect was poor and he did not understand what was said to him. In the face of the differing evidence, the trial at Owen Sound ended in a disagreement of the jury and the case against Helen Findlay was dropped by default. George Green's pitiful death went unpunished, and the public wasted little sympathy over the tragedy. The press were too busy re-examining the whole question of the importation of waifs. As one report said, if Green was an example of what Barnardo called the 'flower of the flock', then Canada wanted no more of it.

The *Toronto Evening Star* said that the revelations in connection with the death of the Barnardo waif, Green, should form the basis of a strict investigation by the Government.

> There is a general belief and strongly defined suspicion that Green was not a solitary instance of children with tainted blood having been brought into Canada, notwithstanding the denial of Dr Barnardo, and no law too strict can be framed to prevent these waifs, handicapped by heredity, from mingling with the pure and healthy children of this country and becoming a burden upon Canada. Such contact cannot fail to result in the moral and physical injury of succeeding generations.

Other editors used even stronger language and the *Owen Sound Times* said the 'greatest crime is being perpetrated by the dumping of the diseased off-scourings of the hotbeds of hellish slumdom of England among the rising generation of this country'. D.J. O'Donoghue was not slow to make use of the tragedy and at their meeting in December the Trades and Labour Council recorded once again their opposition to a system under which 'Dr Barnardo and other so-called "philanthropists" have been burning the candle at both ends', as they quaintly put it in their report, 'getting large sums in England for maintenance and care, while on the other hand, [they have] made Canada a common dumping ground for large numbers of the vicious, the lame, the halt and the blind.'

The publicity attendant on the Green case worried others including Lady Aberdeen, the energetic and intense wife of the Governor-General, who wrote to A.M. Burgess, at the Department of the Interior asking for information about the juvenile emigration movement. Ishbel Aberdeen was a remarkable woman and deeply religious. Her concern with social and moral reform led her to play an important role in Canadian life during the five years she was there, and her involvement with the National Council of Women, which was to become the most important women's organisation in Canada, led on to her establishing the Victorian Order of Nurses, her most notable achievement.

Burgess wrote back soothingly.[19] It seems strange that his letter, coming after the highly publicised death of a Barnardo immigrant child, made no mention of the conditions under which the immigrant children lived. It was designed rather to reassure her, and through her the women's organisations in Canada, that the children were remarkably law-abiding and in no way constituted a threat to the communities in which they lived. A copy of Mr Justice Street's speech, made at the time of the Brandon case, was included and the figures Barnardo had provided were quoted with approval. Burgess sent Lady Aberdeen more figures for her use. These showed that out of the 3,725 children placed out by the Quarrier Homes only seventeen were on record as having committed any offence, while figures for Bowman Stephenson's children showed only 0.2 per cent in any kind of trouble. The average for the Macpherson, Fegan and Birt children was somewhere in between the two. The most notable exception, not surprisingly, was any mention of Maria Rye's children, since, once placed, those children were left to fend for themselves.

However, since many of Maria Rye's children came from the workhouse, the figures produced by the Department of the Interior with regard to the pauper children under their surveillance have some relevance in this context.[20] The Department, unlike the voluntary agencies, had no need to defend their record, and their figures were less reassuring. Of the 12,000 pauper children who had come out under the auspices of the rescue homes from 1883 until 1893, 2 per cent were shown to have died and 1 per cent to have been criminal, a much greater percentage than those admitted to by the homes.

The Dominion Government did not see any necessity for involving itself further in the juvenile emigration movement; they were paying $2 a head for each child who entered the country, except in the case of workhouse children, but for them they were providing a rudimentary supervisory service. The Ontario legislature, on the other hand, to whose province most of the children had come, felt impelled to take action to reverse the wholesale condemnation of the movement. An act to regulate the Immigration into Ontario of Certain Classes of Children was passed in 1897 which, it was hoped, would mollify public opinion. Under the act the work of each agency was to be inspected four times a year; careful supervision over the children was to be maintained by all the agencies involved until they attained eighteen years of age. It was further provided that all agencies were to maintain proper homes for the reception of the children and for their shelter in time of need. Sections eleven and twelve, put in to refute further allegations that Canada was being used as a dumping ground, stipulated that no child would, in future, be permitted to leave the old country without a certificate from an examiner that the child was the right class to come to Ontario. It was made an offence to bring into Ontario any child who was defective of intellect or who had any physical infirmity or any child of known vicious tendencies or who had been convicted of crime. The action taken by Ontario was soon followed by Manitoba, Quebec and New Brunswick. Finally, the Ontario Act appointed Joseph John Kelso Inspector of Juvenile Immigration Agencies.

J.J. Kelso was only thirty-three at the time of his appointment, but he had already shown himself to be a passionate defender of the rights of children. By profession a journalist, he was working on the *Globe* in Toronto when he became aware of the number of young children involved in prostitution in and around Yonge Street. Whether he was inspired by the success of his fellow journalist, William Stead, in bringing the matter before the public in England, or if this played any part in his decision to make the evils of child prostitution a major crusade, is not known. However, his interest in child welfare was known and when the speaker to the Royal Canadian Institute failed to appear, J.J. Kelso was invited as his replacement.

He seized his opportunity and spoke so forcefully on the need to prevent cruelty to children and animals that a group was formed which eventually became the first Children's Aid Society with Kelso as its president. Five years were to elapse between his speech and government action. A bill for the protection of children was passed in 1893. But if he had longer to wait than Stead for legislative action, his involvement with children was to be of far more importance and benefit to children than anything Stead achieved. Kelso was almost immediately invited to become the Superintendent of Neglected and Dependent Children of Ontario. Although neither directly involved with nor responsible for the juvenile emigrants from Britain until the passing of the Ontario Act, his new duties nevertheless made him aware of the problems their arrival had created. His position also provided him with a yardstick by which to judge the performance of the rescue homes' work in Canada.

Almost his first action after his appointment as Inspector of Juvenile Immigration Agencies was to write a special report on the immigration of British children. If Doyle can be seen to have been prejudiced against emigration and in favour of workhouse education for the poor-law children from the start, so Kelso seems to have had no thought but that emigration must be beneficial to the majority of the children, and the whole tenor of his report is directed toward the calming of Canadian fears. While Doyle methodically carried out a systematic inspection of the children and methodically noted cases of abuse, the system had grown too large for Kelso to do more than make general statements on the subject while pinning his faith on the efficacy of the new Ontario Act to eliminate 'grave abuses and radical defects in the work of some of the agencies' and to eradicate the shipments of 'vicious and sickly children'.

Where both Doyle and Kelso were of one mind was in their wholesale condemnation of the work of Maria Rye. Kelso thought it only fair to say 'in justice to the other agencies, that

I consider this home responsible for a good deal of the odium that now attaches to child immigration in this country'. Maria Rye had just retired and had handed over her work to the Church of England 'Waifs and Strays' Society who had suspended the work of the agency. His report is short and sharp.

As a result of my inquiries it appeared quite evident that the work had not been properly handled in the past and that some radical change would be necessary before it could be considered satisfactory from a Canadian standpoint. The arrangements – if there could be said to be arrangements – for the supervision of the children after going to foster homes and situations were far from adequate. Miss Rye, during the period in which she was engaged in this work, did not make any effort to have the children personally visited after leaving her care, and she is credited with the statement that the other homes were going to an unnecessary expense in maintaining a staff of visitors.

The agreement in use did not seem sufficient to fully protect the children, and altogether the work gave evidence of poor management in the past. No formal agreement had been entered into between the Home and those receiving the children beyond signing the application form; no personal visitations were made after the child left the Shelter, and the correspondence between the child and the Home has always been of the most meagre character. The consequent danger is that the child soon realizes the lack of interest that is manifested in its welfare and the foster-parents see that they are not likely to be interfered with if they overwork and otherwise take advantage of their young charges. These four thousand children have gone to all parts of Ontario, but probably a large proportion find homes in the Niagara district.[21]

Kelso seemed to be hedging his bets when it came to reporting on Annie Macpherson's work, now being carried on in Canada by her nephew William Merry. It was now clearly impossible for Annie to visit all her children as she had done in the past, even though Kelso dutifully noted the fact that 'it has always been the policy of Miss Macpherson to personally visit each child yearly'. He ends his report,

While it would be impossible to say just what proportion of these children have turned out well, in the absence of evidence to the contrary it is fair to assume that a reasonable proportion, at least, have grown up to worthily discharge the duties and responsibilities of citizenship.... With increased care in selection and closer supervision in their new homes it is likely that good result will follow the work of this agency.

Kelso did not visit Louisa Birt's Home at Knowlton but simply printed a letter he had received from the Chairman of the Sheltering Homes concerning the management of the work. He did call at Marchmont and talked with Annie's old friend Ellen Wallace and her husband. Again in the report on Marchmont there is the same questioning tone, as though Kelso is not really satisfied that all is well, yet cannot put his finger on what is wrong: 'It is much easier to trace those who have done well than those who have turned out badly, since the latter wander away and are lost sight of, but the earnest contention of Mr and Mrs Wallace is that the proportion of those who have utterly failed is a remarkably small proportion of those assisted.' Later on in the report he almost seems to be asking for confirmation that all is well. 'I have invariably heard the Marchmont Home and its work spoken of in terms of the highest respect, and surely if in all these years poor work was being carried on extensively the matter would have attracted the attention and adverse comment of leading citizens!' (The exclamation mark is Kelso's.)

The Marchmont children came from three sources, the Manchester Boys' and Girls' Refuges founded by Mr Leonard Shaw, the Saltcoats Orphanage in Glasgow and the Canadian Emigration Home in Bristol. Shaw was only one of several workers among the children who were totally opposed to the Ontario Act and saw it as a threat to their work. None opposed it so strongly as William Quarrier from Scotland. In vain Kelso pointed out that the act was to protect children from ill-usage and neglect as well as to protect Canada from undesirable immigrants. Quarrier saw it as completely unacceptable and in a furious letter to the *Globe* he made known his feelings.

On March 31st of this year there was put on the statute book of Canada, a law for regulating the immigration into Ontario of certain classes of children which is anti-British in enactments and alien in its character. It lays hold on a voluntary Christian work supported by British money and puts it under the control of a Government which does not contribute one cent toward its keep. It prohibits any philanthropic individual or society from bringing into Ontario a child under

William Quarrier

eighteen years of age without a licence from the Government, while at the same time any immigrant – criminal or otherwise – may enter the country with his children.... I say without fear of contradiction that it was hastily enacted, and is the most inquisitorial law that was ever put on the statute books of a British colony.

He argued that no government had the right to interfere with religious work which it does not support, that he had spent hundreds of thousands of dollars in conducting the work; that he was one of the pioneers who had brought more than 5,000 trained and tested children and young people into Canada and less than 2 per cent had ever become criminal or chargeable on the municipality. He saw the new act as a personal affront and said he felt he had been unjustly treated and that an unmerited stigma had been put on his work.

Arthur Hardy, the Premier of Ontario, tried to placate him, writing, 'As you doubtless know, there is a strong public prejudice against the importation of children, owing partly to the work of placing and supervising not having been properly attended to by some agencies ... as you can readily comprehend on a little reflection, it would be absolutely impossible to discriminate in law between one agency and another.... Mr Kelso, who will have the direction of this department, will always be prepared to cooperate with your representatives.' He ended by urging him to comply with the terms of the act, not only for the protection of the children, 'but in assuring the Canadian public that every precaution is being taken to guard against the moral or physical deterioration of our people'. If Quarrier could not exercise the absolute power to which he had grown used the only effective protest he could make was to refrain from sending his children to Canada and this he proposed to do. Kelso ended his report on Quarrier's by expressing the hope that when Quarrier understood 'the spirit in which this supervision is entered upon he will withdraw any objections', which in time he did.

Autocratic though Barnardo was, he saw the act, not as a threat but as vindicating the principles upon which his work was established. Because Barnardo's work, as Kelso said, had attracted more attention and criticism than that of any other agency due to its size and its aggressive advertising policy, Barnardo was more aware of the widespread prejudice against the children and had a better understanding of its damaging effect on the lives of the young immigrants. He therefore welcomed any action that reinforced what might be called his 'only the flower of the flock' principle. The way in which Kelso presented Barnardo's work was designed to be entirely reassuring. Alfred Owen was quoted as saying that 'never where we have been able to avoid it, has any child been left to become a burden on the institutions or municipalities of the country'. The history of one of the 1884 party of boys does show to what lengths Owen went to implement this policy. The most unusual boy in that group was Charles Barnard. He had referred himself to the homes on Christmas Day in 1883 giving his age as sixteen. He was subsequently discovered to be nineteen and sent to the Labour House, Barnardo's home for older boys, and from there sent to Canada the following March. Owen had just written to Barnardo in March 1896 saying he was 'returning this young man per the ss *Laurentian* which leaves Portland on the 23rd'. He continued, 'It may seem rather a preposterous case that we should be spending money on a man of this age who has been twelve years in the country,' but Barnard was in an advanced state of consumption. He had become destitute and the municipality had refused to assist him further. Owen had thought that he might possibly be maintained in the Canadian House of Industry (workhouse), but he feared that as soon as it became known that he had come out under the auspices of the Barnardo organisation, 'every effort would be made to throw him on our hands and we should be more or less in collision with the authorities as long as he remained on their hands, of course bringing a certain amount of discreditable publicity'. It was just this kind of publicity that Barnardo was most anxious to avoid. Owen was anxious to highlight the positive aspects of the emigration policy as well, and he pointed out that each child came to Canada with an outfit worth $35 and that the payment of boarding-out fees in Ontario alone came to more than $60,000 a year.

Kelso had begun his report by admitting that there was widespread prejudice against child emigration which he hoped the Ontario Act would remove. He accepted there was no means of computing its success, apart from Barnardo's figures. Throughout his introduction he showed himself to be aware of the grave injustices that had been done to the children by sensational accounts appearing in the press of crimes committed. He gave as an example the case of a girl, said to be an English waif, who had tried to poison the whole family with whom she lived and who had then disappeared. Numerous editorials followed, all denouncing child immigration, yet on investigation he discovered the original offence was trifling and the child a native-born Canadian.

He recognised that the agitation had been 'tremendously hurtful' to the children and many of the girls had been exposed to the base designs of disreputable men because of the constant reference to 'slum' and 'outcast' children. The second-class status of the children is underlined again and again by Kelso. He cited the case of a girl who had been grossly ill-used and a prominent member of the community made the remark, 'as a sort of extenuating circumstance, that the girl "was only an English girl"'. Although he said it would not be fair to say that those taking children belong to an inferior class, 'this much may be said – that the best class of people, as a rule, seek native-born children for adoption, while the element of work, present or prospective, enters largely into the calculations of those applying to English agencies'.

Aware of the hazard to which the children were exposed through lack of adequate supervision, the dangers of rapid placement which meant they would not all get proper homes, the possibilities of exploitation because of the obviously superficial nature of much of the inspection, Kelso's final conclusion was that 'unfortunately there have in the past been cases brought to light forcibly illustrating the need for vigilance in protecting the children from cruel task masters, but there is hardly sufficient ground that this is the prevailing condition'. Kelso's main consideration was, however, not what was best for the children but what was best for Canada. He knew there was a 'genuine demand' among farmers for the services of the children and he thought 'briefly, that child immigration, if carried on with care and discretion, need not be injurious to the country'.[22] He asked only that the children should be free from disease or taint of criminality, their treatment should be such as to surround them with every desirable safeguard and that opposition be withdrawn until the Ontario Act had been given a fair trial.

Nine

FROM SALVATION TO EMPIRE: LETTERS FROM SOUTH AFRICA

> Far as the breeze can bear, the billows foam,
> Survey our Empire, and behold our home.
>
> BYRON

THE slow evolution during the nineteenth century of Britain's position at the centre of a world-wide empire might be said to have culminated with the exuberant celebrations that marked Queen Victoria's Diamond Jubilee in 1897. With hindsight the occasion can now be seen as a high-water mark and Britain's imperial role, since then, as one of long slow decline. To those alive at the time the prospect must have looked very different. There was an illusion of permanence; there was confidence that loyalty to the crown, the symbol of imperial power, would continue to hold nations as different as India, Australia, Canada and South Africa together. The Boer War was two years off. When it was painfully won, a small army of ill-equipped but determined Boer farmers, keeping the imperial forces at bay for three long years, would reveal just how vulnerable were the links that bound the Empire together.

The historian J.R. Seeley aptly described the British Empire as 'having been acquired in a fit of absence of mind' which neatly took account of its random origins. Its possessions had been acquired for different motives, for profit, for markets and raw materials, to protect trade routes; there had also been a desire to do good. By the 1890s there was a real belief that the extension of the Empire was good, not only for Britain, but for those who came under her sway. Seeley had been one of the first to point to Britain's changed relationship with her colonies. In his Cambridge lectures, published in 1883 under the title *The Expansion of Britain*, he linked poverty and unemployment with the concept of imperial expansion through his advocacy of widespread emigration of the pauper population to the 'white' colonies.

The British were, in any case, a restless people and more of them had left the British Isles in the nineteenth century than had gone from any other European country. Disasters like the Irish famine in 1845 and the periodic depressions in England caused the numbers to vary, but by the 1890s some 200,000 were leaving annually, in some cases to avoid actual starvation. Few can have had any thought of furthering the imperial cause. They wanted security for themselves and a chance to earn their livings. For the working man the colonies were not particularly attractive: convict settlements in Australia were still in the recent past; Canada was less attractive than the United States; South Africa had little need for unskilled labour.

When gold was found the picture changed. Poor people joined the rush with adventurers from all ranks, moving from gold-strike to gold-strike. Such emigration was essentially unplanned and had little to do with the dreams and aspirations of the social imperialists. They saw emigration as a way of ridding the country of unprofitable and costly citizens and at the same time as a way of strengthening the ties between Britain and her Empire. Lord Brabazon's plans for state-aided colonisation as a remedy for the unemployment problems of the 1880s had never materialised because it was soon realised that urban-bred casual labourers would never make good farmers, nor would the colonies be willing to receive such emigrants. Gold-rush fever did little or nothing either to relieve the chronic poverty of the great cities or to further emigration.

But when William Booth, of the Salvation Army, published his solution to the problem of poverty and destitution in 1890, his book, *In Darkest England and the Way Out*, was an immediate best seller. Briefly, his idea was that the chronic poor, 'the submerged tenth', as he called them, should be settled on depopulated land in 'farm colonies' in Britain where they would receive both moral teaching and instruction in agriculture. Thus prepared they would be moved overseas to the colonies where they would settle in new 'farm colonies'. Booth wrote, 'It would be absurd to speak of the colonies as if they were a foreign land. They are simply pieces of Britain distributed about the world, enabling the Britisher to have access to the richest parts of the earth.'[1]

Booth had relied heavily on William Stead's journalistic skills in writing the book and it was a partnership which was to cost him a lot of support. The leaders of the juvenile emigration movement, who might have been expected to welcome this new initiative, were hostile, although because of their respect for the work of the Salvation Army, their criticism was muted. *The Christian* quoted a passage Stead had written in support of Booth: 'eighteen millions may be regarded as the cash value of the endowment erected by the Salvation Army out of nothing in twenty-five years. A tolerably substantial miracle this, compared with that of the loaves and fishes but a small affair.' The editor commented on it with 'pain and shock' and said:

> In *In Darkest England* the voice is the voice of General Booth, but the hands are the hands of Mr Stead. We greatly admire the benevolence of Mr Stead, but we fear, and feel, that his preponderating influence is leading the originator of the Salvation Army away from the principles on which the movement was based.[2]

There was another reason for alarm. Booth had announced that he would need at least £1,000,000 to implement his scheme. Much of the finance that supported the juvenile emigration movement came from readers of *The Christian*. It warned, 'Let not a shilling contributed to this scheme be permitted to lessen the subscriptions to agencies which are already in the field, doing this very work on a smaller scale, with proved efficiency; and it certainly is not desirable, even if it were possible, that all these should be swallowed up in one great organisation.'

But although Booth's ideas gained neither the support of Parliament nor the approval of the evangelicals and his plans were the cause of yet another COS investigation, none the less the numbers of adults and children emigrated by the Salvation Army increased significantly. By the end of the century the number of children being sent to Canada made it one of the largest agencies in the field of child emigration.

The growing importance of the social imperialists, the influence of social reformers like Brabazon and Samuel Smith, and Booth's book all helped to give those who believed in juvenile emigration a broader base on which to make their appeal. Barnardo, always the most publicity minded of the philanthropists, was not slow to make use of the imperial theme in his advertising. Referring to his children as 'bricks for empire building' and 'precious freight' he wrote articles with titles like 'How to think Imperially' to raise funds for emigration. He would have liked to enlarge his personal empire and to create opportunities for his children in Australia and South Africa as he had done in Canada.

Throughout the 1890s Barnardo had been receiving requests from Australia, New Zealand and South Africa for trained boys and girls, requests which on the whole he had ignored, fearing the dangers that would face youngsters on the long journey out and knowing that he would be totally unable to give them any support once out there if things went wrong. Occasionally this rule was relaxed, when for instance a whole group of lads sailed on the *Charlotte Padbury* and landed at Fremantle in Western Australia in 1883. The happy coincidence that Lord Brassey, who was president of the Barnardo Homes, was appointed Governor-General of Western Australia in 1896 enabled Barnardo to test the strength of the support he might expect from the colony. Lord Brassey had offered him land from his own holdings in Western Australia to enable him to set up an industrial farm like the one he had in Canada, but before Barnardo could accept he needed to know how much financial support the government of Western Australia was likely to offer him.

A debate was initiated in Parliament by Mr Cooksworthy, the Member for Sussex, who was an admirer of Barnardo's work and thought the importation of his trained boys and girls would be advantageous to the colony. The motion debated was, 'That in the opinion of this House, it is desirable that the Government should put themselves in communication with Dr Barnardo with a view to his sending young people to the colony.'[3] The debate neatly illustrated why juvenile emigration was a less attractive proposition to Western Australia than to Canada. William Stead had recently written an article in the *Review of Reviews* extolling the virtues of Barnardo's work in Canada, and

Mr Cooksworthy quoted from this. He said he had already ascertained that the emigration of children could not be done on a small scale as it would be too expensive, but he felt that the Government only needed to give Barnardo some assistance for a large number of boys and girls to be introduced into the colony.

He was supported by Mr Illingworth, the Member for Nannine, who said that there was 'no scheme in Great Britain, or in all the British-speaking colonies that was doing a greater work than that of Dr Barnardo's'. He went on to say that grave objections had been raised against the idea of a colony of the Salvation Army being established, but these objections failed if they were directed against the young men and women who came from the Barnardo Homes as 'the work was complete in all departments, most perfect men and women being turned out under the system, and out of the worst possible material'. Looking at the advantages Canada had gained, and weighing up the advantages of importing trained children as against trained adults he produced the rather unusual argument that it 'costs £200 to produce a full grown man, and if they could land on these shores a number of these young people, each of whom had cost £200 to produce, they would by that means increase the wealth of the colony considerably'. Mr Illingworth ended his speech by saying that the children had been 'taught to work, taught to recognise the position in life in which they had been placed', by which he presumably meant that the girls would not look for fulfilment beyond domestic service or the boys beyond farm labour. 'They had been taught to do their work with spirit and energy and were the kind of men who would build up the national life in the best possible way.' Barnardo himself could not have put it better.

It was left to the Premier, Sir John Forrest, to spell out the fact that no government could be sufficiently altruistic to import children for the sake of giving the children a better life; only where there was a genuine need for child labour could juvenile emigration really succeed. He pointed out that at this time there was a great influx of people into the colony, that the Barnardo boys were not taught agriculture and were strictly artisans, and, touching on a delicate point, said 'there was no doubt that a little prejudice existed in Australia against the introduction of people who had some little taint.... The feeling to which he referred was probably an improper feeling; and for his own part he thought it was, but it existed and they could not altogether ignore it.' He also pointed out that only Canada of all the self-governing powers had entered into negotiations with Dr Barnardo, and 'if the advantages were so very great there would have been a rush by all the other self-governing colonies to obtain the services of his young people'.

The Commissioner of Crown Lands then chose to draw attention to the fact that there was a great scarcity of female servants in the colony and that it might be no bad thing if Barnardo could send out some of his trained girls. Since no one could deny that such a need existed it was agreed to let the motion stand as it committed no one to anything at all. It was not until after the First World War that any Barnardo children came to Western Australia. They came then under very different circumstances, as part of a new wave of emigrant children, sent to Australia to live and work at the Farm School in Pinjarra. It was a school founded by Kingsley Fairbridge, whose vision of the future transcended the simple notion that child emigration provided a means of salvation and a fresh start; he saw the children, growing to adulthood in the Australian bush, as forming part of the very fabric of the Empire.

Fewer children were sent to South Africa than to either New Zealand or Australia. This could have been because Barnardo's work might have been better known in Australasia, where in 1891 he had sent a party of 'musical boys' accompanied by the Reverend W.J. Mayers to make known the work of the homes and to raise funds. As a result of the musical entertainment provided by the boys £10,000 was raised for the work. This publicity may well have resulted in supporters in Australia knowing of friends and family who would be willing to accompany children out to Australia. For the children who were sent to South Africa there was no organisation to which they could go in time of trouble. Of the children who went to South Africa, in at least two cases Barnardo had cause to believe that they would be better off out of the country, and there were reasons why it was not appropriate for them to be sent to Canada.

In 1885 Barnardo had been approached by a Mrs Boyden who asked him to admit her godson, Henry Crick. Henry's parents were separated. His father, who at different times had run eel pie and tripe shops with a notable lack of success, was said to be always in debt and a 'shifty customer'. His mother was recorded as being a drunken and dissipated woman. Mrs Boyden said that if Henry were returned to either of his parents it would lead to his utter ruin, so, aged fourteen, he became an inmate of the Stepney Home. He had suffered from bad eyes since the age of two and his record shows that while he was at Stepney he was constantly in and out of the infirmary on account of eye trouble. Afraid of what might happen if he returned to either of his parents and unable to send him to Canada because of his medical condition, Barnardo sent him to Natal with another lad named Frederick Greer.

There seems no particular reason why Frederick should have been selected to go to South Africa unless Barnardo had received a specific request for two boys and sent Frederick as part of the deal. His parents were poor but respectable. His father had been a porter at the Nine Elms goods station but he had died in 1882. As a porter he had earned one pound a week and out of that had managed to insure with the Prudential Insurance Company. When the £4 12s insurance was used up his widow could only make six shillings a week by needlework and was forced to sell off her furniture to maintain herself and her family. Before Frederick was admitted, a very thorough investigation was made of all her relatives, of which she had many, to discover if any one of them could help: of the two grandmothers, three uncles and four aunts identified, all were too poor or had too many children of their own to be able to help.

A strange quirk of fate sent William Cassell to South Africa. Had he not destroyed some bills he had been given to distribute by the Boys' Brigade in Gateshead, where he had been an inmate for eighteen months, he might never have gone overseas. His mother had died when he was thirteen and his father, who was described as a 'lazy, worthless man', was in the Gateshead workhouse. Although the superintendent of the Boys' Brigade described William as 'an Irish lad full of devilment', he had never been in trouble until the incident with the bills. The superintendent decided, however, to make an example of William and expelled him from the Brigade and thus William came to Barnardo's. Both William's parents were Roman

Catholic and Barnardo had not long since been in trouble with the law and the Roman Catholic hierarchy for sending Catholic children to Canada. On the other hand, William was said to have 'too many doubtful associates to be likely to prosper' in Gateshead, so he too was sent to South Africa in response to yet another request for a boy.

The year was 1898. In Rhodesia Kingsley Fairbridge, a year younger than William, was living with his father, helping to open up the country. It was in 1897 that Kingsley, walking home, half starved and miserable, had had a vision of the empty veld covered in farms and peopled by emigrants from England whom he had heard about. He was never to lose that vision which was to lead to a new initiative in child emigration, not in Rhodesia as he had hoped, but in Western Australia where Barnardo had just failed.

Since the debate in the Western Australian parliament had led precisely nowhere, Barnardo began to think more seriously about the possibility of starting an organised emigration scheme to South Africa. After the débâcle of the Jameson Raid Joseph Chamberlain, the Colonial Secretary, who was to make imperialism the central plank of his political career, sent Milner to be British High Commissioner to the Cape and Governor of the Orange River Colony. Milner, complex, clever, had described himself as 'a civilian soldier of the Empire'. His assignment in Africa was no easy one. Since the discovery of gold and diamond mines in the Transvaal, which had made fortunes for Rhodes and Alfred Beit, the importance of establishing British supremacy in South Africa had taken on a new dimension. The disastrous raid – led by Dr Jameson, financed by Rhodes and Beit and connived at by Chamberlain – which had been designed to wrest political power from the Boers in the Transvaal, ended in ignominy, and British authority was gravely weakened. Jameson served a prison sentence, Rhodes resigned from the premiership of the Cape and from the chairmanship of the Chartered Company, the British South Africa Company, granted a Royal charter in 1889.

Milner, who admitted that he 'was cursed with a cross-bench mind' said at the party given for him before he left to take up his duties in South Africa that, in spite of that, he could not understand the arguments of those who questioned imperial unity. Milner shared with Chamberlain and Rhodes the belief that the Empire would not grow of itself but had to be 'urgently manufactured'. Milner was not long in reaching the conclusion that the only way not just to restore the position, but to open the way for the future unity of South Africa under British rule, his ultimate objective, was to fight and vanquish the Boers. Relentlessly he drove Kruger, their stubborn leader, into a position where he had no option but to stand and fight.

Thus in 1899 began the Boer War and Barnardo was forced to defer his hopes of finding homes and work for his children in South Africa. The war finally ended in May 1902, but the peace at Vereeniging had been dearly bought in terms of men, money and materials. As the country struggled back to normality no one knew how many men, women and children had lost their lives in the field and in the concentration camps. Kitchener's scorched-earth policy had left the Boer homesteads devastated and their stock killed. Rhodes had died before the peace was signed, before the imperial government had started to implement, under Milner's guidance, plans for the re-settlement of the country. Arrangements were made for thirty-five million pounds to be borrowed for investment, plans were made for large-scale irrigation channels to be dug and for a network of railways to be constructed. But before any of these plans could bear fruit Barnardo decided that the time had come for him to investigate the possibility of extending juvenile emigration to South Africa.

There was no question of Barnardo making the journey himself: he was a sick man with a dangerous heart condition. His eldest son, Stuart Barnardo, however, was willing and qualified to act on his behalf. Stuart had shown no desire to follow in his father's footsteps and had trained as a mining engineer. He had accompanied his father on more than one occasion to Canada and was well aware of the nature and needs of Barnardo's work. It was from the farm in Manitoba, which Barnardo had visited for the last time in 1900, that Stuart had gone on to the Yukon. This venture proving unprofitable, he had returned to England and was happy and willing, for a small salary and expenses, to go to South Africa, where he hoped to find work in the gold and diamond mines for himself after he had accomplished his mission for his father.

Although Barnardo appears to have had little understanding of the political situation in South Africa he gave Stuart very precise instructions as to his needs. The Duke of Argyll, a former Governor-General of Canada and an advocate of juvenile emigration, had become president of the homes. He had interests in South Africa and, like Brassey before him, had offered Barnardo 1,500 acres on any one of the twenty farms that Hendersons, the land agents, were supposed to be holding for him. Stuart was to visit the farms and select the most promising. He was to find out if the Government would be willing to make money available both for the erection of farm buildings and for a home for girls; he was to see if he would get help with fares, both on the journey out and on the railways; he was to inquire as to the chances of being given educational grants; and he was to assess the chances of the children finding work once they had been trained. Stuart was provided with a formidable list of letters of introduction. Given the state of the country and the tight financial budget on which he was expected to operate, it was a daunting assignment.

Stuart set out in August and for four months he travelled the length and breadth of South Africa. His letters to his father, in which he dutifully described how he spent each day, whom he met and what they said, have an interest which transcends their seemingly circumscribed intention. They provide an extra dimension to our understanding of the juvenile emigration question and put it in a different perspective. Although Stuart believed that his father would be able to build up a system of organised child emigration to South Africa on the same lines as he had done in Canada, at the same time his letters reveal the many crucial differences between society in South Africa and Canada. It was these differences that effectively prevented the development of organised child emigration to South Africa in spite of the almost hysterical demand for white domestic servants and the imperial ambitions of the British High Commissioner, Lord Milner. Stuart's letters provide a picture of a country at a critical stage in its development. The point of view is unusual but the special interest of the letters lies in Stuart's analysis of the situation in the country, which points out, all too clearly, trends which have led to South Africa's present isolated position in the world.

RMS *Scott*
Aug. 4 1902

My dear Father,
I got away safely on Saturday last and up to the present have not much news to tell, except that the Bay has for once in a way been calm like a mill pond. The boat is very inferior to what I expected and not to be compared in any way to the Atlantic ships, as the table and attendance are very bad indeed. We have only got about 60 passengers on board amongst whom are Dr Jameson and Alfred Beit, the S. African millionaire, but they have not been on deck much up to the present. The rest of the passengers are mostly young fellows who are going out to S. Africa for the first time. . . . We reach Funchal, Madeira, tomorrow (Wednesday) morning at about 6 o'clock and the mail has to be made up tonight. After leaving there I believe everything improves and gets more sociable as up to the present nobody has spoken to anyone hardly at all, the general tone of all being that the voyage does not begin till after we leave Madeira.

Yr, Affte. Son,
Stuart

Stuart made good use of his opportunities on board as is shown by his second letter, when he had managed to get into conversation with both Alfred Beit and Jameson who were on their way back to South Africa not only to look after their own interests but to implement the terms of Rhodes's will. Jameson, the disgrace of the raid forgotten, was to become Prime Minister of the Cape within two years.

Aug. 6 1902

My dear Father,
Since posting my last page I had a conversation with a Mr Battery special correspondent for the *Daily Mail* who has been out in S. Africa for two years, partly before and partly during the War on the *Johannesburg Miner and Diggers News*, who is now on his way to Madeira to meet Botha and others of the late Boer leaders. From him I gathered that the first question to be considered in the Transvaal and S. Africa in general is that of water and that without some scheme of irrigation such as is now advocated by Lord Milner, the question of whether farming can succeed must be answered in the negative. . . . He also thought that the native was much superior to a white man as a farm labourer or indeed for any kind of work in the open owing to the climate. With regard to house servants he also thought the native superior and to be preferred by most settlers, even in the towns, as

they are more amenable and easier to keep. But the great question he thought was that of an increase of the British by children born out in S. Africa and that any agency which could and would help that on by providing girls who might in the near future be the wives of the colonists and the mothers of the next generation would be heartily welcomed and helped. Of course he was only speaking from the standpoint of a journalist.... Dr Jameson and Mr Beit have kept very much to their cabins up to the present but I hope if they emerge from their retirement to get their news.... Mr Justice Mason from Durban is going out with us, his father was a Wesleyan Minister and he takes an interest in all work of this description.... Mr Justice Mason is going to introduce me to Mr Beit....

Mr Beit seemed very interested in the scheme when I had a talk with him this morning and asked for some literature on the work.... He thinks Sir G. Sprigg [Prime Minister of Cape Colony] may do something for us and if not, that the Transvaal or Orange River Colony are likely to look favourably on the scheme. In which case he is of opinion that the government would aid by grants. He also tells me that in his opinion white labour will be in demand on the farms of the two new colonies. If I am not very successful in Cape Town he would like me to call on him there and he will do what he can by letters to his partners in Johannesburg etc. to help me. I did not have much chance of questioning him as he seemed anxious to do most of this himself. Still he is now on deck reading the report.... He particularly wanted information on the Canadian work which I gave him to the best of my knowledge....

Dr Jameson who is now on his way out to S. Africa to put through, if possible, an emigration scheme in accordance with Mr Rhodes's Will, had a talk with me this morning. He holds views similar to Mr Beit, but thinks that while white labour will never take the place of native, yet boys such as you might send out will readily find places with farmers as apprentices and will then when men be fit and able to take up land for themselves either from the government or from private individuals. Dr Jameson thinks that we are more likely to find assistance in the Transvaal and Orange River Colony than in the two older colonies, owing to the very keen interest Lord Milner takes in the question of emigration.... Dr Jameson's idea is to start industrial farms in S. Africa and send out boys of the workhouse class most probably....

Stuart arrived in Cape Town on 19 August and immediately got busy making inquiries. He had an interview with the editor of the *South African News* who confirmed Dr Jameson's feeling that the Orange River and Transvaal Colonies were more likely to give aid, 'as they are now being run as Crown Colonies and the people have not to be consulted in the matter at all as they have here'. Stuart called on Sir Hely Hutchinson, the Governor, and his wife. Lady Hely Hutchinson's views on emigration were typical of many of her class. She was only interested in one aspect of the problem, the getting and keeping of domestic servants. Self-interest rather than genuine philanthropy motivated a lot of the powerful support given to the work of the rescue homes.

Aug. 22

I called by appointment on Sir Hely Hutchinson this morning at 11 o'clock and was received very kindly by him. He is very keen on getting boy and girl emigrants to the Colony, chiefly the former, but he said that unfortunately the Governor of the Colony could not do whatever he wanted like Lord Milner in a Crown Colony.... Lady Hely received me in a very gracious way. She is a charming woman and beautiful, and takes a very keen interest in the subject of domestic servant emigration. From her I gathered that domestic servants are a crying want in the Colony, but not owing to the fact that none come out. Indeed she thinks that too many are coming out and that the Colony is now being flooded with women of that class ... they will not remain as servants for any length of time and are marrying young men of the better class, not farmers. She thinks it unadvisable that the mothers of the next generation should be domestic servants. Servants here are not much use until they reach the age of 18 and when they reach that age they refuse to be servants any longer, but go to the restaurants, bars etc., or marry young men who ought to have wives of a higher class. She thinks that the farms would be quite unsuitable for your girls as they are mostly owned by the Dutch who have no regard to their proper care.... If you could only arrange some scheme by which the girls you send out might remain as servants, for some time at any rate, you would, in her opinion, be doing a great and lasting good to the country and would be going far in solving the domestic servant question. I suggested that a similar law might be passed, giving you the power of guardian as you have in Canada; but Lady Hutchinson thinks the age ought to be at least 21....

The following day Stuart called on the Prime Minister, Sir Gordon Sprigg, leader of the Progressive Party, a party which had been financed by Rhodes. Sprigg enjoyed power and was unwilling to do anything to offend the powerful Dutch opposition, represented by the Bond. 'Sir Gordon heard me out to the end and then said he was not prepared at present to say what the Government would or could do, in fact he was not even prepared to say that he was in favour of child emigration such as ours at this juncture.' Sprigg knew full well that the Dutch Bond were totally opposed to any form of emigration from England. However, Mr Pillans at the Department of Agriculture, to whom Sprigg sent Stuart, was more forthcoming.

I met with a much more hopeful reception from Mr Pillans who told me he had met you in London about 1885 and had then tried to get you to send out some of your boys and girls to S. Africa, but that you would not fall in with his wishes. I explained the reasons against sending out isolated children or even a number of children until we had some settled organisation by means of which we could exercise supervision over them. I then laid before him the conditions we thought to be essential to success. He thought that the time had now come for you to do something and gave me the assurance privately, that even at the present moment the Government are preparing in the estimates to put aside a sum of money to help emigration, but this is being kept very dark owing to the fear that the Dutch would oppose it tooth and nail if they found it out before the proper time came....

Dr Muir, the superintendent-general of education, had a more realistic approach to the situation than Mr Pillans:

Dr Muir also told me the same as others, that it is no good trying to get any aid to emigration of English children from the Dutch side of the House and that the present Government is kept in power and are hoping to pass their measures by aid of the 'Bond', who much as they dislike the idea of voting money towards emigration of any kind yet can hardly refuse or give their true grounds of refusal viz., dislike of England, since they are now loudly proclaiming their loyalty. Dr Muir says aid to emigration is purely a political position and has to be treated as such by the Government.... I have seen enough to already realise what a keen political question emigration is. The Dutch are absolutely against it except for an isolated girl or two whom some families want for their own convenience, but which is quite different from an emigration scheme aided by the Government.... And the Government, who are looking to the 'Bond' side of the House to carry their measures and not to their own party, are very unwilling to do anything to alienate the Dutch or to in anyway bring to a head the racial question by asking openly for money to help bring out English settlers and thus increase the British element at the expense of the

Dutch. Still I now mean to try and get to know some of the leading Dutch in Cape Town and see what they think of emigration.

Stuart found it more difficult to meet with members of the Bond and it wasn't until early September that he managed to meet Dr Beck at the Salvation Army farm at Rondebosch, which was being run mainly by men recently released from jail.

Sept. 5th

I went out to Rondebosch today and had lunch with Dr Beck and his wife. He is a Dutchman but told me he considered himself a 'Dutch Britisher', is also a member of Parliament and one of the chief men in the 'Bond'. He thinks highly of your work and of the idea of sending out children, but he thinks it ought not to be entered into lightly and without getting a thorough idea of the country and its ways of life. That the native everywhere enters into competition with the white girl as a servant and that it is next to impossible to employ them both. The servants in a house must be either all white or all black. That the country is in such an unhappy state of turmoil and seething discontent at present that it is almost impossible to get a fair unbiased opinion of the wants of the country as a whole.

That the British element is crying out in a hysterical manner for English servants, chiefly because they wish the British to be in the majority, and who in calmer moments would most probably take a quite different view of the question. Also that the Government have got a most serious problem of their own to consider, viz the Poor Whites. That this question was a serious one before the war, although much had been done for this class, but that now it had assumed large proportions through the number of farmers who had lost their all and through the children and widows of men who had died fighting on one side or the other. That the Government must provide for their own people first before aiding a scheme having as the object of its work the bringing out, training and finding employment for children who will enter into competition with the Colonial children mentioned above.... He does not think the Government would be justified at present in promising aid until the more acute questions have been decided and the country has settled down with the Dutch and English living peaceably side by side and not as they are at the present time, flying at each others throats.

Dr Beck seemed to me to be a thinking and honest man, who really has the good of Cape Colony and S. Africa at heart and who would sincerely like to see the two races friendly and contented. And I think his opinion is worth more than that of a large number of the intensely pro British I have met out here.... I think I have done all I can in Cape Town at present, so am leaving for Bloemfontein by tonight's train. Unfortunately we start at 9 pm so I shall miss seeing the country round Cape Town. I am sending this off here tonight as I should miss the English mail which leaves here on the 10th if I delayed posting till I got to Bloemfontein.

Yr. loving son, Stuart

Stuart had had to obtain special permission to travel outside Cape Colony and considered himself lucky to have obtained a pass that allowed him to stop where he wished. The journey to Bloemfontein, the capital of the Orange River Colony, took nineteen hours and he was lucky to find a hotel to stay in.

Sept 8th

I found when I went to bed that I had to share my room with another man, still I had a bed to myself and must congratulate myself on faring better than some other people who came up by train and had to sleep in the station wherever they could lie down. The town is frightfully crowded at present, partly owing to the military and partly to the returning Boers who are coming back by the train load every day.

This morning I called on Mr J.G. Fraser, uncle I believe of the ex-President Mr Steyn, an Englishman by birth, to whom I had a letter of introduction ... a far seeing, level headed and fair minded man who did his best to avert war but when it came accepted the situation.... In his opinion the country is at present ruined and the farmers who are going back to their farms find their homesteads burnt and their land desolate. It will be some time, perhaps 3 or 4 years before the country reaches the prosperity it had before the war and that until this time comes it would be quite out of reason to think that the farmers could afford to hire boys or girls as servants.

There were other reasons why Mr Fraser did not think it would be right to send children to South Africa, reasons which Stuart was to hear repeated many times. Stuart continued his letter:

The natives make most unreliable servants in his opinion, but it would not do to let your girls go to families except those who keep only white servants. He tells me that white girls who go as servants to families who keep native servants also, always quickly deteriorate when they find that there are servants lower than them and become quite useless. Also that the majority of the Boer farmers would not be suitable people to send your girls to, not because they would illtreat them.... The average Boer farmer and his family treat a servant (white) as one of themselves, but they live in an untidy, dirty way and quite unfit a girl for service elsewhere.... Sometime in the future, when the country is prosperous, he thinks the boys would be welcomed on the farms and would do well as the native labourer would not interfere with them.

Stuart saw the Governor, Sir Henry Gould-Adams, but he was no more encouraging than any of the other people he questioned in the Orange River Colony who all thought there would be opportunities for placing boys, but not for three or four years when the country would be more settled. Conditions were difficult.

Bloemfontein is at present the reverse of healthy as far as the water is concerned ... [it] is not fit to drink unboiled, and as I cannot get boiled water in the hotel I have been forced to drink soda water. I have no room to pack anything more or I would get a kettle and spirit lamp and boil my own. Also it is almost impossible except in the large towns to buy spirit and even here it is frightfully expensive. In fact just at present everything is at famine prices. Eggs are worth here four shillings a dozen and in Johannesburg seven shillings and sixpence, so you can imagine we do not get a chance of eating many.

Stuart did not find things any easier when he tried to see the farm at Mooiplatz, journeying to Winburg for the purpose. It took him two and a half hours by train to travel the last twenty-eight miles, and then he could not hire a horse to ride out to it.

Sept 11th

I have just arrived in Winburg after an awful journey.... The wind was awful and the dust and sand so bad that I could hardly put my head out of the refreshment room without getting choked with dust so as to be unable to breathe.... The train took two and a half hours getting to Winberg and when we did get there the storm was worse than ever. I had to leave my baggage and fight my way to the only hotel in the place, about half a mile off.

Sept 12th

This morning the storm is as bad as ever, grit and dust are in everything. I have sent a boy down for my baggage to the station.... This afternoon the wind has dropped with consequence that the rain has come and it is simply pouring down in torrents.

Sept 13th

I have tried to hire a cart and horses but have been unable to do so. You can have no idea how terribly scarce horses are now all over the country. What few there are, are in the hands of the police (the S.A.

Constabulary) and this is one of the great drawbacks to a rapid re-establishment of the farmers on their old farms.

Sept 14th

This morning I went to the Dutch Reformed Church, but as the whole service was in Dutch I could not understand much. There is an English Church here but the parson was away.

By 18 September Stuart had arrived in Johannesburg. He was somewhat comforted to find that even if he had succeeded in getting to Mooiplatz Farm his journey would have been useless. He wrote to his father:

The arrangement between the Duke of Argyll and Messrs Hendersons seems to have been drawn up very badly. No mention is made of which 1,500 acres of land on Mooiplatz Farm is meant and as far as I can gather there is nothing to prevent Henderson's from selling or renting all the best land, leaving the Duke of Argyll with 1,500 acres of the poorest. And so with most of the farms mentioned in the list you gave me, you only have choice of a portion of the land making up each farm and there is nothing definite about this even. In fact from what I can gather, about half the so-called farms are not even worth going to see as they are so far away from a railway or from other farmers. Mr Pott (of Henderson's) will not be able to let me have the plan of Mooiplatz Farm till next week.

Now began Stuart's long wait to see Lord Milner who was away from Johannesburg when he arrived. Milner had recruited a group of young men, known as Milner's 'kindergarten', eager to share with him the task of reconstructing South Africa's war-torn economy and of bringing about the unity of the country so as to become truly part of the British Empire. Lionel Curtis was the most prominent member; others included John Buchan, whose book *The Thirty-Nine Steps* would bring him fame, and Oliver Walrond.

This afternoon I spent from 2 pm till 5 pm waiting to see Mr O. Walrond, private secretary to Lord Milner, to whom I had a letter. Mr Walrond, when at last I saw him, could only give me a few minutes but wrote a letter for me to Mr Buchan, Lord Milner's secretary for emigration, asking him to do his best to get me an early interview with Lord Milner. Mr Walrond, however, tells me that I may have to wait a fortnight before I can see Lord Milner as he is very busy and full of engagements for some time to come. I hope I have better luck though than that.

Still I shall not be surprised if I have to wait some time, as everybody out here seems to be born tired. They do not seem able to get a hustle on even in this town where one would think everything would be bustle and hurry. But the mines are scattered for a long distance and the energetic men mostly live out at the mines. The whole country also is in a sort of paralysed condition, waiting like Mr Micawber for something to turn up and there is I am told very little business being done in Jo'burg at present. Thousands of men are out of work and the streets are full of loafers. Living is very dear and all the hotels are full and have put up their prices. £1 a day is the lowest one can get decent accommodation for.

Sept 19th

... After lunch I called on Mr Buchan, whom I have already mentioned and had a long talk with him. At first he was inclined to pooh-pooh the whole idea, but I found that he had a very mistaken idea of your scheme. He thought you proposed to take up a very large grant of land and on it place a large number of boys as permanent settlers....

After Stuart had disabused Buchan and put forward Barnardo's scheme there was a change in attitude.

Mr Buchan thereupon expressed unqualified approval and asked what help you expected to get from the Government.... He tells me Lord Milner will be back in Jo'burg on Sunday and that he will try and arrange an interview for me sometime next week. He also said that your boys, after they had been out here two or three years and then had gone to situations, would be perfectly qualified in his opinion to take advantage of the 'Government land settlement scheme' by which stock, land, implements and a loan of money are advanced to intending farmers on easy terms by Government in localities where there will be a number of British farmers within a small radius.... Mr Buchan also had a list of the farms which the Duke of Argyll has given you a choice of, and told me that you ought to very closely look into the deed by which the option of these farms is given to the Duke as Henderson's are notoriously very close and hard people to drive a bargain.

Stuart remained worried about the number of farms he was supposed to visit and wrote, 'I shall see all that I possibly can ... the expense of going to see some of them would be enormous, at least £5 a day for a cart, even if I could hire one which is doubtful.' He continued to call on a wide variety of people to whom he had introductions, canvassing opinions as to the viability of Barnardo's scheme. Mr Cook, the manager of a large wholesale merchants, was very much in favour of girls being sent out. Stuart wrote:

> The great field for you is in providing of domestic servants for the better class families in the large towns of Jo'burg and Pretoria.... Servants cannot be obtained at any price, even the natives refuse to work now since the war as they are rich and do not need to work for the next few years at any rate ... Mr Cook tells me that for the last four months his wife has had to do all the ironing of clothes for his family although he has offered £5 a month to a native woman just to do the ironing and washing. She refuses to do this as her husband, who is working for Mr Cook, makes £7 per month which is riches to them.

When Barnardo was introduced to Mr Carr, the Deputy Chairman of the City Council, he had a rough reception.

> Mr Carr immediately said I am a Roman Catholic and if Barnardo's Homes are going to work on the same blackguarding lines in this country like they do in England I shall oppose their coming to S. Africa tooth and nail.... I told him that what you wanted to do was to establish ... institutions as in Canada to help carry out the emigration of boys and girls to act as servants etc. Mr Carr then said he should write to Cardinal Vaughan to see if you could be trusted ... I then gave him an outline of the scheme as at present thought of. Mr Carr said, 'I suppose you are going to flood us with criminals.'

While waiting to see Milner, Stuart called on the brother of Ellen Bilborough of the Marchmont Home in Canada. A stockbroker, he had 'very distinct and settled views on emigration'.

> He thought you would be most ill-advised to think of sending either boys or girls out to S. Africa. That the boys would certainly not be taken on by any of the Dutch farmers.... That the native would stand in the way of the boys getting on, as native labour is almost exclusively used on the farms and that even if the boys were employed they would have to work alongside the native. That this would lead to moral retrogression on the part of the boys who would, like all white men, when they sink to the level of the native, go still lower down than even the native himself. That the native is not, and will never be in his opinion, anything but a rather superior sort of beast, being dirty and vicious in his habits. That as to the girls ... it is very hard to find among the well-to-do-class a family where the girl would be subject to Christian influences and that in his opinion you would simply be helping them to a worse state than that from which you had rescued

them by sending them out here. In addition to this most families keep natives to do the rough work, such as washing dishes which the white servants refuse to do after they have been out here a short time, and that it does not do for many reasons to mix them. One must either keep all native or all white servants. That for similar reasons the girls could not be sent to farms.

On 27 September Stuart went again to see Buchan in the hopes that 'he might be able to arrange for an interview with His Excellency, even if only for a few minutes. Mr Buchan, however, said that Lord Milner was so very busy that . . . he was afraid it would be several days before he could . . . make an appointment.'

Johannesburg,
Sept 29th 1902

My dear Father,
I have just returned from seeing Lord Milner, who listened carefully to what I had to say and when I had finished said that he would very much like to see you succeed out here, but that there were very many things against your doing so. With regard to aid from the Government he said that the aid we wanted would have to come through the Executive Council of the Colony and that they were so busy at present, one man trying to do the work of six, that they would want something definite, he thought, to go upon. That they would want to know the exact amount of money we should require for buildings, also the exact locality we intended to settle in and the name of the farm. . . . That the Colony was only just making a start from the very bottom of things (three months ago) and that while they wanted emigrants, yet there was a limit to what they had the power or money to do. . . . That the Dutch would not take our boys at all and that there were so few British farmers at present it was very hard to say where would be a good place to settle on. . . .

But he frankly said that both with regard to the boys and girls the Colony wants artisans and servants, but that the Government, he thought, would at the present state of affairs rather import the finished article than go to the great expense of getting out children and paying largely for their training and maintenance until they were fit for service. . . . Also that the people out here were rather aristocratic and the danger of bringing out children of the lower classes was that by doing menial work, which the whites do not do, they might fall to the level of the native, a most undesirable state of affairs. . . . That owing to the very high price of living out here it would be a very expensive thing to maintain these children for one to three years and he was afraid the Government would not be able to see their way to give any promise of support....

Two weeks later Stuart wrote that his own impression of the Transvaal was that his father would not get much help from the Government as the country was so unsettled. Although there was a great need for domestic servants the Government had given their support to the Women's Emigration Society, which Stuart categorised as a 'society fad, with Lady Lyttelton as the prime mover'. Edith Lyttelton, the wife of Alfred Lyttelton, who was to succeed Chamberlain as Colonial Secretary, had come out to South Africa with her husband when he came to assist in the preparations for peace. He thought the Government would not be 'likely to welcome any rival in the field at present. Most likely they will tire of this (the Women's Emigration Society) and then you may get help.' Stuart was hardly cheered by his visit to Pretoria where he was told by the Lieutenant-Governor, Sir Arthur Lawley, who was later to be an ardent supported of Fairbridge's Child Emigration Society, 'that the Government did not feel able to help in any way'. He wrote to his father that he did not think the Transvaal was ever likely to be a great agricultural country like Canada and America.

The trip was proving not only arduous but also a great deal more expensive than had been anticipated. In reply to a letter from his father he wrote: 'I note what you say with regard to money ... Although I have kept everything down to the lowest notch, yet the cost of everything is so great that my expense sheet is very terrifying and it seems to mount up every day no matter how I try to keep it down.' But at least he got a free pass and a permit to visit Natal, although he had to pay from Johannesburg to Charlestown, the first station on the Natal line. In the train on the way to Pietermaritsburg he met a farmer who told him that the great curse of the country was the importation of coolies from India, who came out under indentures for five years and when their time was up, instead of being sent back, were allowed to settle down in the country, and as a result Natal was being overrun with coolies who now equalled the whites in number. It was the refusal of the native population to work that had led to the importation of coolie labour. When Stuart saw the Colonial Secretary, the Hon. C.J. Smyth, he confirmed what the farmer had said, that farmers would not hire boys when they could get native or coolie labour for much lower wages.

With regard to the girls he thought the cry for white domestic servants was largely a parrot cry and brought about by the fact that during the last three or four years native servants could not be got for £1 a month as formerly, or even at £2 per month. But he thought people would rather have the native than the white servant. That the white servant cost so very much more both for wages and 'keep' and the accommodation had to be superior. While the native or coolie lived in any tin shanty at the back of the house and only had mealie or rice rations, white women or girl domestics required more looking after in every way to get them to stop in situations. He thought that eventually the natives would come back to work in the towns at the old rate of wages.

Mr Smyth 'did not want to throw cold water on your scheme in any way', wrote Stuart unconvincingly. After visiting Durban, Stuart took the steamer to East London, where the ex-mayor, Mr Lambert, thought that if Barnardo wanted an institution for his girls he should apply for some of the magnificent buildings put up for the Boer concentration camp. It was Kitchener's policy of sweeping the veld clean that brought about the need for 'refuges' for the wives and children of Boer soldiers. But between twenty and twenty-eight thousand Boer civilians died of epidemics in these concentration camps and the holocaust stirred the conscience of Britain and proved to be an enormous political blunder, leaving a 'gigantic scar across the minds of the Afrikaners'.[4] Stuart described his visit to the camp:

After lunch I took a cab and drove out to the Concentration Camp about two miles from town. It lies on the top of the hill overlooking the Buffalo River and is, I should say, very healthy. The buildings are laid out in streets parallel to each other and consist of one-storey bungalow buildings of corrugated iron, lined with match lining. Each building is divided into nine rooms not connected with each other, but each having a door opening onto the street of the camp. There are four rows of buildings and at the top is an enclosure in which lie the hospital buildings, school house and offices, including kitchens. The hospital buildings are of the same nature except that they are not divided into rooms like the other buildings.... I think the majority of these buildings will be removed and sold, but those in the hospital enclosure would I think do excellently for your purpose. They are good substantial buildings and could easily be altered to suit your requirements.

Further up the Buffalo River Stuart visited King William's Town where there was a convent farm run by German nuns of the Dominican order. About ninety-five orphans attended the school, the girls being taught domestic work while the boys went to situations in the towns, the Mother Superior telling Stuart that it was no good trying to send the boys to farmers as they were quite satisfied with Kaffirs. 'The convent is self supporting, the farm on which it stands being worked by the nuns themselves. It looked very odd to see the nuns in their usual costume, except for a large sort of apron overall and a large straw hat on top of their ordinary head gear, working in the fields, hoeing, harvesting and ploughing.'

On 20 December Stuart wrote his final letter to his father saying that he had now completed his tour round South Africa. He reminded his father that the situation was very different to that obtaining in Canada and that the four colonies with their own officials, laws, parliament, aims and ambitions were only bound together by the somewhat vague influence of a common flag.

Throughout all South Africa the racial question has to be faced in a way that it has not in Canada. In the first place in S. Africa the great bulk of the population is black, and the majority of the native races, instead of dying out like the North American Indian, are increasing in numbers very rapidly. Neither do they appear to be degenerating physically by their contact with the whites. Then the white population in S. Africa is divided into two chief classes, the British and the Dutch. These latter, as a general rule, are absolutely opposed to all British aims and influence, and what these bring, viz. progress. They are quite content with life as it was a hundred years ago and do not see any advantage to be gained by going in for progressive methods. The country Dutch are uneducated, dirty, and without any of the ordinary refinements of speech or living. In fact their morals, or want of them are very peculiar....

Then again up to the present the servant has almost universally been a native 'boy' or woman who lived in any shed or lean-to and simply fed on mealies with an almost nominal wage. The consequence of the employment of natives as domestic servants is that the great majority of the houses have no suitable accommodation for girls....

Then again there is the peculiar fact that young white emigrants have almost always in the past, owing to some unexplained cause, been very apt to deteriorate morally after being out here a short time. This is the universal opinion. You must remember that no matter what the social rank or position of whites in the country where they originally came from, yet as soon as they set foot in South Africa they find themselves one step higher in the social scale owing to the native population. This in a great number of cases causes them to look down on and refuse to undertake hard work of the kind they have previously been quite willing to do and indeed accustomed to.

With regard to South African emigration as a whole, I think it would be successful if you were careful. But you would have to be extremely careful in selecting both boys and girls who should be of as superior class as possible in view partly of the fact that white servants of both sexes have not proved a success when brought out here in the past, and also that the South African colonist is an aristocratic person, or thinks he is, and does not want to be saddled with children of the criminal class. This latter point has been much insisted on to me wherever I have gone.

The first of these reasons makes it necessary that you should keep the most rigid control over all children brought out by you until they grow up. The general opinion is that both boys and girls should be about the age of 16 years when placed out in situations. I should not recommend your keeping them in the institution out here longer than six months before going out to situations, as the cost of living is so great that you could probably keep at least two children in England at the cost of one out here. . . .

Another point that cannot be too much insisted upon is that the boys and girls sent out by you must be absolutely kept away from mixing with natives in any way and you must not send out children who have the least trace of colour in them, or at any rate these must be sent out quite separately from the rest, as the great danger with young emigrants to South Africa is that of getting down to the native level and forgetting they are whites and consequently the superior race.

Stuart ended his long series of letters simply with the words, 'I hope I have done satisfactorily. I have done my best for you out here and I think you will meet with success.' He then went off to Johannesburg to follow his own career as a mining engineer, doubtless facilitated by the contacts he had made while about his father's business. There was one last letter from South Africa on the subject of juvenile emigration. It was from Milner to the Duke of Argyll.[5] Barnardo had obviously decided as a result of Stuart's letters that his dream of having a training farm in South Africa was impossible. He thought, though, that there were openings for his girls.

8.6.03

Dear Duke of Argyll,
I have received your letter of 5th May with reference to Dr Barnardo's proposal to immigrate girls to W. S. Africa. While I am most favourable to Dr Barnardo's scheme's and know the good work he has done in the Colonies, I do still hesitate to greatly encourage his sending girls, of the class for whose advancement he labours, to the new colonies (Trans Vaal and O.R.C.) at the present time. The enormous cost of living, which is bound to come down in a few years, and other circumstances peculiar to the social and economic position of S. Africa at the present time, seems to me to involve objections to his scheme, which do not exist in the case of Canada.

I should be the first to welcome and indeed invite such immigration as he proposes as soon as it appeared to me that this special obstacle had ceased to exist. But at this particular moment I cannot conscienciously urge the govt. of either Colony to actively support a scheme which seems to me premature.

Believe me, Yours very faithfully,
Milner

Thus ended the only other attempt to emigrate children to South Africa since Captain Brenton's Children's Friend Society ceased operations more than sixty years before. By 1905 Barnardo was dead and the parlous financial situation in which the homes found themselves precluded any new initiatives of this kind.

Ten

AN IMPERIAL INVESTMENT

I looked, and beheld. . . .
The brown of the veld, the unending immensity,
League after league of the houseless and homeless,
The smokeless, the gardenless wealth of the desert,
The rivers unfish'd and the valleys unhunted,
An empire peopled with nothing – a country
Abandoned to emptiness, yearning for people,
A mother well fit for the birth of a nation.

KINGSLEY FAIRBRIDGE, *Veld Verse*

KINGSLEY FAIRBRIDGE, the last of the great exponents of child emigration, is perhaps the one who came nearest to creating a system which combined the most positive and well-thought-out approach both to the rehabilitation of the children and to the economic practicalities of the situation. It is almost strange that this should have been so, for Fairbridge did not start from the premise that there were children in need of help. His vision was of the empty veld which needed populating; his first aim was to find the men and women who would bring those farms, which he saw in his imagination scattered over the veld, into existence. His intense loyalty to England and his idealistic espousal of the cause of Empire made him look to England for emigrants to people the farms. It was only when he visited London as a young man and saw the children of the East End that his compassionate concern for their plight became fused with his vision of populating the empty lands of the Empire.

He saw that if he could take the children to a farm school where they could complete their education while at the same time be taught the rudiments of farming and become acclimatised to their new country, they would eventually provide the population for 'the empire peopled with nothing'. The youngsters thus trained would have imbibed the same loyalties, be fired by the same vision, and would grow up to be citizens of both their adopted country and the Empire. The idea of merely removing a child from institutional care and placing it out with a farmer, with only intermittent support from the home, held no appeal for him. The idea of farm schools had originally been suggested by Andrew Doyle in his report of 1874, an idea which had never been taken up and of which Fairbridge was clearly unaware. Barnardo's industrial farm in Manitoba had perhaps come nearest to Doyle's idea, but the Manitoba farm was for older lads and they stayed only a year.

There was something slightly chilling about the farm in Manitoba in spite of undoubted success in giving hope and work to many unemployed lads from England. True it was beautifully sited and when Lord Aberdeen visited it as Governor-General in 1897 he reminded 'the fine healthy looking lads' of the advantages they enjoyed in the 'great, free, fertile country'. The buildings were well kept and the produce of the creamery was noted for its excellence for miles around. But besides the fine buildings the visitors always noticed the two windowless rooms with barred doors which served as jails.[1] One visitor allowed himself to be closed in 'for the space of just about a minute and that minute was quite enough for him. And yet,' he said, 'the housemaster informed him that he has known boys endure that dark narrow confinement for two and three days at a stretch, before they would yield to some trifling point of discipline.' As the visitor dutifully noted, 'such dogged obstinacy, when applied against legitimate authority of course had a bad look,' but he comforted himself with the thought 'that such strength of will would probably be an invaluable asset in a man who had to make his way in the world'.

In 1908, the year before Fairbridge's Child Emigration Society was founded in Oxford, Barnardo's farm in Manitoba was closed for financial reasons. No one bought it and it remained empty for years. A descendant of one of the pioneering families of the district, whose father remembered it being built, described how the huge vacant home appeared to her 'as a benevolent mother whose great frame had enfolded hundreds of

Manitoba Farm in its heyday. A visit from the Governor-General, Lord Stanley of Preston

needy boys who had come over a mighty ocean and across half a continent to find refuge in her arms. The empty windows seemed infinitely sad like eyes that had witnessed the passing of a great hope.'[2] But as one hope faded another venture was beginning.

Kingsley Fairbridge was born in 1885 in South Africa. His father, Rhys Fairbridge, was a land surveyor to the Cape Government, and much of Kingsley's early childhood was spent either travelling by wagon through South Africa with his father, surveying the terrain, or trekking over the veld. His mother, Rosalie Fairbridge, who is scarcely mentioned in his autobiography, had a hard, rough life with few comforts. The only school Kingsley attended was St Andrew's preparatory school in Grahamstown which he left after three years to accompany his family to Umtali. Umtali was then a raw, new settlement in the northern hinterland which even the young Kingsley, then eleven years old, found 'pretty beastly'. His father had called their home Utopia. From Kingsley's description of the two buildings made of mud, the house thatched, the kitchen with a galvanised-iron roof, this might have seemed a misnomer.

> The windows were made of calico, tacked across a frame. . . . There were two rooms, both very small, divided by a partition. A low bed stood in one room, and a hammock was slung in the other. On a table made of rough poles and packing cases lay a quantity of tin plates, some black handled knives and forks, two or three enamelled mugs of different sizes and a number of jam and kipper tins with their edges carefully knocked down.

The jam tins, Kingsley discovered, made excellent cups, while the kipper tins, being long and shallow, could be used either as vegetable dishes or as porridge plates.

Kingsley's constant complaints about life in Umtali drove his father to give him two alternatives: either to go back to school or to stay and help with the work of surveying. Kingsley didn't hesitate, and with his father's help built a hut of his own, raising an old wagon and building stones up round the wheels and pitching a tent on top, so that the bottom compartment could serve as an office and the top as a bedroom. This ability to improvise, learnt from his father, was to be an invaluable asset to Kingsley during his long hard struggle to establish his farm school.

Not long afterwards Kingsley's father offered him ten pounds to build two small pondokies for him on his Gold Belt property about eight miles distant. It was while he was walking back from this assignment that Kingsley first had his vision. The incident shows how inextricably bound together were the two aspects of Kingsley's nature, the poet and the visionary allied to an iron determination and a steely will. Kingsley had set off with his dog and his 'boy' Jack, a middle-aged man of the Senna tribe, who carried his blankets and provisions. In seven days the poles had been erected, the grass cut for the thatch and the huts almost completed. Food, however, had run short and the natives would not sell to a boy of twelve with no rifle except at an exorbitant price. Kingsley refused to trade though the rains came and they discovered they had not cut enough grass. For three days they fasted, as hungry, sodden and tired they struggled to finish the huts. At about three o'clock on the third day the sun came out as they finished, rolled up their blankets and started back for Umtali. Kingsley wrote his autobiography while he was at the farm school he founded in Australia and the memory of that walk home remained vividly with him:

I felt dreamy and far-away; my body seemed light, but I breathed heavily as we breasted the great slopes. Suddenly the thought came to me, 'Why are there no farms? Why are there no people?' It came to me again and again, 'Why are there no farms *here*?' I remembered having heard my mother say that her father had been concerned in settling the emigrants who came from England to the Cape. 'Why are there no emigrants here?' I thought. I found myself picking out little plateaux on the grassy slopes, and thinking 'There is room there for a farm.' Sometimes I spoke aloud and Jack thought I was speaking to him.... So the vision came to me when I was starved and miserable: I spoke it aloud: 'Some day I will bring farmers here.' Jack stopped and looked at me, 'Bass?' he said. 'Let us go on,' I said, 'it is nothing.'

Not only had his grandfather been concerned with the settlement of English emigrants, his great-grandfather had been a member of the committee of the Children's Friend Society, who, if the Society had not ceased operations, had had plans to establish a farm school at Wynberg.[3] Kingsley did not know of this link any more than he knew about the stream of children crossing the Atlantic each year or about William Cassell, the boy Barnardo had sent from Gateshead to work in South Africa.

Kingsley was with his father when he met Cecil Rhodes, a legend in his lifetime and to Kingsley a heroic figure. It was an unhappy time for Rhodes: following the Jameson Raid he had resigned all his offices and the rebellion of the Matabele and the Mashona tribes in Southern Rhodesia had inflicted heavy financial burdens on his Chartered Company. The young Kingsley regretted that he had not had the wit to ask Rhodes to take him into his service and remembered him as 'strong and quiet, as he looked out over the land – great spaces washed with sun

– that he had won for the empire'. Shortly afterwards Kingsley volunteered to join the army and hoped to take part in the Boer War, but he was turned down on account of his age. Instead he had a varied career, working first as a bank clerk and later as a market gardener. He visited England when he was seventeen. The country had a profound effect on him. He wrote, 'I love England. She cured me of a bitter sickness, of bitter hatreds, of bitter ignorance.' The visit confirmed his sense of mission. He made the inevitable comparison between the overcrowded cities and the lack of population in South Africa, but he also realised that it would not be possible simply to transform a clerk or a casual labourer into a competent farmer. He had already decided to try for a Rhodes scholarship to get to Oxford, where he would be better able to promote his ideas, when it came to him that if he took children and gave them training in farm training schools, not only would he be benefiting them, they would then become the farmers of the future. Kingsley had had no schooling since he left Grahamstown, and nothing illustrates better his dogged determination to get to Oxford than the effort of will needed to prepare himself for the examination and to be undaunted after three successive failures. Kingsley had not only one battle to fight but two. While working for his father he had gone down with malaria, 'the great grey thief' as he was to call it, and for the rest of his life the disease was to remain ready to pounce whenever overwork or stress tired him.

At Oxford he began to write of his ideas. He shared his dreams with Ruby Whitmore to whom he had become engaged, but it was two friends, Frank Day and Alec Johnson, who persuaded him that he must speak. It was arranged that Kingsley should address the Colonial Club at Oxford on 19 October 1909. He had hoped to be able to tell his audience that he had been given land on the Rhodesian high-veld for the first farm school and was bitterly disappointed when the British South Africa Company wrote saying that they considered Rhodesia too young a country in which to start child emigration. None the less he spoke with passionate eloquence on the appointed evening: Great Britain and Greater Britain are, and must be, one – we are interdependent. The colonies have the land for the landless men of Britain. Britain has the men, but they are not always of the type needed in the colonies, therefore we should take the orphaned and poor children and train them in schools of agriculture in the colonies. This will not be charity, but an imperial investment. There will be no pauper stain – every child will be worth far more than the price of his training to the colonies.

Kingsley's private dream had become public property and every one of the fifty men present became founder members of the Society for the Furtherance of Child Emigration to the Colonies. From then on there was no rest for Kingsley. He and his friends and his future wife wrote literally hundreds of letters to anyone who they thought might help. Earl Roberts, Viscount Milner, the Archbishop of Canterbury, Andrew Carnegie, William Stead, the Duke of Argyll, Lord Brassey and Lord Northcliffe were among those who received letters, together with all the Boards of Guardians and the mayors of every town. Among those approached was Sir Edward Morris, the Premier of Newfoundland, who offered Kingsley fifty thousand acres which Kingsley accepted gladly. He was soon disabused by Lord Northcliffe who wrote:

> The only people who could possibly succeed in Newfoundland in my opinion and in that of those who have been working there for five years, are married agriculturalists – preferably Scotsmen – willing to work under very lonely circumstances in a climate that has six months winter and a very intense summer.... As for sending children there, you may not be aware that there is often a considerable amount of starvation among the inhabitants in winter.[4]

Kingsley's ignorance about other schemes for juvenile emigration was soon brought home to him. Charles Kinloch Cooke, emigration's parliamentary champion, wrote stiffly:

> You will excuse me if I say that because you assume, rightly or wrongly, that there is no association in existence which carries out the views, which you, in common with myself, entertain, this assumption does not in itself, as you seem to suppose, give you, or those working with you the right to claim a monopoly, in the matter of child migration.[5]

Kingsley was also an innocent when it came to working with others already in the field. The years before the First World War had seen a great upsurge in the numbers of children sent to Canada in spite of the Ontario Act, which had had little effect in practice. Barnardo's alone was sending over a thousand children annually and for several years before 1914 the total numbers of children sent overseas exceeded two and a half thousand. At one time more than forty-seven different agencies were engaged in the work. One of these had been started in 1902 by Mrs Elinor Close, a lady of formidable energy and with great powers of persuasion. Her idea had been to acquire farms in Canada to which the poor and sickly children from the workhouse would be sent to be brought up in invigorating surroundings. She wanted the scheme financed by Boards of Guardians and saw thousands of children benefiting. Having established one home in New Brunswick at Nauwigewauk she wrote, on paper headed 'The Children's Farm House Association', asking the Canadian Government for more land, claiming her scheme had been taken up by the City of London 'from an imperial point of view'.[6]

Kingsley had met Mrs Close and had gladly subscribed to her scheme. She, apparently unaware that he was intending to work in the same field, kept him informed of her work. But when she discovered that he had circularised her supporters with information about his own scheme and asked for their support she, not unnaturally, became annoyed. There is an inbuilt competitive element to charitable fund raising which Kingsley had not recognised. He thought her philanthropy suspect because although she was friendly to his face she attacked him behind his back, holding him up 'as an example of misguided youth'. Kingsley was particularly vexed that she had gone out of her way to convince his friends that Newfoundland was not a suitable place for a farm school.[7] Unsuitable though Newfoundland undoubtedly was, it was the only offer of land Kingsley had until Sir John Scaddan, Premier of Western Australia, wrote in March 1912 offering land to the Child Emigration Society. The Oxford committee decided to accept the offer, and Ruby and Kingsley Fairbridge found themselves, rather to their surprise, sailing to Western Australia later that year.

There was no time for Kingsley to find land, clear it and erect buildings, for the Oxford committee were anxious for action in order to have something concrete to report to their supporters. The Fairbridges had to take the first available property. Kingsley found a run-down farm of 160 acres, four miles out of Pinjarra, and the Fairbridges moved to the simple four-roomed house which, by one of those strange coincidences, had been used, without success, as a training farm for boys sent from the Liverpool ragged school.

The farm school was officially opened on 7 August 1912 and the Fairbridges' first child, Barbara, was born the following month. The first year was a test of strength for both Fairbridges, and one cannot but admire Ruby's courage and fortitude. Unlike her husband she was unaccustomed to the hard life of a pioneer and the primitive conditions that went with it. Besides the house, of the usual colonial packing-case style of architecture with a lean-to kitchen, there were sixteen acres of neglected orchard, a flourishing collection of hens, two starved pigs, one cow, and one worn horse together with a cart. That first Australian summer was particularly hot and trying, but Kingsley managed to prune the orchard, build some makeshift accommodation for the boys, cope with attacks of malaria and deal with the Oxford committee. Their demands on his time and strength were the most exhausting. They had no idea of the hardships under which the Fairbridges were struggling, and requests for answers to thousands of irritating questions tried his patience to the limit.

The first party of twelve children arrived on a pitilessly hot day in January 1913. They had been equipped by the Guardians for life in the workhouse, and when she saw them Ruby Fairbridge said it would have been hard to imagine a more incongruous, desolate little bunch of humanity.[8] Each boy clutched an evil-looking overcoat and a dirty canvas bag whose contents defied description. They were wearing dusty thick-nailed boots, woollen stockings, cheap smelly suits with trousers half-mast to allow for growing, and tweed caps. Kingsley had rashly allowed the boys to swim at Fremantle and when the time came for them to undress most were sunburned and many in tears with pain from the blisters. One poor child was blistered from shoulders to waist and Ruby wrote, 'I wrapped the whole of his back up in cotton wool and eventually even he stopped crying.'

After the arrival of another twenty-two boys five months later no more children came to the farm school until three years after the war. Even Kingsley, with all his extraordinary resilience and determination, could not have succeeded in keeping the farm school going during the war years without the devoted help given by his wife. From the very start he had been unable to get the Western Australian Government to honour the agreement to provide education for the children. Although the Premier, John Scaddan, was in favour of the work of the Society, as Kingsley reminded the Oxford committee, 'You must not forget that he represents the Labour Party which is dead against emigration of any kind.'[9] The Fairbridges had been made aware of the feelings of the Labour Party from the very beginning when they were taxed with introducing child labour into the country by the Labour Women's Organisation the moment they arrived in Perth. The refusal of the Government to provide either a building or teachers for the children put an extra burden on Kingsley. He read to the children from Fletcher and Kipling's *History of England* and gave them an hour's boxing instruction a day but this was on top of all his other work on the farm.

With no further children being sent to Western Australia it became increasingly difficult for the Oxford committee to raise funds to send to the farm school and they thought the financial situation so grim in 1915 that they wrote to the Premier saying that unless the Western Australian Government would subsidise the farm school during the war years they would have to wind up their work. Scaddan was in favour of the farm school, but he could not step too far out of line in his support. The Colonial Secretary, R.H. Underwood, who was asked to investigate the situation of the farm school, stated categorically that he had no intention of recognising the children as ordinary Australian orphans, as it would be very unfair that the people of England should send the boys to Australia and then expect the State to keep them. He was voicing the same fear that had prevented Parliament thirteen years previously doing more than make a gesture of goodwill to Barnardo. Kingsley, in a desperate attempt to gain support, decided to ask for half the normal capitation fee and to absolve, temporarily, the Government from responsibility for providing school buildings. The request was granted in August 1915, but in spite of escalating prices the sum was never increased and it became increasingly hard to make ends meet.

The Government's ambivalent attitude to the farm school

is well illustrated by their action in June 1918 when Kingsley requested the transfer of five or six orphans from other institutions to keep up the numbers of the children at the farm school in order to retain the teacher who had been allocated by the Government at the school. The three boys who came had been receiving eight shillings at the orphanage. The Government cut their capitation fee down to six shillings when they arrived at Fairbridge Farm School, thus making clear their disapproval at finding themselves responsible for a British-based institution, even though they had initially encouraged its setting up in their country.[10]

While Kingsley's children were being trained to become the colonists of the future, who would farm the lands of Western Australia, another group of immigrant children, whose training had been very different, was making its way in New Zealand. In 1910, at the railway station in Christchurch, ten lads aged between thirteen and fourteen had said goodbye to the two men who had accompanied them on a musical tour of Australia and New Zealand, raising money for Barnardo's Homes. The Rev. W.J. Mayers, Barnardo's chief deputation secretary, had been on a similar tour in 1891, but on that occasion the 'musical boys', as they were called, had all gone back to England. This time, given the choice, all the boys elected to stay in New Zealand. So, on the station platform, before leaving to return to England, Mayers presented them all with Bibles, signed by the then chairman of the Barnardo council, William Baker, gave them each a watch and ten pounds, and allowed them to keep the bagpipes they had played with such success on the tour. They deserved them, for the tour had been staggeringly successful in financial terms. They had landed at Fremantle in 1908 and spent a year in Australia, giving performances nearly every day when they were not travelling.

The tour was formidably well organised. The musical party was preceded by an agent who made the bookings and saw to the publicity. Mayers opened the proceedings with a religious talk, which did not always go down too well with Australian audiences, and gave an account of the work of the homes. Then the boys played and sang. They were particularly proficient with the hand bells, but they played the bagpipes and ocarina as well. They succeeded in raising £10,000 in Australia before going on to New Zealand where they repeated their success. As Mayers's train steamed out of the station the boys, with their bagpipes, made their way to the farms round about where they had all been found jobs.

Jo Tate, one of these 'musical boys', lived in Christchurch until his death in 1981.[11] He still kept the Bible and the photograph he was given, but the watch and the bagpipes were sold long ago. He had little idea of what lay in store. At the farm he was welcomed by the farmer's wife who told him to make himself at home. This Jo did, sitting down at the piano in the front room to play. But that was not exactly what had been meant and Jo got his ears boxed and was sent to the kitchen. He stayed at the farm just three months.

Jo came to Barnardo's in 1902 when he was nine. He remembered that occasion well too. He came up on the tram from Victoria with his mother, sixpence and a bag of sweets in his pocket. His father had recently died, and the memory of the death of his twin sisters and of his mother placing halfpennies on their eyelids, was still vivid in his mind; he knew what it was to feel hungry. Leopold House in the Burdett Road, where he was sent, seemed a wonderful place. There was plenty to eat and he enjoyed the companionship of the other boys. The high walls that surrounded the building did not bother him. He had learnt how to beat the system. He had acquired a roller skate and, when he could, he hired it out at the rate of a halfpenny a time to his companions. Then, having made an arrangement with the local ice-cream man, he let down a tin can containing the money on a string. The man removed the coin from the tin, filled it with ice-cream, and Jo hauled it back over the wall.

It was always counted a privilege to be selected for the boys' band for it meant getting out and about. It was even more of a privilege to become one of the 'musical boys' for that meant travelling round the country and often staying in the houses of the people who had arranged the entertainment and being not a little spoiled. Jo was pleased when he was accepted for musical training. Since 1890 the Albert Hall had been taken by Barnardo for his Annual General Meetings. Jo remembered these occasions as special red-letter days. The mandatory speeches and reports were enlivened by the children who performed elaborate musical and military drills; a series of tableaux of astonishing diversity illustrated the range of the work done in the homes; boys and girls already selected to go to Canada came on stage dressed for departure; and when they marched off stage the leading boy and girl hoisted a banner with the word 'Good-bye' written across it while the band played suitably rousing music and the rest of the children waved white handkerchiefs in a gesture of farewell. Jo remembered how much these occasions were enjoyed by the children who took part in them.

In 1905 Barnardo died. Jo remembered his visits to Leopold House, sometimes accompanied by Mrs Barnardo. Jo was selected to be one of the contingent of sixty boys who would march through the streets of the East End of London behind the flower-covered hearse. People in their hundreds stood in the streets to honour the man who had done so much for children, some weeping, as the sad procession slowly wound its way from the Edinburgh Castle, which housed Barnardo's mission church in, Limehouse to Liverpool Street Station where a train was waiting to take the body to its last resting place, the Girls' Village Home, Ilford.

Three years later Jo was selected to go on the tour to Australia and New Zealand – there wasn't much choice about it, Jo recalls. The boys had special khaki suits made and the buttons had the initials EEJM on them. The East End Juvenile Mission was the original title chosen by Barnardo for his work. The boys referred to themselves as the East End Jumping Monkeys. At the end of the tour and after Jo had decided that the farming life was not for him he tried pretty well everything in the way of jobs. Once, when times were hard, he saw the film *Rob Roy* advertised at the local cinema. He persuaded the manager that it might help to attract customers if, for a small fee, he stood outside playing the bagpipes, which he still owned at that time. The manager agreed, but Jo was rather startled to find, when he turned up the following day, a large placard outside the cinema which read, 'Boy Wonder from the Albert Hall will perform on the bagpipes'.

Jo volunteered to join the army when war broke out, but he was turned down so got married instead. He was twenty. He joined the ranks when conscription came in and was sent to France. He was one of those unlucky ones who were gassed during the war. When he came back to New Zealand to convalesce he took up boxing to pass the time. One day he was matched against a big coloured chap. Suddenly there was a shout of recognition – 'Jo Tate!' And Jo to his astonishment recognised his opponent as one of his erstwhile companions from Leopold House, who had also made the journey to New Zealand. When their connection was discovered they were disqualified from fighting each other. Seventy years after he arrived Jo learnt that Barnardo's was working for New Zealand children. Grateful for what the organisation did for him when he was a child in London, Jo became a supporter of Barnardo's New Zealand.

When war came Kingsley, his loyalties torn between patriotism and the struggle to keep the farm school going, put patriotism first, and he too tried to enlist but was turned down because of his health record. Had he succeeded it is certain that the school could not have survived and his dream of farm schools in every state of every Dominion would have had to be abandoned. The war years were very hard, but Kingsley accepted that as the price he had to pay and planned for the future. In 1919 he and his wife and their four children sailed to England so that Kingsley could revitalise and re-inspire his supporters.

His bitterness at the lack of energy shown by the Oxford committee spilled over into a letter he wrote to one of them.[12] 'I have a fear that the English Committee look upon Child Emigration as a hobby or something non vital that is a "good idea" and "ought to be done". I have written so fully to try to show you that this is not the case: that the work is vital and urgent.' He continued most uncharacteristically on a personal note: 'I have lived for seven years as a poor man, unable to give my wife the smallest decencies or to educate my own children, in the passionate hope that my own sacrifice may make others think. I have heard our work described as my "hobby" – a cruel and bitter jest.' His next sentence showed more clearly than anything else he had said the difference between the ideals he was working for and the objectives of the other juvenile emigration agencies: 'I do not care if I never see an immigrant boy again in my life, but I do care to know that my Empire is not drifting . . . is not . . . neglecting a helpless part of its own people.'

While still in Australia Kingsley had been in touch with Leo Amery, the Under Secretary of State for the Colonies, who was very much in sympathy with Kingsley's objectives. He was also chairman of the Imperial Government's Overseas Settlement Committee and arranged for Kingsley to meet the Prime Minister, Bonar Law, and a deputation of MPs. Kingsley did not have Barnardo's expertise in fund raising, nor did he have much tangible evidence to show for his work over the last seven years. True, he had trained thirty-three boys whose services were being eagerly sought by the surrounding farmers. But many thousands of children, some with little previous training in England, some with none, had found work on farms in Canada at far less cost.

However, Kingsley believed so passionately in his ideal of a farm school that his eloquence won the day. No one else could talk of 'young British orphans fighting, many thousands of miles away, to subdue for peaceful and productive purposes the empire's outpost, Western Australia'. He talked of the children having consecrated their young lives to work for the prosperity and strength of the Empire. Devoted to Kingsley as the children undoubtedly were – they had volunteered to stay on and run the farm while he was away at half the wage they might have been earning elsewhere – it is not certain that they saw their lives in those terms.

The Overseas Settlement Committee made a grant of £15,000 towards restarting the work, and Kingsley spent most of the rest of his time in England raising money. The grant he had obtained enabled him to negotiate with the Western Australian Government. However, the assisted emigration schemes that had been put into operation after the war had not been well thought out and a lot of the British people brought out to settle the land had drifted back to the cities. So although Fairbridge's plan was logical and well conceived there was a certain amount of disillusionment over immigration and also, it must be said, some ill-feeling in government circles toward the Fairbridge Farm. Several Members of Parliament took exception to the fact that the State was paying for the upkeep of children who remained outside the control of the State Children's Department. But Underwood, who had attacked Kingsley before, made a series of such personal attacks on Kingsley that public opinion rallied to his defence. A letter in the *West Australian* noted that 'Kingsley Fairbridge does more in a year of his practical work than could be produced in a lifetime from the apparently endless speeches of many would-be social reformers'.[13] Finally, partly because they were afraid of losing the money the Fairbridge scheme was attracting from the Overseas Settlement Committee, the Western Australian Government agreed to £6 passage money for 150 children plus 4s capitation until each child reached fourteen.

To accommodate so many children, a larger farm was obviously necessary and a property of 3,200 acres, ten miles from the first site, was chosen for the New Fairbridge Farm School. The new site was beautiful: to the east were the Darling Ranges, and the land sloped down to the Dandalup River, but it was virgin bush and huge jarrah and great red gum trees would have to be felled before any work could be done. Kingsley's enthusiasm overrode all difficulties and the new farm school opened in 1921. Kingsley was a visionary, but unlike many visionaries he had an iron determination which enabled him to overcome what might have proved to be insuperable difficulties. The obverse of these qualities was a certain dogmatic and unyielding aspect to his personality which caused trouble between him and his committee, now based in London and chaired by Sir Arthur Lawley. Sir Arthur, one of the minor proconsuls of Empire, who had abruptly dismissed Stuart Barnardo's ideas for a training farm when he visited him in Pretoria, now gave Fairbridge his total support. Difficulties about the size and splendour of the house Kingsley had built for himself and his wife were ironed out when it was pointed out that for years the family had lived in the greatest discomfort and that the cool and elegantly proportioned house with its vine-covered stoep would provide a central facility for both the children and the community. Staff also found that, unless they shared the same ideals as their head, working conditions were tough. The children lived in cottages whose very names, Shakespeare, Raleigh, Livingstone and Rhodes, reflected Kingsley's pride in the motherland. In the 1922 report one of the nurses was quoted as saying, 'I am leaving because I am not a missionary, and one needs to be that to stay here.' The Fairbridges had visited the Girls' Village Home at Barkingside before they first came to Western Australia and Kingsley remained convinced that the cottage home plan was superior to any other, and while the Perth committee sometimes queried the expense, Kingsley adamantly opposed any other way of working. When Percy Roberts, Barnardo's chief emigration officer, visited the New Farm School he was very impressed with what he saw and told Kingsley that he was fifty years ahead of his time.[14]

Australia had lost over 60,000 men in the First World War and although there were doubts in Western Australia about the cost of the Fairbridge Farm, New South Wales, a wealthier state, took a very different view of the question of child migration. The Millions Club had been formed after the war with the object of encouraging immigration from Britain and it had as its slogan 'a million migrants for Australia'. Some of its members saw no reason why Canada should be the only country to benefit from the influx of juvenile emigrants from the rescue societies who, since the end of the war, were again crossing the Atlantic in their hundreds. A Barnardo committee was set up with the object of getting boys to New South Wales from the Barnardo Homes.

Forty years earlier Barnardo had written about the difficulties of sending children to Australia. Although, when personal friends could be found to take charge during the journey, children like Thomas and George Andrews – whose parents were dead and whose relatives all opposed their being sent to Canada – were sent to Australia, the dangers to the children on the journey were too great for large numbers to be sent. Now the New South Wales Barnardo committee started to raise funds, and within two months the *Sydney Morning Herald* was able to report that the effort to bring boys from Barnardo's Homes as part of an immigration campaign was bearing good fruit.[15] Sir Denison Miller, Governor of the Commonwealth Bank, contributed largely to the scheme. Appeals were made in factories and to the wealthy farmers. Sir Arthur Rickard and Sir William Vicars between them put up the money to purchase Scarborough House as a receiving home and the scheme was to be run on the same lines as in Canada. It seems ironic that Fairbridge had to struggle so hard for funds to finance his farm scheme, while money was raised with little difficulty to finance a scheme that was already being questioned by those concerned with child welfare, both in Canada and Britain. But the answer was not far to seek: it cost so much less to bring the children out to

Australia and put them straight out to work than it did to train and educate them first.

In 1921, at the same time as the fifty-eight children were sailing to the Fairbridge Farm, forty-nine boys, aged between nine and eleven, were sailing to Sydney under the auspices of the Millions Club. The boys were given lessons on the poop deck and boxing and wrestling were allowed to help pass the time on the long voyage. When the ship called at Adelaide they were given a welcome at Government House and a homily by the Governor.[16] 'You are going to live in the country as God made it . . . you must remember the 61,000 men who gave their lives for Australia in the late war. You will help replace them and I am perfectly sure you realise what your duty to Australia is.' They were also given a piece of advice in a more homely vein and told, 'Don't swank!' The children's duty to Australia was spelled out to them again in Sydney where they were addressed byLordNorthcliffeatGovernmentHouse,cf617'Whilebecoming good and patriotic Australians ready to fight for Australia if she needs it, you must never forget little mother England.'

The imperial theme was never long absent from the rhetoric that surrounded child emigration in the twenties, but whether the young migrants, many of them war babies and the children of war widows, understood or appreciated the role it was hoped they would play, seems doubtful. Australia was even further from England than Canada and the farms to which they were going were just as isolated as the Canadian farms and the sponsoring organisation more interested in their potential as workers than their welfare.

The work of the self-styled New South Wales Branch of Barnardo's Homes was brought to a sudden halt by the London council in the following year after the arrival of a further hundred boys. The council objected to the way the committee had been set up, they were unhappy at handing over responsibility for their children to a group of people over whom they had no authority and finally they were very unhappy at the methods used to raise funds. The committee was told sternly that Dr Barnardo never felt free to support his work by means of dances, whist drives or lotteries. The Barnardo emigration scheme in Canada had been very tightly controlled almost from the start and the London council did not want the same abuses to creep into the scheme as had happened in Canada in some cases.

A new committee was set up with Sir Arthur Rickard as chairman. Mr A.W. Green was appointed superintendent of Scarborough House and London was asked to accept legal liability for the home. Feelings had been ruffled by the way in which the efforts of the Australian committee had been criticised and two members resigned in protest. Once these difficulties had been ironed out the committee had to face what had almost become the standard objection to this form of immigration. In September 1923 an article by Dr Campbell appeared in *Smith's Weekly* questioning the wisdom of juvenile emigration and saying that it took 'generations of environment to overcome hereditary traits', and that 'no Barnardo boy or girl should be permitted to land in Australia without a certified medical and personal history sheet'. Barnardo had often had occasion to answer this particular objection, usually put forward by a member of the medical profession. His reply was equally often quoted, 'I have myself proved over and over again that a new and healthy environment is more powerful to transform and renovate than even heredity has been in planting and evolving taint.' The organisation could also point to its policy of picking only the flower of the flock for emigration to the overseas Dominions.

Both Barnardo's and Fairbridge were struggling to establish their work in Australia at a time when the whole concept of child emigration was coming under increasing criticism in Canada. In the spring of 1924 a British Parliamentary delegation had gone to Canada to investigate the whole system of emigrating juveniles overseas and two years later the Canadian Council on Child Welfare were to conduct their own critical survey of the movement. An emotive article, entitled 'Child Slaves of Greater Britain', in which the children were referred to as the 'Oliver Twists of the Empire' pointedly asked 'what boy or girl would knowingly agree to accept the condition of life as it is on many a farm in the Australian backwoods, the wilds of Canada or the sun baked veld of South Africa? Climate, work and general pursuits – these are all unknown to the average British child.'[18]

There was so much opposition to sending children out to Australia that Howard Williams, who had succeeded William

Baker as chairman of Barnardo's, questioned the wisdom of continuing with the venture. The children could only stay for a week in the home which was proving expensive to maintain and there was trouble with some of the older lads who did not want to stay on the land. The Australian committee wanted a regular supply of boys and girls, they were thinking in terms of a hundred girls a month and fifty boys every two months, so that enthusiasm for the project would not wane. Girls were in greater demand than boys since more boys were coming to Australia under different schemes including the Dreadnought Scheme, which during the forty years it was operational sent out over 5,000 boys.[19]

The first party of girls sailed to Australia in May 1923 on the ss *Euripides*, under the watchful eyes of the three ladies who accompanied them. The Barnardo children were asked whether they wanted to go to Canada or Australia and were given lectures to help them make their choice, a choice some of them had never expected to have to make. Charles Zakharov, one of those who were to sail to Australia, had certainly never even heard of Canada or Australia nor can the idea of emigrating to either land have entered his head until he heard the matter discussed by the staff at Barnardo's.

Charles, whose real name was Shalva Guigolachvili, was born in Gori, Stalin's birthplace, in Georgia in 1905. His parents disappeared during the revolution and Shalva was put in a children's asylum. He ran away from the asylum and lived in the mountains around the city of Tiflis, homeless, hungry, frightened and bewildered by the tragedies he had witnessed, both within his own family and in the world around him. Georgia's declaration of independence and the establishment of a German protectorate in May 1918 was followed, immediately after Germany's defeat, by a temporary British occupation. Thus 1919 found the 99th Brigade, Royal Field Artillery, camped outside Tiflis awaiting demobilisation and sailing orders. Shalva, who was living like a stray animal, sometimes came down to the camp to pick up scraps of food. He would occasionally play football with the soldiers, but was unable to communicate with them because of the language barrier.

Private Freddy Felks, who was to become his lifelong friend, described Shalva as he first saw him, 'aged about thirteen, bright brown eyes, round face, dark hair, and he was a good looker, almond complexion and a lovely smile, he stood there dressed in a shabby worn overcoat, no hem at the bottom, all jagged like a broken piece of wood, sacking round his feet for shoes, hair hanging down his shoulders'. He was filthy and covered in lice. One day Felks really sat up and took notice of the strange child. 'I watched. I saw him pick up an empty bully beef tin, and he put his fingers in the tin, wiped round the inside and then licked them. This went on for some time, and he was evidently enjoying it, but what really struck me more was when he began to eat potato peelings thrown out of the window by the cook.' This really shook Felks and he called the boy over to him.

It was then that he realised that the boy was homeless, hungry and alone. Felks didn't hesitate. He got hold of an iron hospital bed and a couple of palliasses and let Shalva sleep in an alcove off his room. Shalva was quick to grasp anything Felks told him and to pick up both language and pronunciation. Felks, who was batman to a major in the brigade, taught Shalva to polish the Major's boots and Sam Browne belt; he cut his hair with some horse clippers and threw away his verminous clothes, finding him a tunic, a spare pair of drill shorts, puttees, a haversack and a kit bag. Finally he told the Major about Shalva, by then nicknamed Bee-Bee, who said simply 'Look after the lad, he evidently needs some protection from the Bolsheviks'. A cap was found and stuffed with paper to make it fit and Shalva was taught how to recognise an officer and to salute. The boy was delighted and burst out, 'Folkes, me good Onglisky solder.' When finally all was ready he was taken to see the Major. Felks described the scene:

> We went in to the Major and he stood beside me and saluted, and the Major saluted back, and said, 'All right Bee-Bee, let's have a look at you!' He understood, and showed himself off like a prize dog at Cruft's. The Major wanted to know why he had no boots, and after my explanation he said, 'Very well – tell the Quarter Master to indent for a pair his size.' I said to Bee-Bee 'Salute the Major' – which he did after drawing himself up straight. Then he smartly right-turned and away he went.[20]

To remind the citizens to keep the peace, when Tiflis became more unsettled than usual, the army would parade through the streets with what guns, firing battery wagons and limbers they had left, the main armament having gone to aid the White Russians. Shalva wanted to ride a horse like Felks, or at least to sit on a gun, but in the end was more than satisfied to sit on the firing battery wagon. Felks described him 'looking the part of an "Onglisky solder" sitting bolt upright, arms folded, so proud of himself. The day was his, there he sat, stern, not a smile on his face, riding past his subjects, guns in front of him, guns behind him, with two battalions of Indian troops marching four abreast ahead of him.'

Soon after that, news came that the brigade was to go to Constantinople on the first leg of the journey to England. Felks said that he would take responsibility for Shalva in England and after a lot of difficulty permission was granted for the boy to leave Tiflis. Shalva wasn't too happy about the idea of no longer being an English soldier and after Felks had tried to explain what life in England with his parents would be like Shalva said, in his fractured English, 'Me Onglisky solder, me no understand you good, Foulkes, but what for no solder?' However, before Shalva had to come to terms with life in England, there occurred one of those brief idyllic interludes that leave an indelible memory behind.

The brigade was moved to Haida Pasha, opposite Constantinople on the shores of the Sea of Marmara where the English soldier and the Georgian boy discovered a paradise. Felks wrote, 'I had never seen such a wonderful place, so peaceful ... it looked magnificent, silver sand gently ruffled by the sea, sun hot, and not a footstep to be seen; it was untouched by humans; it could have been a sea attached to the garden of Eden, but Adam and Eve were missing and only Bee-Bee and I were there.' Fig trees and almond trees fringed the shore and Shalva was soon up the fig trees, like a monkey; he taught Felks how to eat figs, squeezing the ripe yellow fruit until the delicious contents came oozing out. They stripped to bathe, and with Shalva sitting on Felks's shoulders they would rush into the lagoon, both falling head over heels into its blue waters. Shalva was a good swimmer and left Felks, who had been gassed while in France, gasping for breath. Then Shalva would gather almonds in his army cap which they would sit down to eat.

At the end of the week came the unwelcome news that only

an officer could take Shalva to England. It was arranged that the Adjutant, who was travelling home in eight weeks, should take the boy as his servant, and that once in England Shalva would rejoin Felks. Photographs had to be taken for the magnificent document which was finally issued by the Netherlands consulate requesting in the name of the Queen:

toutes les autorités tant civiles que militaires des Princes & Etats, Amis & Alliés de Sa Majesté non seulement de laisser passer le sujet russe, Guigolachivili Chalva, fils de Nicolas, se rendant en Angleterre par voie de mer avec ses bagages, mais aussi de lui donner ou faire donner, au besoin, toute aide et secours.

A photograph, showing Shalva, resplendent in his army uniform, complete with lanyard and swagger cane was attached to the left-hand corner. Before he left, Felks obtained a rubber tobacco pouch, cut it down, and wrote his name and address in indelible pencil on it and sewed it in between the facing and the forepart of Shalva's tunic. On 8 January 1920 Shalva arrived in Plymouth, where the immigration officer made the Adjutant responsible for his repatriation should he leave his employment.

Now began a desperately unhappy period in Shalva's life. The laughter and songs of the returning soldiers on the ship reminded him at every turn of all he had left behind him. 'Merriment, joy of these soldiers was more than I could bear. Many of them approached me and patted me on the back saying to me – come on Bee-Bee, smile, don't be so sad. I knew they were going to their mothers' relatives, wives and beloveds. Not me, I thought, I am running away from mine. I couldn't smile, but I was pleased to be going with them.' In an attempt to cheer the boy the Adjutant gave him a 1918 service medal and while the men were anxious to be rid of their uniforms Shalva gained comfort by wearing his with his medal pinned to his chest. He was still only fourteen, though having seen and experienced so much he felt he had the mind of a man, but he could explain none of this for, 'I could not speak good Russian nor could I speak good Georgian and I could not speak English at all.'

Arrived in England the Adjutant took the immigration officer's injunction all too literally. Shalva could hardly speak English; neither could he read or write it and was therefore totally dependent on the Adjutant, who was not slow to make use of him. His name was changed to Charles and he was put to work on the family farm, taking his meals with the servant girl, Alice. Miserable and unhappy he was virtually a prisoner. Eventually he confided in Alice who helped him write a letter to Felks, whose address he still had stitched to the inside of his tunic. Felks's letter was intercepted and Charles became desperate. He found the frame of an old bicycle and with the five shillings he received as his weekly wage he started to rebuild the bike. One day, instead of going to church, he started to cycle to London to find Felks. It was too far and he was forced to return. The Adjutant, discovering what he had done and where he had been, reached for his riding whip and thrashed the boy unmercifully.

The following morning the Adjutant's mother and sister, who lived in the same house, asked Charles if he would like to go to a boarding school where he could learn English properly and be taught a trade. Charles accepted promptly and was taken to Stepney Causeway where, in his own words, he 'was born again. Watching the boys walking in twos, laughing, playing and chasing each other. I looked for a friend. It wasn't long when I start to learn to smile. I chummed up with the smallest boy in the school my age.[21] Neither was it long before his dearest wish was also granted, permission to visit Felks. The homes had no idea who Felks was nor how Charles had met him, but when the story was checked, Charles, who had subsequently kept Felks's address in the sole of his sock, finally met up with his friend.

Felks described the meeting: 'Imagine my surprise, when one Saturday Charles turned up in person at Highbury Hill. He was welcomed with open arms. He was speaking very good English, and he had come from Dr Barnardo's Homes, Stepney, to which he had been sent by the Adjutant. He was now Charles, and was full of everything to tell us; how he was unhappy and wanted me; how he could not get on with the Adjutant's family. He seemed lonely, but thank GOD we thought of putting my address in his tunic. He was settling in the Home very well, learning good English, writing, plenty of games, football, exercises in the big room, good food and plenty of fun.' Charles visited the Felkses every weekend, for Freddy Felks was now married, and discussed with them the question of whether he should go to Canada or Australia. It was Felks who more or less persuaded him to go to Australia, for he thought it was a country that needed young men as pioneers. Just before leaving for Australia Charles paid his friend a final visit, a visit which was to have unforeseen consequences.

All leave for the boys sailing to Australia had been stopped owing to an outbreak of smallpox in London. When Charles's visit to Felks in London was discovered he was taken off the sailing list to his immense distress. As part of the campaign to give the emigration movement a truly imperial flavour the presence of royalty was often sought to underline the imperial character of the venture. Queen Mary had agreed to receive a party of girls at Buckingham Palace before they sailed and the Prince of Wales, the future Edward VIII, came to Goldings, the Barnardo technical school, to farewell the boys who were leaving for Canada and Australia. It was an important day for the boys, but for Charles it was just too much. Only telling Gloyns, his little mate, where he was going, he took himself off to his garden hut and shut himself up with his misery. The Prince, never one to put up with formality, was soon mixing freely with the boys, and from Gloyns he heard the story of the Georgian boy. He insisted on seeing him and in spite of Charles's initial hostile response to Gloyns: 'You go to devil and take Prince of Wales with you', the Prince promised Charles if he came out of his cubby-hut he would personally see to it that Charles's name would go back on the list of those who were to sail to Australia. So a few weeks later Charles found himself sitting on the back of a horse-drawn dray on the quayside at Sydney, watched by a few curious onlookers, on his way to the Sandringham hostel.

Charles remained in Sydney and for most of his life has worked as a taxi driver and a master mechanic. At seventy-five he still works for private clients and takes his cab out once a week to keep his hand in.

Life was not easy for any of the boys and some remain bitter at the way in which they felt they were exploited in their youth. But Charles is grateful to Barnardo's for bringing him to Australia. He is proud of his five Australian grandchildren. His main regret is the lack of a proper education which he feels to have been a major handicap. He has been back to England to see Freddy Felks and Barnardo's. An experience he will never forget was a visit to his homeland, Georgia, when he was seventy, fifty-five years after his departure. He was only sure the strange man to whom he was introduced really was his cousin, Alexei, when he asked about his uncle's hand. When Alexei described his father's crippled finger Shalva knew that the people who had come to meet him in Tiflis from Gori, Tskhinvali and Mejvriskhevi really were his nephews and nieces, their children and grandchildren. His old home was gone and the place where the British army had been encamped was the site of a Palace of Sport and a complex of research institutes of the Georgian Academy of Sciences. Charles Zakharov, who had once been Shalva Guigolachvili, could no longer speak his native language. His interpreter wrote afterwards, 'I saw how happy he was. His sparkling eyes, which looked young again, were telling this. I looked at this man and tried to understand the feelings of his soul. . . .'[22] But Charles knew that no outsider could imagine what his feelings were.

Eleven

IN DEFENCE OF CHILDHOOD

> Juvenile immigration is a direct response to what humanity pleads, patriotism wants and Christianity demands – giving the younger generation a chance. It is an imperial back-to-the-land movement.
>
> T.E. Sedgwick, *British Town Lads on Imperial Farms* 1924

Juvenile emigration in the nineteenth century had been started largely owing to the concern of three women – Maria Rye, Annie Macpherson and Louisa Birt – for the welfare of homeless and destitute children. It had been taken up and developed by others: Quarrier, Fegan, Barnardo, Boards of Guardians and the Salvation Army. It had been gently encouraged by both Canadian and British Governments and made much of by social imperialists. The demand in Canada for the services of the children seemed unlimited; in the years before the First World War up to 30,000 applications had been received annually. In the first part of the twentieth century women were again to play an important part in focusing attention, this time on the condition of the emigrant children, and their concern for the welfare of these children would radically affect the development of the movement.

The movement had so grown in size and complexity that it was practically impossible for an objective assessment to be carried out, and, even if money had been forthcoming to fund such a project, the resistance shown by the rescue societies to any outside interference with their work was such as to make it very difficult to obtain the necessary information. Canadian objections in the 1880s and 1890s had been concerned mainly to protect the national interest. With public opinion united, for many different reasons, in extolling the virtues of juvenile emigration nothing short of a catastrophe, it seemed, could stop the flow of children leaving the shores of Britain.

In pre-war years no voice in Canada was more influential than that of J.J. Kelso in matters pertaining to the welfare of children. He was a strong believer in the value of fostering children in families and his opposition to institutional care was well known. He considered his greatest achievement to have been the finding of good homes for thousands of neglected and dependent children. He could not, therefore, quarrel with the policy of the rescue homes, which effectively removed children from institutional care and gave them the experience of family life.

There was another reason for Kelso's reluctance to question the work of the rescue homes. Although Kelso had become a government employee, his relationship with Government was always ambivalent. He did not believe the Children's Aid Societies, which he had established throughout Ontario, should be entirely Government funded. Indeed, he was strongly in favour of voluntary funding and voluntary involvement in the work of the societies, feeling 'the inevitable tendency of large government grants is to limit the personal activities of good people and thus destroy what we regard as the triumphant feature of the work,' although this inevitably meant that he was never able to do all he wanted because of lack of funding.[1] In an assessment of his own work, written toward the end of his life, Kelso reflected on this dichotomy and came to the conclusion that he had been in the wrong place in government service. 'Philanthropic and social work of all kinds is better in the hands of private organisations than under government control', he wrote.[2] Then in a passage which reveals a more personal reason for his support for the juvenile emigration movement he wrote of his great admiration for Dr Barnardo and his envy of the freedom under which Barnardo operated. 'My hope, desire and aim was to carry on great Christian rescue work, somewhat similar to that of Dr Barnardo in England, and had I only got started right there is no doubt that I could have raised hundreds of thousands of dollars for such a worthy cause. No one would give money to a government enterprise and the Government was not interested enough to vote the funds necessary to ensure efficiency. . . . Had I my life over again it would not be as a government official.' However, Kelso was a government official and his approval of the juvenile emigration movement reinforced the efforts of his contemporaries in the Department of Immigration and Colonisation to popularise the movement in the early 1920s.

Even the Local Government Board, after years of uncertainty, started positively to encourage Boards of Guardians to send children overseas, saying in 1903 'that emigration affords one of the best means for providing satisfactorily for the orphan and deserted children', and in 1909 that it was one of 'the surest means of extracting children from pauperism and the influence of evil surroundings'. Mrs Despard, of the Lambeth Board of Guardians, was one of those to voice disquiet at the way in which juvenile emigration had developed. She was an advocate of women's rights and had been to Canada in 1903, where she not only visited farms in the relatively more populated parts of Ontario, but also went to Manitoba. She described how, leaving her companions at Brandon,

> I spent the whole day, from dawn until dusk, in visiting this one farm. The drive over the wide prairie, the sense of exhilaration, the fragrance of the air, the extraordinary promise and latent potency of the land, it would be impossible for me to put into words. To give you some idea of the distance – I drove that day 50 miles out and 50 miles back, and for the most part over roadless country. The farmhouse, which we found with considerable difficulty, was a poor bare struggling place. Our child seemed in good health, but the home was not such as I should have chosen for him, nor would I have spoken of it in the terms which were used by those who had inspected it. This was also the opinion of my driver, an exceedingly shrewd Canadian, who said, 'They are kind enough folks, but I wouldn't put a boy of mine there.' A day or two later I visited several other farms. . . . There were still the immense distances, still the great isolation and apparent poverty of the farms – still the same overpowering impression on my part of what these farms, so isolated in the summer, would be in the depths of a Canadian winter.[3]

Mrs Despard spoke to other Canadians who said that they objected to these homes, not because the children, in the main, were ill-treated, but because they had no chance of learning good farming and had little prospect of making a good start by and by. She also heard terrible stories of ill-treatment of boys on the isolated farms, of one farmer being punished for his cruelty and of another turning a boy out into the bleak winter cold.

She made the point that not all boys were suited to farm life, but they had no choice in the matter. She stressed the point still more emphatically in the case of girls.

> Why must we send all our girls to domestic service? It is a common idea that girls of a certain class could all be servants, but for a peculiar perversity of judgement, but for a vicious desire for liberty which wise friends ought to combat. Now I dissent from this. Had I been born of working-class parents, I should have preferred any poor life to the comforts and so called refinements of domestic service. Moreover our poor girl-children have sometimes gifts and talents which no domestic service will develop.... Why should not our girl emigrants who object to domestic service ... be placed in Canada ... where they can develop their gifts?[4]

The answer was, unfortunately, all too simple: Canada wanted them only for their skills as domestic servants. Florence Despard was ahead of her time, and the men who directed the rescue homes saw no reason to allow girls any choice over the future direction of their lives.

Seven years later, in 1910, the Chorlton Board of Guardians sent another lady, Olga Hertz, the chairman of their Cottage Homes committee, to Canada to follow up the careers of a large group of children who had been sent from their union to Marchmont and placed out by the Wallaces. Although Miss Hertz criticised the lack of educational opportunity available to the children and recommended that a woman should be added to the staff of supervisers, she was so impressed by the physical well-being of the children that she came back to Chorlton convinced that emigration to Canada was 'giving them happier and healthier surroundings than we can provide for them at home'.[5] However, the Board of Guardians took a more critical look at the situation and noted that the children placed out by the Wallaces were often as young as seven. Only Barnardo's and the Catholic Emigration Association paid boarding-out fees to cover the expenses of children under ten, and since it was no secret that the children were wanted for their labour, the Board of Guardians concluded that many poor-law children 'were sent to work for their livelihoods at an age which would not be tolerated' in their own country. They were also unhappy about the terms of the indentures which they thought looked more like forced-labour than free-labour contracts. A letter to the *Manchester Guardian* from one Board member brought the whole issue into the open, although carefully refraining from blaming Canadians.

> We socialists do not condemn (and never have done) Canada nor emigration there; what we do condemn is the robbing of young children, because they are poor, of their childhood, the depriving them of the educational advantages of their native country.... No one can deny that the policy is one of economy bought at a fearful price – the price of a child's toil, for their work is compulsory, and therefore differs entirely from that of the child who in its play hours works in its own home.[6]

Although the Chorlton Board had decided by the autumn to cease sending school-age children to Canada, and their example had been followed by the Guardians of St Mary's Islington, it was the First World War that effectively put a stop to juvenile emigration to Canada as it had to Australia, but the stoppage was only temporary. The fact that 10,000 former emigrant boys had joined the Canadian army was seen as the strongest possible proof of the success of the movement. G. Bogue Smart, as chief inspector of British immigrant children, wrote 'that the promptness and loyalty of our old-country born boys in voluntarily giving up their profitable situations and comfortable homes ... to enlist and serve with the Canadian army in the great war has impressed the public mind of Canada and Great Britain more than ever of the truly imperial character and advantages to the Empire as a whole of juvenile emigration'[7]

Barnardo's were the first to restart their emigration programme and a party of boys and girls arrived at St John's Halifax, on board the ss *Sicilian* in March 1920. They were soon followed by the other rescue societies. Seven of the children who sailed on the *Sicilian* have been traced by Phyllis Harrison who has recorded their stories in her book, *The Home Children*.[8] The three Bates brothers, who travelled out together and hoped to stay together, were almost immediately parted. One of them, William, remembers how alone and afraid he was as he drove away from the home sitting on the back seat of his employer's car, although he says he can laugh about it now. Another boy,

Len Weston, was very eager to go to Canada but afraid that he might not get a job because 'he was so very small for eleven'. However, the farmer who accepted him allowed him to help in the house instead of doing farm work and he later described the family as 'the only parents he had ever known' and 'their home as his home'.

One girl was so happy with her foster mother in England that she never got over the shock and distress at being parted from her. She found it painful even to recall her early life in Canada. Her chief memories are of the constant change of place, the indifference with which she was treated, the knowledge that she was only wanted as cheap labour and the superficial nature of the inspections. All her life there remained a deep loneliness and longing for England which never left her. Gladys Hunt, another girl, ended her story simply by saying that she had always been glad that her mother had sent her to Dr Barnardo's where she was looked after and had a good Christian training. Charles Gilkes was one of those boys who did what the homes so often wrote about: eighteen years after coming ashore from the *Sicilian* he became the owner of his own farm and married the granddaughter of his employer to boot.

But although all the agencies restarted their emigration programmes, the number of children coming to Canada reached nowhere near the pre-war levels. George Bogue Smart was disturbed that Canada was unable to attract enough young people to meet the needs of her farmers and householders; his awareness of the competition from Australia only served to increase his desire actively to promote juvenile emigration. He obtained permission to visit Britain to publicise the superior advantages that Canada offered to young people. He was very pleased to have obtained the services of a journalist, Gordon McLennon, who managed to place twenty-three different articles in the newspapers with titles like 'The Lure of Empire' and 'Fine Canadian Assets'. He even managed to get the department to pay McLennon for his services. The MP, Charles Kinloch Cooke, through his weekly journal, *Empire Review*, also continued to champion the cause of juvenile emigration. The greatly increased cost of transatlantic travel was another factor which militated against the speedy build-up of numbers after the war. Without some government help it would have been almost impossible for the rescue societies to restart juvenile emigration on the same scale as before. The Canadian side of their work had suffered badly during the war and all the receiving homes needed money spending on them.

It was government policy which was responsible for the short-lived boom in child migration after 1922. The Overseas Settlement Committee, which had been set up under Milner, now Secretary of State for the Colonies, had as one of its duties to keep in touch with overseas governments and representatives of the Dominions. When the conference of Prime Ministers from Canada, Australia and New Zealand met in London in 1921 it had to consider a proposal, put forward by the Overseas Settlement Committee, that:

> His Majesty's Government in the United Kingdom cooperate with the overseas Governments in a comprehensive policy of Empire Land Settlement and Empire directed migration extending over a period of years and to this end to contribute up to a maximum of £2 million a year in any year in respect of schemes of land settlement, assisted passages, and such other kindred schemes as may commend themselves to the Governments concerned.

This proposal was accepted by the conference and in 1922 became part of the Empire Settlement Act which was passed by Parliament. Following the act, agreement was quickly reached between the British and Canadian Governments that each would pay the equivalent of $40 *per capita* toward the cost of transporting to Canada children nominated for emigration by the voluntary agencies and accepted as medically fit by the Canadian immigration authorities. It was confidently hoped that, under these new arrangements, some five thousand children might be emigrated to Canada annually, a far greater number than ever before. However, before the arrangements under the new scheme had time to take effect, a series of tragedies involving cruelty to children gave the opponents of the juvenile emigration movement an opportunity to make their protests heard; the publicity surrounding the scandals increased the feeling of general unease over the whole question of child emigration.

Charles Bulpitt was only one of three boys who committed suicide in Canada during the winter of 1923–4, but his case received widespread publicity and the circumstances surrounding his death were reported in *The Times*.[9] Charles had been sent to Canada by the Southampton Board of Guardians under the auspices of the Liverpool Sheltering Homes. He had been sent to the farm of a man named Benson Cox in Huron County. There he had been so beaten and mistreated that he hanged himself in a barn on the farm. His employer was charged with assault and beating the boy. The jury linked his death to his loneliness which had been made unendurable as a result of the beatings he received and Cox was sentenced to two months' imprisonment. A particularly disquieting aspect of the case was that the defence admitted the frequent whippings but claimed the right of punishment on the ground that the boy was an apprentice. The magistrate ruled that the boy was not an apprentice but hired at $75 a year and that Cox had no right to lay hands on him. From this judgement it would seem that if the boy had been younger he would have had no redress.

John Bull took up the story of another child under the headline 'Appalling Child Slavery' in an article which started, 'Hearts will grow heavy and eyes will blur with misty tears in reading of this sad story of cruelty to a helpless little immigrant.'[10] Bogue Smart, writing to a colleague, referred lightly to the story as being in the 'usual exaggerated style of that publication'. *John Bull* had already carried the story of the death of Albert Cartner, an immigrant boy who had died in an emaciated state in a dark cellar on a farm. The present story concerned Laura Elman, who had been sent, at the age of seven, to work on a farm near Brandon for a family named Goring. As a punishment Mrs Goring is alleged to have stripped Laura naked and sent her into the snow to draw water at the well which she then threw over the child, sending her back to fetch more water. Laura was said to have lost her toes and two fingers through frostbite; her body was said to be covered with scars and there were ulcers on her legs. The article described not only the physical sufferings of the child, but drew attention to the mental torture she had endured which, it was said, had left her a nervous wreck.

The Gorings were brought before the court, but the magistrate imposed only a suspended sentence. *John Bull* stated that there was great local indignation at the sentence since it was through the Gorings' neglect that Laura had been left a cripple for life. Whether the details were exaggerated or not in this case, there is clear evidence that a significant number of children on Canadian farms suffered physically. The suffering was not only physical: the abrupt change in their circumstances, the parting from friends, foster parents and familiar surroundings, left many with an aching sense of loss; for others fear added to their sense of isolation and loneliness. The psychological damage inflicted by these traumatic early childhood experiences left many former children with memories too painful to be willingly remembered.

Another matter which gave rise to adverse publicity was the suspicion, fuelled by one or two rare cases, that the Indians were taking some of the children. In an article in the *News Mirror* under the heading 'Slavery of the worst sort exists on Ontario Farms', there was an eye-witness account by a Toronto lady of an encounter she had had with a little white boy who appeared to be living with a family of Indians.[11] 'It is an outrage', she wrote, 'to place white children with Indians in Canada.' In fact, at this time, unbeknown to her, John Thomas, now a grown man, had lived with the Indians as one of their own ever since he ran away from the farm where he had been placed by Barnardo's as a small boy.

The experiences of John Henry Thomas provide another of those strange and unlikely stories which give the history of the emigration movement a special fascination. John was born in Cornwall in 1887 and he came into Barnardo care through a referral from the NSPCC.[12] His father had died and John and his mother went to live with a gypsy who knocked him about. He ran away and when he applied to the workhouse for admission he was clothed in rags, covered in bruises and swarming with vermin. Two days later he was removed by his mother, crying bitterly. His stepfather treated him brutally, and when his mother attempted to interfere on his behalf she received the same treatment. The NSPCC, hearing of the case, located the gypsy camp and removed the boy. A magistrate committed him to the care of Barnardo's. Aged eleven and a half he had never been to school and was totally illiterate. Less than a year later, in 1899, he was sent with a party of boys to Canada. His first employer returned him to the home on account of his bad habits. He absconded from a second placement, was found, and sent to yet a third farm from which he also absconded. From 1900 nothing further was heard of John until an article appeared in the *Prairie Farmer* in 1952 giving an account of his life among the Indians of North-West Canada.

John absconded from his third farm because the man was 'real mean'. He expected the boy to rise at four in the morning and kept him at work until ten at night. When he left he was penniless and being small for his age was unable to get another job. He wandered around with the idea of somehow making his way back to England, sleeping rough and finding odd jobs. He found his way to Lake Winnipeg and with a companion made a small boat. He tried to get to the River Nelson, which flows into the Hudson Bay, but made very little progress that summer because he was afraid of the stormy weather on the lake. His companion had left him, having found regular work, and he had little to eat except fish. When autumn came early, with frost and snowstorms, as it often does in central Canada, he ran out of food and took shelter on a small island on the lake. There he was found by Indians, and John Robert Dunn, a Saulteaux Indian with a wife and six children, took pity on the youngster and took him into his family. John went with his new friends to the Fort Alexander Indian Reserve.

From the Indians John Thomas learnt to become an expert trapper; he learnt to speak the language and to think like an Indian. His face became leather hard and dark skinned so that he even came to look like one of his Indian 'brothers'. A man of medium height, he had great vitality but remained shy and reserved all his life. According to John himself, during the first thirty-six years he spent with the Indians in the bush he never laid eyes on a white man. He said, 'When I first saw my own kind again I was so shy of them I couldn't even look them in the face.' He became known as 'English John' and when he was twenty-four he married an Indian woman, older than himself and selected for him by his Indian foster father.

John inherited a trap line from his Indian family, which under Manitoba's registered trap-line system meant that John was licensed to trap on his own line for as long as he lived and no one else was permitted to trap by law in his designated area. John who has been described as 'walking through the forest with the seeing eye and listening ear of a native' had a line which was 'just crawling with fur bearers' and he caught everything from silver fox to marten and fisher. In his time John also ate most things, including caribou, fish, beaver, squirrel, lynx and hawks, 'but I backed up on night owls and skunks', he said, 'that was just too much for me'. When there was no wild stuff to eat he went hungry, sometimes three or four days on end. His friend, Stanley Fryer, wrote of him,

> In many ways John Henry Thomas was a credit to the Barnardo Homes, he never became famous or wealthy, but he was reputed for his integrity, and as some old people of an earlier generation said of him – he was 'a perfect gentleman'. In other ways he was a rugged individualist, like many Englishmen of his generation, he never sought welfare assistance or expected it. He became a lonely man, and we used to regret that he never had a happy home life in his married years.

Apart from the moral that it was the Indians and not the white men who cared for John Thomas, his story does illustrate some of the very diverse problems with which the emigration agencies had to deal. When he was sent to Canada, less than a year after being admitted illiterate and verminous, John could hardly be said to have received training. But the homes could not afford to train all the children they admitted, nor, once the children were overseas, could they afford the staff it would have needed to make sure child and employer were compatible. It would have taken time to find John a farmer with the understanding necessary to help him adjust to Canadian life after his searing childhood experiences. Since there was no time the agencies, perforce, had to operate their system of placements in a somewhat hit-and-miss manner.

By the 1920s Canadian social workers were questioning many of the old methods of child welfare. Kelso's influence had declined noticeably and the new generation of social workers were critical of the standards of child placement. Kelso's policy of using voluntary help to run the Children's Aid Societies was no longer accepted. Mills, the Director of the Toronto Children's Aid Society, felt particularly that there must be a more professional approach and that simply to love children did not of itself suffice. With this more professional attitude to social work and to fostering and adoption, Canadian social workers began to question the practice, followed by all the emigration agencies, of placing children in homes which had not been personally investigated first. At the 1924 convention of the Imperial Order of the Daughters of the Empire, Charlotte Whitton, Director of the Canadian Council on Child Welfare, spoke on the subject of child immigration:

> Why are so many children being brought to Canada? . . . The only fair inference is that juvenile immigrants are being sought for placements in homes and on conditions which the Canadian authorities will not accept for our children. It does not redound to the credit of Canada that in an official publication of the Dominion Government we should speak of getting farm helpers from ten to thirteen years of age. Do not these facts bear out a contention of a cheap labour demand, a cheap labour that approaches perilously near a form of slavery?

With so many contradictory signals coming across from Canada and with opinion divided in Britain as to the merits of the juvenile emigration scheme the Government had already decided, before Charlotte Whitton spoke, that it needed first-hand evidence about the whole child emigration movement. With no party in the House of Commons able to command an over-all majority under Ramsay MacDonald's leadership, Labour had accepted office for the first time in January 1924, after Baldwin's resignation. For Labour, with its close links with the Trades Union movement, the policy of emigrating juveniles had always been slightly suspect. There had been regular protests by both the Canadian and Australian trades unions on the grounds that the children were simply a form of cheap labour, taking jobs which otherwise would have been available for their members. To continue officially to support child emigration without an impartial investigation into the whole question could have become embarrassing for a Labour Government.

Margaret Bondfield, who had just been elected Member of Parliament for Northampton, was actually chairing a General Council meeting of the TUC when she was notified by Tom Shaw that he wanted her as his Parliamentary Secretary at the Ministry of Labour. When the decision was taken to send a delegation to Canada to obtain information regarding the system of child migration and settlement in that country, it was a woman, Margaret Bondfield, who was chosen as leader. She was well equipped to fill the role: not only was she the first woman to hold ministerial office; she had her own experience in the labour market as a young girl to remind her of what it meant to be overworked and hungry.

Having left home at fourteen she had worked as a shop assistant in Brighton. Through the exercise of rigid economy at the end of five years she had saved five pounds, and with this small fortune she came to London. She was nearer starvation in the next three months as she searched for work than at any other time in her life. She learnt the bitterness of a hopeless search for a job and wrote in her autobiography, 'even today those first months in the great city searching for work carry the shadow of a nightmare'. When eventually she found work she discovered that conditions as a shop assistant were no better than they had been in Brighton. She lived in and worked a sixty-five-hour week for between £15 and £25 per annum. She seized the opportunity of joining a trade union and at considerable cost to herself took on the job of investigating conditions under which shop girls worked. Her reports were used as background material for the Shop Assistant's Act.

Margaret Bondfield's personal experience certainly gave her a deeper understanding of the difficulties the emigrant children had to face in Canada. Mr G.F. Plant, who was a member of the British Overseas Settlement Committee as well as a member of the delegation, said later that he thought Margaret Bondfield had gone to Canada already convinced that children should not be sent away from the United Kingdom until they had attained school-leaving age, a recommendation which was later unanimously put forward by the delegation. Apart from the Secretary, the third member of the party that left England in September 1924 was Mrs Harrison Bell, appointed by the TUC to represent organised labour on the Overseas Settlement Committee, and therefore more likely than not to be critical of the emigration movement. In the event she was so impressed by Canada that she told Mr Plant that had she been younger she would have seriously considered settling there herself.

Because of an unforeseen event the delegation only had seven weeks in which to complete their work. Margaret Bondfield was actually in Edmonton when a cablegram reached her giving the news of the fall of the Labour Government, causing her to hurry home to take part in the next general election. However, the delegation had worked hard and travelled extensively. Bogue Smart had supplied them with lists of all the children in each province and they were taken to see those children they decided to visit. The delegation called at the Barnardo Receiving Home in Jarvis Street in Toronto, a magnificent building which had been bought after the war, largely from money sent by old boys and girls. Here Margaret Bondfield addressed the most recently arrived party of children and some old boys and girls, telling them that they must be careful not to think themselves superior – strange advice to children who had suffered all too often from the stigma of being known as 'Home' children. She did not forget to wave the flag for Britain and the Empire. 'Remember that when you are doing things well here you are helping to hold up the Old Country and helping the Empire, and then if you do win, your great adventure will have been worth while.'[13]

The report of the delegation was presented to Leo Amery, the recently appointed Secretary of State for the Colonies.[14] The delegation came to the conclusion that the migration of children over school-leaving age should definitely be encouraged by the British Government and that the proportion of girls should be increased. They felt that the prospects for the boys and girls in Canada were better than they would have been had they remained in the United Kingdom. It seemed to the delegation, unused to the ways of voluntary organisations, that there was unnecessary duplication of effort and they suggested the amalgamation of some of the receiving homes. They thought that in all cases the home should be inspected prior to placing the child and made several other minor recommendations. They realised that in recommending that only children over school-leaving age should receive government assistance they were making a controversial decision. They knew enough of the situation to be able to discount the argument that the younger children were adopted by Canadian families. They also knew that without exception the older emigration agencies considered that the younger the child came to Canada the more easily it would become adapted to Canadian ways and would be absorbed into the community. Although none of the delegation had met any young children who had complained to them of overwork, they themselves thought that several children were doing more than they should and that their education was suffering thereby. But it was more as a matter of principle than on hard evidence that the decision was made.

They argued that the comparative helplessness of the child made this form of migration the most liable to abuse and that there was always the danger of overwork, and the loss of educational possibilities could not be overlooked. Certain of the Children's Aid Societies had said that they had difficulty in placing some of their children in districts where the migration societies were active. The delegation commented that this argument assumed that the farmer who could not secure a British child would take a Canadian child from a local shelter, and said they 'had reason to believe that this would not always be so'. A special paragraph was devoted to the Barnardo boarded-out children for whom a boarding fee was paid to enable them to go to school in the summer months as well as in winter. The delegation found that in some cases the children had all their spare time taken up with miscellaneous duties about the house and farm and they said, 'Taking the system at its best, boarded-out children transferred from homes in the United Kingdom to homes in Canada do not seem to us to have gained any appreciable advantage.' The recommendations in the Bondfield report were accepted by the Government and children under fourteen were no longer eligible for the assisted passages government grant. The ban was to remain in force for a period of three years when the recommendation would be reviewed. The fact that the ban was for a trial period only stimulated argument on both sides. The division of opinion between the older philanthropic agencies, Bogue Smart and the Canadian immigration authorities on the one side and the various Canadian welfare organisations on the other, became more sharply defined. Over sixty Boards of Guardians sent identical resolutions to the High Commissioner for Canada demanding:

> that the Government of the Dominion of Canada be requested to make it compulsory that all homes in Canada should be examined and approved by Government officials before any children are drafted into them from England and Wales, and that the homes be frequently visited by Canadian Government officials.

Although few children went as far west as British Columbia it was known that some thirty or forty were in the province under no supervision at all as there was no inspector. The NSPCC made known their concern by writing directly to Mackenzie King, the Prime Minister, about the possibility of cruelty to children going undetected.

Not to be outdone by Margaret Bondfield and the British parliamentary delegation, the Social Services Council of Canada launched their own investigation into the history of Canada's child migrants under the presidency of Mrs Plumptre.[15] Besides the Canadian Council for Child Welfare many women's groups gave evidence and the long report, which was carefully researched, came out in 1925. It took a much broader view of juvenile emigration than anything else previously published. Looking at the subject from an international point of view it came to the conclusion that organised juvenile emigration was almost entirely a phenomenon of the British Commonwealth. In most parts of the world, it discovered, children were positively prohibited from leaving their own countries unaccompanied by their families and many states prohibited the entry of young unaccompanied children. It noted that none of the reports on the children ever touched on the causes which led the children into the poor-law or voluntary organisations and remarked on the fact that the ethics of the system of transplanting dependent children from their homeland were never discussed. Canadian social workers, it said, were required to make a minute and inclusive study of the child's family history, the health, habits and standing of his relations in the community, the reasons for his leaving home and his age. All children should have a physical and psychiatric examination before being placed.

None of these principles were very different from the admissions policy followed by many of the homes, and certainly no more thorough than that of the Barnardo organisation, whose records had always been amazingly comprehensive since the earliest days. The trouble was that, in so far as the Canadians were concerned, they never saw those records. A letter from Mr Hobday, who had succeeded Alfred Owen as superintendent of the work in Canada, to Mrs Macgregor, of the Council on Child Welfare, illustrates the difficulty. Without the facts the Council for Child Welfare felt they were unable to make a comprehensive study of the problem, while the homes felt it to be their duty to protect the private lives of their children.

I am in receipt of your letter with reference to records being kept by Dr Barnardo's and note that your suggestion is that these records should in some way be made available to the Council of Child Welfare....

Dr Barnardo's Homes have during many years, developed an arrangement for keeping the records of children under their care. These records we consider to be the very best, but they are compiled with one object alone, and that is for the purpose of assisting, taking care of and protecting their wards. They are the records of the children rather than the records of the Homes and they are certainly not records intended for the public. The view taken by Dr Barnardo's Homes has always been that these, usually humble members of society are entitled to decide that the history of their childhood should be as much shielded from public curiosity as is the history of the more fortunate children who have been brought up in the privacy of their own parents' homes. That being so, we must decline to disclose to any other institution whatever anything which relates to the history of the children, and we desire to make it quite clear that, although we wish to be quite courteous to the Canadian Council for Child Welfare, we cannot disclose these records to other people.[16]

However, it was over the work of actual placement that the greatest difference between the work done by the agencies and the standard of practice now adopted by Canadian social workers was shown to exist. Before the selection of a home, the Canadians said, the child himself must be studied with care and sympathy, and his temperament, his physique and his tendencies considered. Then there should also be a careful personal investigation of homes applying for foster children. Again the temperament of the man and his wife must be considered in relation to the child they might receive; five or six references should be required and continued and frequent supervision must be maintained. From the official statistics in 1923 it could be shown that 37 per cent of the children were not visited that year. The children might have received visits from their own agencies, but the ability of the agencies to provide regular inspections varied greatly.

Sensational claims, made by Dr Eric Clarke, concerning 125 immigrant girls, who had passed through the Toronto General Hospital, all said to have been brought to Canada by Barnardo's between 1917 and 1924, were reported by the National Council for Social Service. Of the group seventy-seven were mentally defective, six suffered from dementia praecox, eighteen had two or more illegitimate children, thirty-six were prostitutes and four had served jail terms. All the girls were between eighteen and twenty-one, which, as the report pointed out, showed that that 'the dangerous ages' are just the years when the children for the first time become independent of the home. Professor Macphee repeated the claims made by Clarke at yet another conference called by the Canadian Council on Child Welfare in 1925.[17] Although Barnardo's sent no girls to Canada from 1917 to 1920 and the figures quoted were shown to be so inaccurate in other ways that Macphee published a complete retraction and apology, his claims were nevertheless very damaging.

Among the speakers at the conference Percy Roberts, Barnardo's chief migration officer, was in effect given the task of defending the policy of juvenile emigration. He relied too heavily on sentiment and the nostalgic evocation of Barnardo's pre-war role in child rescue work to be really effective in the present circumstances. While admitting that a boy could be exploited or even ill-treated for a time, he declared it to be almost impossible under the Barnardo system of after-care. He saw farm work as 'a splendid challenge to a boy and it brings out the best in him'. He said that out of 50,000 children who had come to Canada only 2–5 per cent had failed. He ended:

> I appeal to those disinterested persons present here who love children and have a real knowledge of this Barnardo work and the spirit in which we endeavour to do it; to those who are loyal to the flag, and who wish that every child born under it shall have a chance to make good; to those who believe in our Empire and in the destiny of the English speaking people. I appeal to you to help us and not hinder us in this really great and beneficent piece of Empire building.

This was promptly countered by Adelaide Plumptree who said, 'we cannot look upon child migration as a patriotic British endeavour'. She pointed out that women's organisations in particular, together with Canadian social workers, had been trying to educate public opinion to recognise the fact that Canada had higher standards of social work, methods which were different from those previously prevailing. Playing the numbers game she took Mr Roberts up on the point that he had made that 95 per cent of the children had done well. 'It is not the 95 per cent with whom we are concerned. It is the 5 per cent or the 2 per cent or whatever percentage may be who "went under". The Good Shepherd went after the one that was lost and left the 99. Two per cent even of 50,000 is 1,000 children and it is no attempt at an indictment of the system to strive to learn the destiny of those 1,000 children in Canada.'[18]

Barnardo's had in fact been poised to go ahead as the chief migration agency in the business. Forty-three Boards of Guardians had made use of their services in the post-war years up to 1924: and the Shaftesbury Homes, the Foundling Hospital, the Artists Rifles and Spurgeon orphanages had also used Barnardo's to emigrate their children. Barnardo's in the same period also took over the work of the Liverpool Sheltering Homes, Annie Macpherson's work and the Marchmont Home which had, up until then, been run by the Wallaces. It was not only the British Government who had imposed a ban on assisted passages that made life difficult for the emigrating agencies; the Federal Canadian Government in 1924, by an order in council, had made it effectively illegal for an unaccompanied child under fourteen to enter the country.

An interesting example of the confused thinking that surrounded the whole subject is the surprising involvement of the novelist, John Galsworthy, with the question of juvenile emigration. In a long article in the *Sunday Times* in 1925 dealing with the parlous state of England, he proposed a huge increase in the numbers, not of adults, but of children, to be sent overseas.[19] 'The English adult, in the main is spoiled for this adventure by town life, and the few still on the land we cannot spare. That leaves children. The English child is magnificent material.' He quoted Dr Barnardo's and other small schemes as having shown the way and said there was nothing new about the idea of juvenile emigration. He went on,

> ... why should we not make this a national policy and aim at transferring every year some two hundred thousand boys and girls between the ages of fourteen and eighteen to those great countries who are panting for population ... in seven years time this policy ... would reduce our unemployment to pre-war rate, at least, and pay for itself in the saving of dole. Within twenty years ... the racial unity of the British Commonwealth would be assured.

Yet when Galsworthy came to write about the subject in his comedy, *The Silver Spoon*, book two of the second Forsyte trilogy, there is more than a hint of the comic in his handling of the subject, although the book was published only a year after his article in the *Sunday Times*. Michael Mont, Fleur Forsyte's young husband, makes Foggartism, a system combining child emigration with agricultural improvement, the central theme of his maiden speech in the House of Commons. But, even as he delivers his speech, he is assailed by doubts. 'Is it all right – is it what I think, or am I an ignorant fool?' His visit to Sir James Foggart only underlines the element of the ridiculous. Sir James turns out to be a recluse surrounded by cats, who when Michael raises the question of financing the child migration scheme, breezily dismisses the difficulties: 'Money! There's still a mint of money – misapplied. Another hundred million loan – four and a half millions a year in the budget; and a hundred thousand children at least sent out every year. In five years we should save the lot in unemployment dole.' After having given his views Sir James falls asleep and leaves Michael Mont no less confused. But his views were not so very different from those put forward by Galsworthy himself only the year before. It seems as though the novelist had realised the inherent absurdity of his initial proposal and was using the fictional Sir James Foggart to say so.

Early in January, before the final decision to ban unaccompanied children under fourteen from entering Canada was taken, Howard Williams the chairman of the Barnardo Homes wrote to the Canadian Minister responsible for immigration, Robert Forke, suggesting that he talk to Leopold Amery, who was in Ottawa at that time in the hope of getting a favourable response.[20] He suggested that Canadians were becoming more and more concerned as to the very large percentage of foreign immigrants who were being received into the Dominion. His last argument was that unless the decision to exclude children under fourteen was reversed Barnardo's would have to close down their large establishment in Toronto: 'I dislike the thought of closing it down, but there seems to be no other way open to us if the main stream of our young immigrants is to be stopped.'

But in February Williams received a letter from the Minister saying that although he had had a talk with Col. Amery on the subject of immigration generally they had not had time to discuss that particular question. There is more than a hint in the letter to Williams that had it not been for the pressure from the Canadian provincial authorities the Minister would personally have liked to see Barnardo's and some of the other societies continue their work. As it was he wrote to Williams on 28 February:

> In the matter of child migration, it is unnecessary for me to say much, because you are doubtless familiar with the attitude of practically all the Provincial Child Welfare Associations from the Atlantic to the Pacific. In some provinces the opposition to the migration of young children is greater than in others, but I think generally the situation in Canada as viewed by the provincial authorities dealing with child welfare, may be summed up by saying that they consider the demand for suitable homes in Canada for young children can easily be satisfied by the placement of the waifs and strays that are to be found in various institutions in this country. . . .
>
> There is practically no opposition in any part of Canada to a movement of children of fourteen years of age or over. . . .
>
> After giving the matter a good deal of thought I have arrived at the conclusion that we must continue the present policy, at least for the time being. My own inclination was to try to meet the societies' wishes to some extent and it is only the weighty reasons to the contrary that have finally moved me to decide on a continuation of the present course.

The Minister certainly did not realise that his letter would signal the beginning of the end of the juvenile emigration movement. Four thousand children crossed the Atlantic the following year, but after 1929 there was a rapid decrease in numbers. By 1931 only six girls went to Canada and the figure for boys was under five hundred. The general depression was making life increasingly difficult for the immigrants. By 1932 Barnardo's had practically ceased to send children, and Bogue Smart's annual report showed that quite a number of boys returned to Britain. Other boys found it difficult to settle: taking advantage of the general depression, they preferred to travel about the country rather than stay on the farms for little or no money.

It is impossible to know how many boys and girls returned to Britain during those years but certainly a considerable number came back home. One ex-Barnardo boy who was sent out in

1913 told me recently he returned home because there was nothing to do except cut ice, but that now he wishes he had remained in Canada. John Greenwood was one of those sent out in 1929.[21] He had been brought up by the Foundling Hospital, having been committed to their care as a baby. He was put in a foster home near Cambridge, and although his first foster mother died soon after his arrival, the eldest daughter, May, kept house following her mother's death and proved to be so competent that John was allowed to stay. May Bush became John's foster mother and although she married and is now over eighty and John went to Canada when he was fourteen, John is still very much in touch with her and comes to England to see her every other year. When the time came for John to leave his foster home he was sent to the Foundling Hospital school at Redhill. From there he was given the choice of going to Australia or Canada and he chose Canada as being the nearer home of the two. There wasn't much choice about the question of career: the boy standing next to John was told he was going overseas and only avoided it because he said hastily, 'Please sir, I am only thirteen and a half.' Boys who didn't go to Canada could choose to go into the army – but the boy had to be a bandsman to get in – the fishing fleet, or they could be apprenticed to Monotype.

The Foundling Hospital, understanding something of the wrench that going overseas entailed, alone among the agencies allowed their wards a week's holiday with their foster parents to say goodbye. Some former child emigrants have never forgotten or forgiven the fact that not even their 'auntie', the friend who visited them while they were in the home, sometimes their only contact with the outside world, was told that they were going overseas. After John had said goodbye to his foster family he passed into the care of Barnardo's for four months before sailing. He was sent to Liverpool and there with a group of boys was given a very sketchy introduction to farm life. In groups the boys went to watch work being done on the surrounding farms; they visited the local stables and went camping. Each boy was provided with an outfit of clothes which was packed up in the regulation metal trunks bound with wood. John still has his trunk and his wife now keeps her embroidery wools and silks inside its solid frame. It is opened with care, for John pointed out that if the lid should happen to fall on your fingers the metal rim could do serious harm. The clothes were tough, like the trunk. They were made to last and in three or four years all John had to buy were socks and pants and rubber boots.

John admits that he was one of the lucky ones and he knows of others who were not so fortunate. But everything did not go quite smoothly to start with. He was placed with a farmer who wrote to complain that John did not work hard enough. John received a strong letter from John Hobday, the Barnardo manager, taking a tough, no-nonsense attitude.

> We have today received a letter from Mr Willows which is a cause of great grief and disappointment to us. He states that while you are on the whole, as far as general conduct is concerned, a really good boy, you appear to have no sense of self responsibility nor any ideas of rendering yourself helpful to him....
>
> We are glad to note that you have settled down happily and comfortably and that you appreciate the wonderful country to which you have been brought. However it is absolutely necessary that you strive to realise that you are no longer a little boy of eight or nine years of age who may be excused for playing around and not seeing the work which lies at hand to be done. You were not brought to Canada to spend a holiday nor yet to have a life-long vacation, but so that you might have an opportunity of acquiring knowledge in farming, and eventually become, we hope, a farmer on your own account....
>
> Now, let us warn you, that while we are quite capable of securing you another place, it may not be one where you will receive such kindness and consideration as is your experience now, and no matter where you go *you must work*.

John moved to another farm, where the farmer was used to boys, having had ten successive boys. He was paid less well than at the first farm, but he liked working there because he was well looked after. Three years later he moved to work for Mr Snelgrove's brother-in-law, and in ten years he had five different places. When the Second World War came John left the land, as did many of the boys, and joined up.

When John Greenwood returned from the war he did not go back to farming. Like many others who came to Canada to work on the land the war gave him the opportunity of looking further afield for work. John got a job with General Motors where he stayed for twenty-eight years, retiring when he was fifty-five. He and his wife now live in Oshawa in a charming and comfortable home and John told me he had no regrets about having come to Canada and was proud to have been sent out under the Barnardo emigration scheme.

Twelve

REFUGEES FROM WAR

THE ACT OF EMPIRE SETTLEMENT had been a direct encouragement to the emigration agencies to increase the flow of children leaving Britain for those Commonwealth countries who needed to augment their populations. Although the Bondfield Report was to curtail child migration to Canada, it had little effect on the movement in so far as it affected New Zealand and Australia. It was the economic crisis of the 1930s and its consequences that finally brought large-scale child migration to an end. When children were again sent overseas in 1940 in large numbers, it was for reasons of security, prompted by war-time conditions. The idea of moving thousands of children overseas to safety no doubt owed something to the fact that a long-established tradition of child migration between Britain and the Commonwealth already existed.

New Zealand had been a late starter in the child-migration movement, and, anxious to catch up, gave the greatest encouragement in the 1920s to 'that most important of all immigration policies, juvenile and child migration'.[1] Children were seen as highly desirable immigrants because of their youth: it was felt they would settle more quickly and become assimilated to the country more easily. It was hoped that 40 per cent of all immigrants would be juveniles. With Gibbon Wakefield's theories still very much in mind New Zealand was not content merely to accept children sent by Boards of Guardians and voluntary agencies. The Government did all it could to encourage English public school boys and other young people from secondary modern schools to come to New Zealand.

Owing to the price of wool being fixed during the First World War the New Zealand sheep-farmers had made a considerable profit. In an emotional and generous gesture it was proposed to use part of those profits to buy Flock House and 8,000 acres of land so that the sons and daughters of British seamen, killed or wounded during the war, might be brought to New Zealand and trained to become farmers. The New Zealand Sheep-owners' Acknowledgement of Debt to British Seamen Fund ran Flock House as a kind of living war memorial and from 1924, when the first party of children arrived, about a hundred children made the journey annually, until New Zealand, like the rest of the world, was engulfed by the economic crisis of the 1930s. At about the same time the Salvation Army set up a training farm for boys at Putaruru and the Church of England also made arrangements to send boys to New Zealand, but both these schemes fell victim to the economic difficulties of the thirties.

Canada was as much affected by the unsettled trading conditions in the thirties as anywhere else in the world. The difficulties inherent in the economic situation reinforced the decision, already taken by Barnardo's and the other long-established child migration societies, to cease working in Canada. The newer agencies dealing with child migration, like the Church Army, the British Immigrant Aid and Colonisation Association and the Church of England Council for Empire Settlement, which had all been set up in the 1920s, found it impossible to keep up the momentum with which they had begun operations. The withdrawal of the British-based immigration societies threw an increasing burden on the Canadian juvenile immigration authorities. The older boys who were now coming to Canada were more difficult to settle as the report for 1931–2 makes clear: 'Efforts to get [the boys] settled were not satisfactory as relatively a small number remained in the places to which they were sent and exhibited a disinclination to work, preferring to impose on the sympathy and credulity of the public in towns and cities.'[2] The report can be seen as vindicating the views of those who argued in favour of bringing children to Canada at a younger age, but, as the story of one boy, Charles Davies, makes clear, even those who came to Canada as young children were unsettled by the conditions of the thirties.

Charles, in his autobiography, graphically describes the restlessness he felt, and which was felt by so many boys and girls when their placements ended.[3] He had come to Canada when he was nine and was sent to a foster home where he was happy. When he was fourteen he was sent to work on a farm near Peterborough where he considered himself lucky to have a boss who was kind. None the less, before breakfast he had milked eight cows; after breakfast it could happen that he walked up and down behind two horses for four hours, with no break, until lunchtime; after lunch the ploughing would continue until 6 pm. Although the work was hard, Charles was not unhappy because he found himself becoming tougher and stronger and came to delight in the sight of a well-ploughed field. However, when he was paid his wages at the end of the three years and was out of the jurisdiction of the homes, the first thing he did was to return to England. Nine months later he was back in Canada – but not to work. He wanted to see something of the country instead and decided to 'flag' his way round. He knew the rules of the game. If he arrived in any town after 6 pm he reported to the local lock-up as required. The inmates had to cut some wood, for which they were given a cup of cocoa and a sandwich, but they had to be out of town by 10 o'clock next morning or be arrested for vagrancy. He sometimes begged for meals, but didn't complain when he was only given a bag of biscuits because he knew he was doing it for 'kicks'.

He could have worked had he wanted to. Often as he walked along the highway, farmers would shout, 'Say, Mac, would you work for me?' He always answered in the negative, but says he felt sorry for the farmers because 'a great number of lads were playing to the depression'. Sometimes he stopped the thumbing and worked on a farm for one to three months, and the few dollars he received helped to keep up appearances. When Charles decided to visit the Rocky Mountains he realised he would never get there if he stuck to the road. Compared to hitching, 'riding the trains' was far more exciting and he described his first attempt at 'jumping trains':

I started from Toronto, one evening after dark, all on my own. As I thought to myself, 'I can always have company another time.' I crouched under a board walk jutting out from a long ridge of ground just alongside the track. After three puffs of smoke from the engine, I moved from my hiding place and jumped the train and stood behind the coal tender. The train soon gathered speed and it wasn't long before she started to roll from side to side. I was terribly excited, riding through the night, alone on this monster. After fifty miles she stopped at a small station called Myrtle to pick up mail. 'Oh dear', I thought, 'here goes, railroad cops (or Bulls as they were called) are going to search for fellows like me.' All was fine and away again. This journey is the most vivid in my mind of any as it was my first attempt at 'riding the rods'.

Winter is not the time to be travelling in Canada without money or a job, so Charles got only as far as Winnipeg, where the temperature was 39 degrees below freezing. He quickly decided conditions were too 'rough' and started to look for work.

The Canadian Government offered farm jobs at $5 a month, with board and lodging, but the conditions were hard. There were thought to be 200,000 'transients' like Charles, many of them English, on the roads at that time. Charles thought that the farmers brought their troubles on themselves by exploiting the lads willing to work. He got a job on a farm 160 miles west of Winnipeg. He and his workmate had to be up at five in the morning, Saturdays and Sundays included. They worked without a break, except for lunch, the whole day. The cold was intense. To get the tractor started the farmer had to light a straw fire under the engine; the water trough for the animals had a little wood-burning stove in it and six inches from the stove the water was still frozen. After five weeks Charles and his workmate jumped the milk train and went back to Winnipeg.

Travelling south he got a job on another farm where it was agreed that he should be paid $33 at the end of the year. Charles described his boss as a 'slave driver'. Three days before the end of the year Charles walked out and the farmer refused to pay him anything at all. The farmer worked hard and expected the boys to work as hard as he did. Charles remembered that he rushed everything he did, including eating his meals. 'He literally shovelled his food down, head nearly touching the plate. He shoved his chair back and rushed out of the house to work, saying to me, "Come on, it's a nice day, can't waste time."' Charles commented that there were many times when he was forced to leave his meal unfinished and follow him out. He thought it was conditions like these that drove the lads from the jobs. Charles finally stuck to a farm job for a year and with the $33 he earned was able to get back to England. He joined the army just before the outbreak of war and was one of those who came back from the beaches of Dunkirk.

Apart from New Zealand, which had its own policy for granting assisted passages to juveniles, there were two exceptions to the general ban on the giving of assisted passages to children under school-leaving age. Both Fairbridge and Barnardo's continued to be allowed to send children under school age to their residential establishments in Australia. Kingsley Fairbridge had died in 1924, but not before he had securely established the new farm school at Pinjarra. Even as he lay, gravely ill, in a bed on the stoep of his house, he read to the boys gathered round him from the life of Henry Ford to encourage them to set their sights high. Fairbridge's idealistic concept of farm schools throughout the Empire did not die with him. It was an idea that appealed above all to the rich and powerful. When the worst effects of the depression were over the Child Emigration Society in London launched an appeal for £100,000 taking whole pages in *The Times*[4] and the *Morning Post*[5] to announce that the Prince of Wales had subscribed £1,000 and that Stanley Baldwin was very much in favour of the appeal.

The Child Emigration Society had already sent Miss Leatham, their secretary, to Canada in 1931 to see how the Dominion Government would react to the idea of setting up a farm school in Ontario. With so many young men, like Charles Davies, roaming the countryside the approach met with no success. However, the attention of the Society switched from Ontario to British Columbia when Miss Bostok made a request for a farm school to be started in that province where her family owned a large ranch.[6] She, like Miss Leatham, was turned down:

> We have over sixty years of juvenile immigration experience to draw upon and pretty much all sorts of schemes have been tried out. After talking with Miss Leatham I spoke to the Premier about the minimum age limit and he made it very clear that we will not depart from this limit nor yet give any financial assistance.[7]

The Child Emigration Society refused to give up and, relying on their prestigious support, they tried to influence prominent Canadian citizens in their favour. They finally succeeded when T.D. Patullo, the leader of the Liberals, became Prime Minister of British Columbia. An energetic and optimistic man, he believed that the sooner immigration to Canada was restarted the better it would be. The age rule had never been enforced by anything other than an order in council, and since the Dominion Government had no power to refuse permission for a Fairbridge farm school to be set up in British Columbia, as the province had welcomed the Child Emigration Society's initiative, the rule was waived for the Fairbridge children. It was quixotic that the site chosen for the education and training of British children destined to become Canadian citizens, should have been Duncan, long known as Canada's 'little bit of England transplanted beyond the seas'. At the turn of the century the rolling hills of the Cowichan valley on the eastern side of Vancouver Island had attracted a certain type of gentleman settler, and the 1931 census revealed that 65 per cent of the population were still of English extraction. The quiet English conservatism of the area was a positive asset, and when plans for the farm were announced in 1935 there was almost total local support. Criticism within the province was the exception rather than the rule. British Columbia had had little previous experience of juvenile emigration and had taken no part in the controversies it had aroused in the eastern provinces. The Canadian Daughters' League in Victoria sent a telegram of protest to Ottawa:

> In view of present destitute Saskatchewan settlers asking relief and tremendous numbers of young men in relief camps we strongly protest allowing into Canada British waifs and strays for training in Fairbridge farm school located in Vancouver Island. What guarantee has Canada that these immigrants will never become public charges?[8]

The Provincial Secretary's department, however, was confident that even with the depression 'the demand for farm help of a cheap type cannot be met . . . (and) there is not a doubt in the world that the supply of female household servants is not adequate'.[9] Despite the public-school flavour of the publicity pictures sent from Pinjarra to support the appeal which appeared in the British press, showing the boys playing cricket, bathing in the pool, going to church on Sunday and being addressed by the Duke of Gloucester, their destiny was preordained. They were to be the cheap farm hands and domestic servants of the future.

The year after the school was founded, Colonel Harry Logan was appointed principal. A Rhodes Scholar, Logan had been present when Kingsley Fairbridge made his inaugural speech at Oxford in 1909. His appointment brought tremendous prestige to the school and attracted a large number of visitors. The protests of the child-welfare workers and others, worried at the way the age limit had been disregarded, were lost in the praise given to the school and the Society by most wealthy and vocal Canadians. During the sixteen years of its existence the school became a complete community of its own. Using emigration facilities provided by Barnardo's and Middlemore, 330 children made the journey from Britain to Vancouver, a trip which took two weeks. When war broke out in 1939 the Prince of Wales Fairbridge Farm School found itself facing many of the same problems that had bedevilled the first farm school at Pinjarra. Support for the school had come mainly from Britain and when finance from this source dried up Colonel Logan had to appeal to the Dominion and provincial governments for money to keep the school going. There were other problems apart from finance: rumours of lax discipline and difficulties with staff began to circulate; the first Fairbridgians had left and, with resources stretched, the school was in no position to take on any additional responsibilities. When a seventeen-year-old girl, who had been placed in domestic service in Victoria, became pregnant by an older man who abandoned her in Vancouver, her case was referred by the Vancouver Children's Aid Society to the Superintendent for Neglected Children. The case was not an isolated one.

Since the school now depended on the provincial government for funds, the social workers thought that the farm school should no longer be classed as a private institution. They felt it should operate under a welfare licence like any other residential establishment in the province, and the fact that Colonel Logan did not deign to apply for a licence until eighteen months after the grant had been made further soured relationships between Fairbridge and welfare workers. In any case the whole ethos of the Fairbridge Farm was contrary to what social workers believed to be good child-care practice. The Canadian Council on Child Welfare had unequivocally stated that there was no doubt that a child thrived best in its normal setting – the home rather than in institutional care. In 1943 a new provincial Protection of Children Act specified that a child could not be maintained by a society outside a foster home for more than six months without the written consent of the superintendent. Although this act was designed to protect children who had come to Canada as war evacuees, it nevertheless underlined still further the fact that the school violated most of the principles of Canadian child welfare. An even more serious matter was the way in which Fairbridge children were permanently removed from their parents for reasons other than neglect.

Relationships between the school and the welfare authorities steadily worsened during the war years. Isobel Harvey, the fiercest critic of the school, was superintendent of child welfare when she made her final report on the school in August 1944. Her concluding paragraph left little doubt that she would have closed the school had she been able to do so:

> A child welfare worker viewing Fairbridge is left with a feeling of helplessness. The basic idea, antagonistic to every concept of Canadian Child Welfare, that these children are poor English children and, therefore, different from the ordinary child, is rooted so firmly . . . that there is no use arguing against it.[10]

There is no doubt that the Fairbridge Farm was a separate community, isolated from the mainstream of Canadian life by its curriculum and its location. When comparisons came to be made at the end of the war between those who had spent the war years as evacuees in Canadian families, the Fairbridge children came a poor second.

I was nearly twelve when war broke out and was with my family in France, where my parents had a holiday chalet. I listened to Neville Chamberlain broadcasting the news that we were at war with Germany. My father immediately rejoined his regiment, but it was decided that my mother and we four girls should remain where we were, in Houlgate, a small seaside town on the Normandy coast not far from Deauville. There we children spent a happy eight months during what came to be known as the 'phoney war'. The surrender of Holland and Belgium changed all that and the German invasion of France forced us to return to England. We left after Dunkirk had already been successfully evacuated and we crossed the Channel on 6 June, 1940, sailing from Cherbourg to Southampton on a calm sunny day, eleven days before the fall of France.

Not long after our return my mother said she was arranging for my sister and me to go to Canada for the duration of the war. A trickle of children, whose parents had friends or relatives in America and Canada, had already crossed the Atlantic to escape wartime conditions. Now that the French surrender had left Britain isolated and vulnerable the idea of evacuating children, not only from the towns to the country, but from Britain overseas to the Commonwealth countries, and particularly to Canada as well as to the United States, became both fashionable and popular. The idea of being sent to Canada seemed totally ridiculous to me. If a disaster, such as had happened to France, should befall England why should we two elder ones be spared rather than the little ones, not to mention the baby my mother was then expecting, all of whom, I thought, would be less well able to look after themselves than we two? I did not know how to articulate these thoughts but I was totally opposed to the idea and made use of that childish but effective weapon, tears.

Judging by the number of applications made to the Children's Overseas Reception Board by anxious parents wanting to send their children overseas to safety my feelings were obviously not shared by many thousands of children. But I knew what it was like to be forced to flee before an advancing army: I had watched refugees from Belgium streaming through our small town, their household goods crammed inside and on top of their cars; I had heard the sound of gunfire and had felt something of the panic that engulfed France as the German armies swept through the country. Perhaps it was because I had experienced invasion at first hand that I felt strongly that the family should stay together. The idea of being far from home when the new baby was born doubtless reinforced these feelings. We did not go to Canada.

The organisation of the Children's Overseas Reception Board in the summer of 1940 was a remarkable piece of speedy improvisation. Canada was the first Commonwealth country to offer hospitality to British children, the official offer being made through the Canadian Government on 31 May, but Australia, New Zealand and South Africa were quick to follow suit. The day after we arrived back from France an interdepartmental committee was set up 'To consider offers from overseas to house and care for children whether accompanied or unaccompanied, from the European War Zone, residing in Great Britain, including children orphaned by the war'.[11] The day France fell, 17 June, its recommendations were accepted. It was decided that the tentative offers from the Dominions should be gratefully acknowledged and a scheme agreed for receiving 'children of school age, who had reached five but were under sixteen, from Great Britain'. The threat of invasion and the danger of bombing had swept away the barriers which had been so recently erected to prevent young unaccompanied children being sent to Canada. Schools and private organisations worked alongside CORB (the Children's Overseas Reception Board) to make arrangements to send children overseas. The American Committee for the Evacuation of Children had to persuade the US Attorney General's office to rescind the law that prevented unaccompanied children coming into the United States, a law which had been enacted to prevent the exploitation of foreign children as cheap labour. The committees had to work fast; the fear of invasion was very real and the sense of urgency was increased by the intensification of submarine warfare.

Initial planning by CORB was for a large-scale evacuation, but the overwhelming response to the scheme by anxious parents was something of an embarrassment. There were those who felt, and these were said at the time to have included Churchill, that world opinion would be adversely affected if Britain was thought to be 'admitting her sense of territorial insecurity to such a degree that she was despatching her children to the Dominions'.[12] Letters of inquiry were descending on the Board in such a deluge that night staff had to be engaged to cope with them. When the chairman of the Board, Sir Geoffrey Shakespeare, broadcast an announcement on 23 June that the Dominions were ready to welcome 20,000 children, and that figure could be regarded as a beginning, he also gave a warning that the numbers of children sent depended, not only on the numbers the Dominions could receive, but also on the shipping available: 'When people talk glibly about sending hundreds of thousands of children overseas in the space of a few weeks they do so without authority and without knowledge of the facts. Such talk is both dangerous and stupid.' Such a warning was indeed necessary. A.G. Sainsbury, the president of the New Zealand Small Farmers League had suggested that 10,000 children should come to New Zealand on the *Queen Mary* and be housed in special villages.[13] A suggestion was made that Barnardo's should establish a branch home in the country. By 4 July, when the number of applications to CORB had reached 211,000, it was decided to suspend entries.

Gradually a system was evolved. Parents with children in grant-aided schools were instructed to apply to their local education authority or to the LEA to whose area their children had been evacuated under the home evacuation scheme. Forms had to be completed and returned to CORB together with a medical report, a school report and a teachers' recommendation on the suitability of the child to be sent overseas. An acceptance form was then sent to the parents which constituted a contract between the Board and the parents who thereby undertook to make the same weekly payments as they would have had to pay under the home evacuation scheme. The Board for their part undertook to send the child overseas, to be responsible for its welfare and such education as would be open to it in the Dominion and to bring the child back as soon as practicable after the war. The fact that the final medical examination was arranged by the Dominion concerned followed the practice evolved during the years of juvenile emigration.

The older age limit for the children was lowered from sixteen to fifteen and a half partly because the labour of young people was required in the country and partly because the people in the Dominions did not take kindly to seeing husky adolescents arriving as evacuees. By arrangement with the Dominions the scheme was not extended to Allied refugees or to coloured children, an indication of the exclusiveness of the bond between Britain and the Dominions. Certainly Australia and New Zealand hoped that some of the children would settle permanently in their countries. Hundreds of thousands of offers of hospitality were made in New Zealand with such a 'high sense of feeling and patriotism that would kindle the hearts and minds of all who read of them'.[14] At least 50,000 Canadians were prepared to offer their homes for the accommodation of British Guest Children and there was the greatest interest in the scheme in Australia and South Africa. The first party of children bound for Canada left on 21 July 1940. Children left for Australia on 5 August, for New Zealand on 16 August and for South Africa on 23 August. Owing to the necessity for secrecy it was difficult to let the foster parents know when the children would be arriving. Of the 2,664 children sent overseas by CORB 1,532 went to Canada in nine parties, 577 children went to Australia in three parties, 353 children went to South Africa in two parties and two parties brought 202 children to New Zealand. An escort was provided for every fifteen children and the people chosen had to be able to organise games on deck and to interest the children in singing and handicrafts. The party had usually to be accommodated at the port for two or three days to allow for such contingencies as air raids. The first party to sail to Australia was housed in the Barnardo Homes at Fazackerly in Liverpool.[15] In Canada the Children's Aid Societies utilised their existing organisations for the care of the children without any charge and free homes were offered in such numbers that it was possible to place the British children as guests in Canadian homes where they were treated and provided for as members of the family. As the report for 1941 said: 'It is impossible to speak too highly of the splendid and whole-hearted cooperation that has existed between the Provinces, their coordinating societies, and the Federal Government, and of the high standard of the foster homes offered by residents of Canada.'[16] The practice of keeping the children together for a while after they had landed in New Zealand showed a new understanding of the stress of separation. In recommending that the children should not be sent off immediately, senior child-welfare officers reminded impatient foster parents that the children had suffered a serious separation from their parents; had had a long journey on which they had formed new friendships and associations, and that a further break would occur when they were parted from their friends so they needed time to adjust.[17] Nearly three times the number of children sent by CORB went overseas privately under the auspices of schools and voluntary organisations. The evacuation was not quite all one way. Children from Gibraltar were evacuated to Britain and some came to the Barnardo village at Barkingside which admitted both boys and girls.

The problem of actually transporting the children overseas was becoming increasingly difficult. The United States's decision to withdraw shipping from the 'belligerent seas' reduced the number of ships available; the sinking of the *Andorra Star*, a fast unescorted ship, induced the Board to decide that CORB children should only travel in convoy, and the defection of the French fleet meant there were fewer naval ships available for convoy duty. The ss *Volendam* was torpedoed on 28 August but mercifully there was no loss of life and all 350 CORB children on board eventually reached Canada. There was a certain amount of dissatisfaction in New Zealand at the slow arrival of the children, but they only learnt sometime later of the disastrous voyage of the *City of Benares* which was torpedoed and sunk on 17 September. Ninety children had been on board and seventy-three lost their lives, together with six of their escorts, many dying of exposure in the open boats tossed about by the heavy seas. Two little girls from Glasgow managed to survive by clinging to an upturned boat on which were the bodies of two dead Lascar seamen. Miss M.A. Cornish, a music teacher, received the George Medal for saving the lives of the seventeen children in her lifeboat, keeping them active by making them sing and using musical games to make them move their arms. This tragedy brought the overseas evacuation scheme to an end. Children already waiting in Liverpool to embark for Canada were brought back to London. They arrived at Euston station to find themselves in the midst of an air raid and Mrs Davies, the CORB representative who met them, had immediately to guide them to the nearest air-raid shelter.

It was perhaps fortunate that the intensification of the war at sea made it impossible to ship out the 24,000 children who had already been approved and the thousand escorts who had been chosen to accompany them. Had the children and their escorts sailed in 1940 as planned, this would have constituted the greatest migration of children overseas the world had known. One cannot help suspecting that only Britain, with its long tradition of juvenile emigration, could have inaugurated and put in motion so quickly such an infinitely complex and delicate operation. In the rush to get children to safety the emotional consequences of separation, of the establishment of new relationships with unknown foster parents and feelings of parental bereavement were scarcely considered. A diminished staff at CORB continued to watch over the interests of the children and a special committee was set up by the Board to liaise between parents and foster parents of those children privately evacuated.

Unhappily the end of overseas evacuation did not end the loss of life of those concerned with it. The *Rangitane* returning from New Zealand was sunk by shell fire and six escorts were killed or died from wounds. One became a prisoner of war, and fifteen others, after having been kept for three weeks in appalling conditions in the hold of a prison ship were landed, two seriously wounded, on a remote island of the New Guinea archipelago. When the *Port Wellington* was sunk another eight escorts were captured and taken to prisoner-of-war camps in Germany where one of them died.[18]

All the Dominions had insisted that the children should be placed in private homes and that the hospitality should be free. Canada and New Zealand gave tax concessions to foster parents and in Australia a child endowment grant of 5s a week was paid. Foster parents had to have well-brought-up children of their own and to be in a position to care for, feed, and clothe the children without involving themselves in hardship or a lowered standard of living. Particular care was taken where older children were placed to see that there was no likelihood of the children being exploited, made to do domestic or other kinds of work. As the final report makes clear, 'It was on the selection of foster homes that the success of the scheme really depended ... the forethought and care with which the offer of homes was scrutinised cannot be sufficiently commended.'[19]

This was achieved despite all the difficulties under which the Dominion authorities had to work. Owing to the speed with which the scheme was organised, information about the children and their background was woefully inadequate; reports and comments from their teachers which should have been attached to their papers were often missing. Although the majority of parents had sent their children overseas to escape the bombing and possible invasion, a few had used the opportunity of ridding themselves of their children for a few years for marital or other domestic reasons. The children who developed behaviour problems were often found to have come from such homes, but the receiving authorities had little background information to help them deal with such cases.

In Canada, in particular, there was considerable anxiety over the question of the guardianship of the children. Charlotte Whitton, of the Canadian Welfare Council, thought that the British Government's attitude to the matter was casual in the extreme, and she claimed the United States authorities shared this view.[20] Eventually the British Ambassador to the US, Lord

Halifax, and the UK High Commissioner to Canada, the Earl of Athlone, were appointed legal guardians to those children who needed such representation. For all practical purposes guardianship was exercised by the provincial authorities in Canada. It is interesting to note that in South Africa, where there had been no tradition of child migration, the organisation was of a 'rather more voluntary and unofficial character than in the other Dominions'.[21] In some isolated districts in South Africa the services of the magistrate seem to have been used, as they had been a hundred years previously when the Children's Friend Society had asked that an investigation be made into the conditions under which their children were living.

In spite of the difficulties, owing to lack of information about some of the children, the overall success in the selection of foster homes in Canada was very striking, particularly when compared to the large number of placement changes that were the norm for the pre-war emigrant children. In the first four years 70 per cent of the children remained in their first home and of those given a second home 15 per cent settled happily. The very success of the operation brought with it difficulties of its own. It was hard for the parents left in England not to have any idea to what kind of home their child had gone; it was particularly hard for parents whose children had gone to Australia, New Zealand and South Africa and who had to wait months before they knew where to write. For some letter-writing did not come easily and when the ships carrying mail were sunk the gap in communication caused anxiety and reproach. Inevitably foster parents came to know the children better than their natural parents, but most were careful to keep the memory of home and family in the forefront of the children's minds. In the majority of cases confidence was established and with it 'an understanding strong enough to bear criticism or advice from the other side'.[22]

Inevitably the children were affected by these divided loyalties. Some found their relationships with their own families hard to re-establish; others discovered that the years of separation had left a gap which could not be bridged; most felt themselves somehow to be different. Anthony Bailey, who went to America in 1940 under the auspices of the American Committee for the Evacuation of Children, has explored his reaction to the ex perience with perceptive insight in his recent book, *America Lost and Found*. The advantages of having a family on both sides of the Atlantic are balanced against the difficulty of having to 'learn to cope with and integrate one's double childhood'. The sense of being different has remained with him, even to the extent that he sometimes thinks of himself as being two Tonys. His sense of melancholy or nostalgia for Britain when he is in America or for America when in Britain must be shared by many of the children who spent their formative years separated from their families, growing up in a different country with different customs. Anthony Bailey, as he came down the gang plank, did not at first even recognise the small wavy-haired woman who met him as his mother.

For parents welcoming home children whom they had last seen four or five years previously the difficulty was of another kind. As one parent recalled, 'It was a most dramatic meeting. The small boy I had seen off at the railway station in 1940 had come back a man.'[23] The drama of that particular meeting was much greater than normal for while in Canada Cecil had suffered a brain tumour and as a result had become practically blind. He had studied braille in Canada and came back to England determined to continue his studies and get to university. His father had expected, when he met him off the ship, that his whole life would be taken up looking after him, 'but I soon discovered that Cecil did not need any looking after in the sense I had envisaged. He has a really wonderful philosophy and faces his difficulties in a manner which is an example to me. . . . Those two wonderful people Mr and Mrs M— will for ever be remembered by me for their wonderful care of my boy.'

Both British and Dominion authorities considered that the whole scheme had been an outstanding success. For Dr Wallace, Principal of Queen's University and Chairman of the National Advisory Committee for Children from Overseas, the spirit of the letter that Cecil wrote to his foster parents describing his studies in England was 'sufficient in itself to justify the whole work of the committee, the provincial bodies and the foster parents of Canada. It is a magnificent tribute to the courage of youth and gave one new hope and confidence.'[24] Other letters show that the Canadians were right in feeling that the movement had forged strong bonds of friendship between their coun try and Britain. One father wrote, 'To say thank you seems very inadequate. Our great hope remains that in the future you will hear and maybe see in Bill something which will give you pleasure in knowing that you played a very important part in shaping.'[25] Another said simply, 'There is nothing England or the English people can ever do to repay the generosity of Canada.'

The ten thousand children, mainly from middle-class professional families, who were sent overseas privately, at their own risk, far exceeded in numbers those sent out under the auspices of CORB, although had CORB been able to continue to send children there is no doubt that thousands more would have gone. In Washington Lord Halifax had even discussed the question with the German Ambassador, who had assured him that ships carrying children would not be attacked.[26] It is clear from the reports that were made at the end of the war on the work of CORB that the idea of child migration was far from dead. It was not seen for what it was, a somewhat desperate wartime measure, induced by a relatively short-lived panic as to the ability of Britain to survive the German bombing and possible invasion, a gamble with the lives of children and their families, which somehow succeeded beyond all expectation. The very success of the scheme was taken as representing a new and encouraging development in the long history of juvenile emigration. The official conclusion actually summed up the scheme as 'an experiment in child migration'. There was certainly also a distinct feeling of regret among the Dominions that the overseas evacuation scheme was on a much smaller scale than had been anticipated. They had been willing and eager to welcome far greater numbers of children whom, they hoped, would become not only good ambassadors for their countries, but future citizens.

The great advantage of the CORB scheme was that it was government sponsored and this gave the Dominion authorities freedom to control the placement and supervision of the children, something they had never enjoyed under previous child migration schemes. This power enabled them to follow the children's careers right through and gave them the ability to monitor the development of the scheme. The children were placed in private homes of the citizens and were thus assimilated with the life of the Dominion and not, as on farm schools and other residential establishments, kept separate from the community amongst whom they lived. There was, of course, no question of the children being made to work, or exploited for the sake of their labour. Without the willing co-operation of the British and Dominion Governments the scheme could not have succeeded and while it lasted it created a living link between the countries involved. The identified weaknesses of the scheme had, in the main, arisen from the speed with which it had been implemented.

The Director of CORB, Miss Marjorie Maxse, visiting Canada in 1944, met Ishbel Harvey when she was in British Columbia. The very successes of CORB only served to highlight the weaknesses of the Prince of Wales Fairbridge Farm School. The school needed money from both the Dominion and Provincial Government if it was to be able to continue and Ishbel Harvey, the Deputy Provincial Secretary and three members of the Fairbridge Board were members of a committee set up to try to solve the problems the school posed to the provincial authorities. It was resolved that there should be a change of principle, that children coming to British Columbia should be treated as any other British Columbian children and given foster-home care and trained supervision and that the Provincial Fairbridge Committee must have complete control and responsibility. Isobel Harvey wrote passionately, 'These children belong to both our countries and they have no chance at all. When I look at our lovely CORB boys and girls going back and then look at the Fairbridge ones I could sit down and weep.'[27]

The Fairbridge Farm School in Canada was not alone in finding its work the subject of criticism. Sir Eric Machtig, Permanent Secretary to the Dominions Office, had seen Isobel Harvey's letter and wrote to Malcolm Macdonald, the UK High Commissioner in Canada, about the unfavourable comparisons between the CORB children and the children who had been educated at the Fairbridge School. Sir Eric had also had complaints about the educational inadequacy of the Fairbridge schools in Australia. The farm school in Pinjarra had been joined by two more in New South Wales. He wrote, 'The difficulties that have arisen in Australia are partly educational and partly administrative and seem to be due to the fact that the Fairbridge organisation does not seem able to deal so satisfactorily with what may be called "problem" cases as some other farm schools, notably that run by Dr Barnardo's Home.' Sir Eric went to the root of the problem when he wrote of the rigidity with which the original principles laid down by Kingsley Fairbridge had been adhered to, 'that boys should be trained only for farm work and girls for domestic employment, whereas modern conditions seem to demand a broader range of technical instruction to provide scope for personal aptitudes and for alternative forms of employment'.

These criticisms effectively spelled the end of the Fairbridge Farm School in Canada which finally closed in 1953. The farm in Pinjarra has changed the focus of its work and concentrates on helping one-parent families and their children who wish to emigrate to Australia.

Barnardo's, the most active of the agencies to have been involved in the movement, had already begun to admit Australian children to its residential homes and farm school. The small parties of carefully selected children who went to Australia in the 1950s and 1960s no longer went by ship; they made the long journey by air. Since 1967, when the last party went out, Barnardo's in Australia has worked entirely with Australian children. In 1969 Barnardo's New Zealand was set up to help New Zealand children in recognition of the support New Zealand had given to the work of Barnardo's in Britain in the past.

New Zealand had rejected an offer made in 1947 to establish a Fairbridge farm school, but it was New Zealand who agreed, two years later, to what must be the very last of the many schemes for the emigration of children. Building on what was thought to be the successful experience of the CORB scheme, the Child Migration Scheme was started in 1949 by the Royal Overseas League.[28] Under the scheme, which was to bring 256 British children to New Zealand in thirteen parties of twenty, the Superintendent of Child Welfare was to have the right of guardianship over the children who were to be placed in foster homes until they were old enough to work. The ingrained British tradition of confusing the needs of disadvantaged children with the demands of Empire settlement died slowly. New Zealand came late to the juvenile emigration movement and it is understandable that it should have been the country to give this uniquely British phenomenon one more chance. Welcoming the scheme the New Zealand Government issued a press statement saying that from a long-range point of view children between five and seventeen were the best immigrants a country could have.

On 5 June 1951 the *Rimutake* docked at Auckland with a party of boys on board. In their trunks they each had one woollen blue-check dressing gown, two pairs of grey and one pair of fawn trousers, two cotton shirts, one and a half dozen hankies, one suit, blue with grey pin stripe, and a sports coat, blue with red stripe; a thick red- and blue-check sweater, two pairs of shoes, a pair of tennis shoes and only two vests and two pairs of pants. The contents of the trunks were not so different from those of the tens of thousands of children who had preceded them overseas.

The difficulties inherent in the scheme were not long in making themselves manifest. A system which had worked because of exceptional wartime conditions could not be adapted as a permanent migration scheme. There was no provision for supervision or after-care when legal guardianship passed from the superintendent to the foster parent; there was uncertainty as to the legal situation if the parents of the child themselves came to New Zealand; the children, in spite of many satisfactory placements, became unsettled when their natural parents wrote to them or when they migrated and upset the arrangements that had been made. It was recognised that it was 'not possible to stand in the way of parents writing as they have a natural bond of affection and the child has been sent out to give it the best possible chance in life'.

Criticism was not long in coming. When the National Council for Social Service asked for information about the scheme and how it functioned with no base in New Zealand they were told it was not necessary to have a base as 'the documentary information and photographs we receive from the High Commission for New Zealand is sufficient to enable children to be suitably placed with approved foster parents'. It seemed that nothing had been learnt from the long experience of juvenile emigration to Canada! There was no question of the children being adopted and it was confidently stated that the boys would become successful farmers. A good face was put forward and unpalatable facts were simply not notified.

When the *Rangitiki* arrived on 2 October 1952 it had on board the last party of children sent by the Overseas League. The New Zealand cabinet decided on 14 October of that year that the scheme must end, and it absolutely refused to receive or listen to the protestations of the Overseas League. The Government said, however, that New Zealand was prepared to take orphan children, to which the League replied, 'We will do our best to find some, but there are many difficulties in this country where there is such prejudice against sending orphans overseas.'[29] They were not successful. Public opinion in Britain had finally closed the door to organised child migration.

APPENDIX

1 *Condensed statistical history of the juvenile immigration movement 1868–1928*

society or agency	*year*	*children sent to Canada*
Miss Macpherson and Mrs Birt, London, Liverpool (Canadian headquarters, Marchmont Home, Belleville, Ont.)	1868–1926	14,578
Miss Rye and Church of England (Niagara-on-the-Lake and Sherbrooke, P.Q.)	1868–1928	4,218
Mr (now) Sir J.T. Middlemore, Fairview, Halifax, N.S.	1873–1928	5,109
The National Children's Home and Orphanage (formerly Dr T. Bowman Stephenson, Hamilton, Ont.)	1873–1928	3,206
Mrs Bilbrough-Wallace (Marchmont Home, Belleville, Ont.)	1878–1915	5,529
Cardinal Manning (Ottawa and Montreal)	1880–1888	1,403
Dr Barnardo, Toronto, Ont., and Winnipeg, Man.	1882–1928	26,790
Mr J.W.C. Fegan, Toronto, Ont.	1884–1928	3,080
Mr Wm. Quarrier, Brockville, Ont.	1890–1928	4,340
The Catholic Emigration Association and amalgamated societies, St George's Home, Ottawa	1897–1928	7,237
The Salvation Army	1905–1928	3,149
Dr Cossar, Lower Gagetown, N.B.	1910–1928	711
Captain Oliver Hind, The Dakeyne Farm, Falmouth (near Windsor, N.S.)	1913–1928	110
British Immigration Aid and Colonization Association, Montreal, P.Q.	1923–1928	1,709
The Church Army, Winnipeg	1925–1928	459
Church of England Society, Council of Empire Settlement, Edmonton, Alta., Indian Head and Melfort, Sask.	1926–1928	139
Minor agencies	1897–1928	5,932
Total		**87,699**

Source PAC, Report of the Department of Immigration and Colonisation, 1929, p. 89.

2 *Statement of the numbers of juveniles emigrated to Canada by the principal organisations of Great Britain 1900–20 and the number of applications annually received at their Canadian receiving and distributing homes during the same period*

fiscal year	*children emigrated*	*applications received*
1900–1	977	5,783
1901–2	1,540	8,587
1902–3	1,979	14,219
1903–4	2,213	16,573
1904–5	2,808	17,833
1905–6	3,264	19,374
1906–7	1,455	15,800
1907–8	2,375	17,239
1908–9	2,375	15,417
1909–10	2,422	18,477
1910–11	2,524	21,768
1911–12	2,689	31,040
1912–13	2,642	33,493
1913–14	2,318	32,417
1914–15	1,799	30,854
1915–16	821	31,725
1916–17	251	28,990
1917–18	—	17,916
1918–19	—	11,718
1919–20	155	10,235

Source PAC, Report of the Department of Immigration and Colonisation, 11. George V. A. 1921, p. 46

NOTES

PRO: Public Record Office
PAC: Public Archives of Canada
PP: Parliamentary Papers

1 Early Child Emigrants

1 Banks, *Planters of the Commonwealth*, p. 3
2 Ibid., p. 118
3 Andrews, *Colonial Period of American History*, p. 134
4 Ibid.
5 Pinchbeck and Hewitt, *Children in English Society*, I, p. 94
6 Wertenbaker, *The Planters of Colonial Virginia*, p. 75
7 Historical Manuscripts Commission Eighth Report, II, No. 253; quoted in Andrews, op. cit., p. 135
8 Virginia Company Records, I, 130 (83), quoted in Andrews, op. cit.
9 Andrews, op. cit., p. 135 n. 2
10 Ibid., p. 62 n. 1
11 Wagner, *English Genealogy*, p. 305
12 Davis, *The Ancestry of Phoebe Tilton*; quoted by Wagner, op. cit., p. 306
13 Banks, op. cit., p. 31
14 Ibid., pp. 28–32
15 Pinchbeck and Hewitt, op. cit., p. 107
16 Bateson, *The Convict Ships*, pp. 54–5
17 Brenton, *The Bible and the Spade*, p. 13
18 Ibid.
19 Brenton, *Observations on the Training and Education of the Children of Great Britain*, p. xx
20 House of Lords Sessional Papers, 1835, No. 42, p. 324
21 Report from the Governor of the Cape of Good Hope to the Secretary of the Colonies, relative to the condition and treatment of the children sent out by the Children's Friend Society, 1840, PP XXXIII
22 Ibid., p. 13
23 Ibid., p. 13
24 Ibid., p. 13
25 Ibid., p. 11
26 Ibid., p. 11

2 Opportunities in Australasia

1 National Archives of New Zealand, G1/5 42–52, p. 327
2 *Southern Cross*, November 1843
3 Letter, Book of Superintendent of Guardian of juvenile immigrants, 7 December 1842–29 April 1847,
4 Ibid., 4 July 1843
5 Battye Library, Superintendent of Guardian of juvenile immigrants to Colonial Secretary, 13 April 1847–28 March 1857, 22 June 1847
6 Ibid., 13 April 1847
7 First Report 1848, p. 16, H.C. 1847/8 (963) xxxiii; quoted by Robins, *Lost Children*, p. 200
8 Robins, op. cit., p. 200
9 *Tipperary Vindicator*, 3 January 1849; quoted by Robins, op. cit., p. 203
10 Robins, op. cit., p. 208
11 *Hansard*, Third Series, vol. CXI: Juvenile population, 6 June 1848

12 Shaftesbury's speech to House of Commons on 'Juvenile Population', 6 June 1848, p. 441
13 de Serville, *Port Phillip Gentlemen*, p. 40
14 *Hansard*, Third Series Report, vol. CXI: Emigration of Orphan Children, 28 May 1850
15 *Ragged School Union Magazine*, 1849, p. 52
16 Ibid., p. 52
17 Ibid., 1851, p. 160
18 Ibid., 1853, p. 92
19 Pinchbeck and Hewitt, op. cit., pp. 559–61

3 'Our Western Home'

1 *Niagara Mail*, 17 November 1869
2 *The Christian*, 16 June 1870
3 *The Christian*, 30 May 1872 4 *The Times*, 14 April 1863
5 Report of the Select Committee of the Parliament of Canada on Immigration and Colonisation, 23 June 1875, p. 22
6 *The Times*, 29 March 1869
7 Cruikshank, *Our Gutter Children*, p. 1
8 *The Christian*, 14 July 1870
9 *Niagara Mail*, 17 November 1869
10 Rye, *What the people say about the children and what the children say about Canada*, p. 41
11 Report to the President of the Local Government Board by Andrew Doyle, Local Government Inspector, as to the emigration of pauper children to Canada, 1875, PP LXIII, pp. 26–7
12 Reply of Mr Doyle to Miss Rye's Report on the emigration of pauper children to Canada, 1877, PP LXXI, pp. 495–6
13 Rye, op. cit., p. 45
14 Ibid., p. 51
15 Ibid., p. 50
16 Grainger, *Charges made against Miss Rye*, p. 6
17 PAC, RG 17, vol. 25, file 252: Dixon to Stafford, 12 November 1868
18 Grainger, *Charges made against Miss Rye*, passim

4 To the Land of the Maple Leaf

1 *The Christian*, 1 September 1870
2 Birt, *The Children's Homefinder*, p. 4
3 Ibid., p. 12
4 *The Christian*, 29 December 1893
5 *The Revival*, 4 March 1869
6 *The Christian*, 29 December 1893
7 *The Revival*, 3 June 1869
8 *The Christian*, 19 May 1870
9 *The Christian*, 29 September 1870
10 *The Christian*, 29 September 1870
11 Sutherland, *Children in English Canadian Society*, p. 57
12 *The Christian*, 22 February 1872
13 *The Christian*, 29 February 1872
14 *The Christian*, 30 May 1872
15 Birt, *The Children's Homefinder*, p. 77
16 *Edgbastonia*, a monthly magazine, vol. VII, No. 70, 1887, pp. 17–29
17 *Middlemore, a Family Memoir* (privately printed, 1961)
18 *One Hundred Years of Child Care, the Story of the Middlemore Homes, 1872–1972*
19 *The Middlemore Homes, Personal Report of John Middlemore for 1877*, pp. 13–14
20 Records of the Liverpool Sheltering Homes
21 Ibid.

5 A Setback for Miss Rye

1 *The Times*, 6 June 1874
2 Report to the President of the Local Government Board by Andrew Doyle, Local

Government Inspector, as to the emigration of pauper children to Canada, 1875, PP LXIII, p. 4
3 Ibid., p. 18
4 Ibid., p. 12
5 Ibid., pp. 12–13
6 Ibid., p. 12
7 Ibid., p. 29
8 Ibid., p. 34
9 Turner, *Miss Rye's Children*, p. 181
10 *First Report of the Select Committee of the Parliament of Canada on Immigration and Colonialisation*, 1875, p. 18
11 Ibid., p. 3
12 *Free Press*, 27 March 1875; quoted by Turner, op. cit., p. 184
13 *The Globe*, 6 April 1875; quoted by Turner, p. 187
14 *Montreal Gazette*, 31 March 1875; quoted by Turner, p. 187
15 *The Globe*, 2 October 1875; quoted by Turner, pp. 188–9
16 Miss Rye's letter to the president of the Local Government Board, 1877, PP LXXI
17 Ibid., p. 2
18 Reply of Mr Doyle to Miss Rye's report on the emigration of pauper children to Canada, 1877, PP LXXI
19 Ibid., p. 2
20 Ibid., p. 5
21 Ibid., p. 1
22 Ibid., p. 4
23 Ibid., p. 9
24 PAC, RG 76, vol. 66, file 3115, p. 4
25 *The Times*, 14 May 1878
26 *The Christian*, 20 June 1878
27 *The Christian*, 18 September 1879

6 The Sovereign Remedy

1 *Night and Day*, vol. VII, p. 140
2 Royal Commission on the Housing of the working classes, 1884–5, PP XXX, p. 19
3 *The Revival*, 1 October 1868
4 For a more detailed discussion of the quarrel between Barnardo and Charrington and Reynolds, see Wagner, *Barnardo*, chapters 6–8
5 *Daily Chronicle*, 20 October 1877
6 *The Christian*, 12 August 1887
7 *Night and Day*, vol. III 1874, p. 66
8 PAC, Letter from T.J. Barnardo to Sir Charles Tupper, 26 June 1884
9 PAC, Letter from Tupper to Barnardo, 2 July 1884
10 *Night and Day*, vol. VII, November 1884

7 The Sovereign Remedy in Practice

1 Parr, *Labouring Children*, p. 108
2 Barnardo Boys Canada Party, vol. I
3 First published in *Encounter*, June 1976; reprinted in Lawrence Lerner, *The Man I Killed* (1980). Reproduced by kind permission of Secker and Warburg Ltd
4 P. Harrison, *The Home Children*
5 Bagnell, *The Little Immigrants*

8 'Only the Flower of the Flock'

1 *Toronto News*, 6 May 1884
2 *Toronto Globe*, 9 October 1884
3 Bagnell, op. cit., p. 88
4 Kelso, *Special Report on the Immigration of British Children* (1897), p. 17
5 Report on the Education and Maintenance of children in the Metropolis, 1896, PP XLIII, vol. 2, p. 360
6 *Night and Day*, vol. LX, p. 158
7 *Pall Mall Gazette*, 'The Maiden

Tribute to Modern Babylon', 6 July 1885
8 *The Children's Advocate*, vol. 22, p. 151
9 Parr, op. cit., p. 67
10 *Night and Day*, vol. XX (October 1896), p. 73; vol. XXI (May 1897), p. 32
11 Marchmont Home, Belleville, Ontario, History Book 1892–3
12 For a more detailed account of these cases see Wagner, *Barnardo*, Ch. 13
13 PAC, RG 76, vol. 65; Catholic child emigration to Canada, 1904, p. 10
14 Montgomery, *Anne of Green Gables*, p. 9
15 Harrison, op. cit.; Bagnell, op. cit.
16 PAC, RG 76, vol. 94: Letter from Barnardo to the Secretary of the Department of the Interior, 23 February 1894
17 PAC, RG 76, vol. 194, file 73883
18 PAC, RG 76, vol. 24, file 25933: Manslaughter trial of Helen Findlay in the death of George Everitt Green, 1895
19 PAC, RG 76, vol. 194, file 73883: Letter from A.M. Burgess to Lady Aberdeen, 2 May 1896
20 PAC, RG 76, vol. 194, file 73883
21 Kelso, *Special Report* (1897), p. 35

9 From Salvation to Empire

1 Booth, *In Darkest England and the Way Out*, p. 144
2 *The Christian*, 24 October 1890
3 Western Australian Parliament. Debate on the proposal to import trained boys and girls, 2 September 1896, pp. 599–604
4 Pakenham, *The Boer War*, pp. xvi, 495
5 Argyll Papers, Bundle 858 (Courtesy of the Duke of Argyll)

10 An Imperial Investment

1 *The Colonist*, vol. 2, 1896–7, p. 127
2 *The Banner County*, 'History of Russell and District, 1879–1967', pp. 102–3
3 R. Fairbridge, *Pinjarra*, p. 1
4 Battye Library, Ibid., Letter book of Kingsley Fairbridge, Letter from Northcliffe to Fairbridge, 2 December 1909
5 Battye Library, Letter from Kinloch Cooke to Fairbridge, 3 November 1909
6 PAC, RG 76, vol. 323, file 32973
7 Battye Library, Letter book of Kingsley Fairbridge, Draft letter from Fairbridge
8 R. Fairbridge, op. cit., pp. 66–7
9 Battye Library, Fairbridge to Jefferson, 11 March 1913
10 Le Fevre, Kingsley Fairbridge and the establishment of the Farm School at Pinjarra, p. 21
11 Jo Tate told me his story while I was in Christchurch in February 1981. He died six months later.
12 R. Fairbridge, op. cit., p. 170
13 Le Fevre, op. cit., p. 15
14 R. Fairbridge, op. cit., p. 211
15 Mitchell Library, NSW, Barnardo cuttings book 1921–9, Box No. 3K 33277
16 Ibid., *Adelaide Express*, 17 October 1921
17 Ibid., *Sydney Morning Herald*, 24 October 1921
18 PAC, RG 76, vol. 67, file 3115, part B
19 The scheme was financed by money raised by NSW citizens to buy battleships for the fledgling Royal Australian Navy until there was a change of policy and

the money raised was used to sponsor immigration

20 From an account written by F.S. Felks in 1956, lent to me by Mr Zakharov

21 Gulnara Abashmadze, *Where do I come from?*, an account of Charles Zakharov's visit to Georgia, 1975, lent to me by Mr Zakharov

11 In Defence of Childhood

1 PAC, Annual report of the department of neglected and dependent children, Ontario, 1909

2 J.J. Kelso papers; quoted by Jones and Rutman, *In the Children's Aid*, p. 177

3 PAC, RG 76, vol. 65, file 3115, p. 5: Report of a conference held at the board room of the Lambeth Guardians, to consider the subject of the emigration of poor-law children, June 1903

4 Ibid., p. 9

5 PAC, RG 76, vol. 66, file 3115: Report to the Chorlton Guardians on a visit to emigrated children in Canada, by Miss O. Hertz of the Cottage Homes Committee, 1910

6 *Manchester Guardian*, 19 April 1910

7 PAC, Ontario Sessional Papers, Report of the Department of Immigration and Colonization, Ottawa, 1921, p. 50

8 Harrison, op. cit., pp. 182–98

9 *The Times*, 2 February 1924

10 *John Bull*, 3 November 1923

11 *News Mirror* (undated): PAC, RG 76, vol. 67, file 3115, part 11

12 Sources for John Thomas's story include Barnardo records, an article in the *Free Press Weekly Prairie Farmer* (16 January 1952) and a letter from his friend Stanley Fryer, whose father was the Church of England Medical Missionary to the Fort Alexander Indian Reserve 1911–35

13 *Ups and Downs*, November 1924, p. 13

14 Report of the delegation appointed to obtain information regarding the system of child migration and settlement in Canada, 1924–5, PP XV

15 Canada's Child Immigrants, Annual report of the Committee on Immigration and Colonisation to the Social Service Council of Canada, January 1925

16 PAC, RG 76, vol. 68/3115, part 15: Letter from John Hobday to Mrs Macgregor, 27 September 1927

17 Canadian Council on Child Welfare. 5th Annual Conference, 1925: Problems in Juvenile Immigration

18 Report of inquiry by Miss Gladys Pott and Mrs A.B. Lowry on behalf of the Overseas Settlement Committee into the methods of selecting children in this country for settlement overseas

19 *Sunday Times*, 27 September 1925: 'Is England Done?'

20 PAC, RG 76, vol. 69/3115

21 I am grateful to John Greenwood for allowing me to tell his story

12 Refugees from War

1 National Archives of New Zealand, Annual report of the Department of Immigration, New Zealand, 1926, p. 2

2 PAC, Ontario Sessional Papers, Report of the supervisor of

juvenile immigration, G. Bogue Smart, 1931-2, p. 79

3 Unpublished autobiography of Charles Davies, *Here We Go*, deposited in the Barnardo Library. I am grateful to Mr Davies for permission to use part of his story

4 *The Times*, 6 November 1935

5 *Morning Post*, 3 October 1934

6 Terpsma, Prince of Wales Fairbridge Farm School and Child Welfare in British Columbia

7 PAC Immigration Branch, Fairbridge file: F.C. Blair to W.R. Little, 22 October 1931

8 Terpsma, op. cit., p. 31

9 Ibid.

10 Public Archives of British Columbia, Provincial Secretary correspondence 1934-46, vol. 86, file 503: Isobel Harvey, 'Report on study made of Fairbridge Farm School during month of August 1944'

11 PRO Children's Overseas Reception Board papers

12 PRO, CORB material prepared by Marjorie Maxse for the *Official War History*, 1944

13 National Archives of New Zealand: Evacuation of children and refugees from England, 1940

14 New Zealand Archives, Evacuation of Children and Refugees from England, 25 July 1940

15 Information supplied by Mrs Elspeth Davies

16 PAC, Report of the Department of Mines and Resources for the year ended March 1941, p. 198

17 National Archives of New Zealand: Evacuation of children and refugees from England

18 PRO, CORB papers

19 Ibid.

20 PAC, RG 76, vol. 452, file 693249, part 1: Letter from Charlotte Whitton to F.C. Blair, 24 February 1941

21 PRO, CORB papers

22 Ibid.

23 PAC, RG 76, file 55-36, temporary box 88: British Guest Children Scheme

24 Ibid.

25 Ibid.

26 PRO, CORB papers

27 PRO, CORB papers

28 National Archives of New Zealand, Child Migration Scheme, 1949-53

29 National Archives of New Zealand, Letter from Mr Bavin, Migration Officer, Royal Overseas League, 5 November 1952. I have been unable to study the relevant files belonging to the Royal Overseas League as they are not accessible

BIBLIOGRAPHY

All books published in the UK except where otherwise stated.

Books, Reports, Articles and Pamphlets

Andrews, C.M., *The Colonial Period of American History* (Yale, 1941)

Bagnell, K., *The Little Immigrants* (Toronto, 1980)

Bailey, Anthony, *America Lost and Found* (1981)

Banks, J., *The Planters of the Commonwealth* (1930)

Bans, E., *Catholic Child Emigration to Canada* (privately printed, 1904)

Barnardo, S.I. and Marchant, James, *Memoirs of the Late Dr Barnardo* (1907)

Bateson, Charles, *The Convict Ships 1787–1868* (1959)

Birt, Lillian M., *The Children's Homefinder: The Story of Annie Macpherson and Louisa Birt* (1913)

Bondfield, M., *A Life's Work* (1948)

Booth, Charles, *The Life and Labour of the People in London*, 17 vols (1902)

Booth, William, *In Darkest England and the Way Out* (1890)

Brace, C.H., *The Life of Charles Loring Brace, Chiefly told through his own letters* (New York, 1894)

Brace, Charles Loring, *The best method of disposing of Pauper and Vagrant Children* (New York, 1859)

—— *The Dangerous Classes of New York* (New York, 1872)

Bradfield, W., *Life of Bowman Stephenson* (1913)

Bready, J. Wesley, *Doctor Barnardo, Physician, Pioneer, Prophet* (1930)

Brenton, E.P., *Observations on the Training and Education of the Children of Great Britain* (1824)

—— *The Bible and the Spade* (1837)

Brenton, Jahled, *Memoir of Captain Edward Pelham Brenton* (1842)

The Cambridge History of the British Empire, vol. III *The Empire and Commonwealth 1870–1919*

Carlebach, J., *Caring for Children in Trouble* (1970)

Carpenter, Mary, *Reformatory Schools for the Children of the Perishing and Dangerous Classes and for Juvenile Offenders* (1851)

Carrothers, W.A., *Emigration from the British Isles* (1965)

Chesney, Kellow, *The Victorian Underworld* (1970)

Collier, R., *The General Next to God* (1965)

Copping, A., *The Golden Land. The true story and experiences of British settlers in Canada* (1911)

—— *Smithers, a true story of Private Imperialism* (1912)

Coutts, General Frederick, *No discharge in this war: a History of the Salvation Army* (1975)

Cranfield, Walter, *John Bull's Surplus Children* (1915)

Cruikshank, George, *Our Gutter Children* (1869)
Davenport Hill, Florence, *Children of the State* (1868)
Erickson, Charlotte, *Invisible Immigrants: The Adaptation of English and Scottish Immigrants in Nineteenth Century America* (1972)
Fairbridge, K., *The Story of Kingsley Fairbridge by himself* (1910)
—— *Juvenile Emigration and the Farm School System* (1927)
Fairbridge, Ruby, *Pinjarra: The Building of a Farm School* (1929)
Fuller, T.E., *Cecil John Rhodes, a monograph and a reminiscence* (1910)
Fullerton, W.Y., *J.W.C. Fegan* (1930)
Galloway, C.F.J., *The Call of the West* (1916)
Galsworthy, J., *The Silver Spoon* (1926)
Gibbon Wakefield, E., *A Letter from Sydney* (1829)
—— *A View of the Art of Colonisation* (1849)
Goodall, J., *Suffering in Childhood., The 1979 Barnardo Lecture, Christian Medical Fellowship*
Grainger, Allerdale, *Charges made against Miss Rye before the Poor Law Board at Islington and her reply thereto* (privately printed, n.p., 1874)
Gutherie, T., *Seed Time and Harvest of Ragged Schools* (1860)
Hamilton, M.A., *Margaret Bondfield* (1924)
Harrison, Brian, *Drink and the Victorians* (1971)
Harrison, Phyllis, *The Home Children* (Winnipeg, 1979)
Heaseman, Kathleen, *Evangelicals in Action* (1962)
Hertz, O., *Copy of the report to the Chorlton Board of Guardians on a visit to emigrated children in Canada* (privately printed, 1910)
Heywood, Jean, *Children in Care* (1959)
Hodder, Edwin, *The Life and Work of the Seventh Earl of Shaftesbury*, 3 vols (1887)
Inglis, Brian, *Poverty and the Industrial Revolution* (1971)
Inglis, K.S., *The Churches and the Working Classes in Victorian England* (1963)
Johnson, S.C., *A History of Emigration from the United Kingdom to North America 1763–1912* (1966)
Jones, Andrew and Rutman, Leonard, *In the Children's Aid. J.J. Kelso and Child Welfare in Ontario* (Toronto, 1981)
Jones, Gareth Stedman, *Outcast London* (1971)
Kelso, J.J. *Special Report on the Immigration of British Children* (1897)
Kinloch Clarke, Charles, 'The Emigration of State Children', *Empire Review*, vol. 9 (1905)
Langsam, Miriam, *Children West: A history of the placing-out system of the New York Children's Aid Society 1853–1890* (Wisconsin, 1964)
Le Fevre, Anne, Kingsley Fairbridge 1885–1924 and the establishment of the Farm School at Pinjarra, Western Australia (unpublished paper, 1978)
Longman, Norman, *The Workhouse* (1974)
Lowe, Clara, *God's Answers, a narrative of Miss Macpherson's work* (1882)
McCarthy, D., *The first fleet of Auckland* (1978)
Macnamara, T.J., *Children under the Poor Law. A report to the President of the Local Government Board* (1907)
Magnuson, J. and Petrie, D., *Orphan Train* (1981)
Marriot, John, *Empire Settlement* (1927)

Mearns, Andrew, 'The Bitter Cry of Outcast London: An Enquiry into the Condition of the Abject Poor' (Congregation Union, 1883)
Middlemore, *One Hundred Years of Child Care: The Story of the Middlemore Homes 1872–1972* (1972)
Miles, M.C., Parish of Fulham, Report of Miss M.C. Miles, Guardian of the Parish of Fulham after her visit to children emigrated to Canada by Fulham Board of Guardians (1903–4)
Montgomery, L.M., *Anne of Green Gables* (1908)
Morgan, G.E., *A Veteran in Revival, R.C. Morgan* (1909)
Morris, James, *Farewell, the Trumpets: An Imperial Retreat* (1978)
—— *Heaven's Command: An Imperial Progress* (1968)
—— *Pax Britannica: The Climax of Empire* (1973)
O'Brien, T., *Milner* (1979)
Orr, J. Edwin, *The Second Evangelical Awakening in Britain* (1949)
Owen, David, *English Philanthropy, 1660–1960* (1965)
Pakenham, T., *The Boer War* (1979)
Parr, Joy, *Labouring Children – British Immigrant Apprentices to Canada 1869–1924* (1980)
Pinchbeck, Ivy and Hewitt, Margaret, *Children in English Society*, 2 vols (1969 and 1973)
Plant, G.F., *Overseas Settlement: Migration from the United Kingdom to the Dominions* (1951)
Powell, E., *Joseph Chamberlain* (1977)
Robins, J., *The Lost Children* (1981)
Rye, Maria, *What the people say about the children and what the children say about Canada* (1871)
St John, E., *Manning's Work for Children* (1929)
Scholes, A.G., *Education for Empire Settlement* (1932)
Sedgwick, T.E., *Town Lads on Imperial Farms* (1911)
Seeley, J.R., *The Expansion of England* (1883)
Semmel, Bernard, *Imperialism and Social Reform: English Social-Imperial Thought 1895–1914* (1960)
de Serville, P., *Port Phillip Gentlemen* (1980)
Sims, George R., *How the Poor Live* (1883)
Smith, A.G., *Colonists in Bondage: Emigration from the United Kingdom to North America* (1947)
Smith, Samuel, 'The Industrial Training of Destitute Children', *Contemporary Review*, vol. 13 (1883)
Stroud, John, *Thirteen Penny Stamps: The Story of the Church of England Children's Society (Waifs and Strays) from 1881 to the 1970s* (1971)
Sutherland, Neil, *Children in English-Canadian Society: Framing the twentieth century consensus* (Toronto, 1976)
Tallack, W., *Peter Bedford, The Spitalfields Philanthropist* (1865)
Terpsma, B., Prince of Wales Fairbridge Farm School and Child Welfare in British Columbia (MA thesis, University of British Columbia, 1979)
Tiffin, Alfred, *Loving and Serving: An Account of the Life and Work of J.W.C. Fegan* (undated)
Turner, Wesley, 'Miss Rye's Children', *Ontario History*, vol. 68, no. 3 (1976)

Wagner, A. R., *English Genealogy* (2nd edition, 1972)
Wagner, Gillian, *Barnardo* (1979)
Waugh, Benjamin, *The Goal Cradle – Who Rocks it?* (1875)
Webb, Sidney and Beatrice, *English Poor Law History* (1906)
Wertenbaker, T.J., *The Planters of Colonial Virginia* (1922)
Williams, A.E., *Barnardo of Stepney, The Father of Nobody's Children* (1943)
Williams, H.D., *The Keys of Paradise* (1927)
Woodroofe, Kathleen, *From Charity to Social Work in England and the United States* (1962)

Archive Collections

Argyll Papers

Barnardo Archives
Barnardo Boys Canada Party, vols 1–99, 1882–1935
Barnardo Girls Canada Histories, in bundles

Liverpool Sheltering Homes
Canada Migration, Liverpool, vols 1–18, 1872–1916
Liverpool Sheltering Homes 'Band' books, vols 1–20, 1873–1925

Macpherson Homes
Canadian Migration, London history books, 33 vols, 1882–*c.* 1920
Emigrant Register, Home of Industry, Commercial Street (undated)
Home of Industry Register, 1877–1884
Home of Industry, Spitalfields history books, vols 1–10, 1870–1924
Macpherson Home Stratford, 1871–73

Marchmont Homes
Canadian Migration, Marchmont Home, history books, 28 vols, 1870–1914

Reformatory and Refuge Union
Minutes of management, circulars, cuttings and letters pasted in 1856–1924

Public Archives of Canada
Source: RG 76:

Annual Report of the Committee on Immigration and Colonialisation to the Social Service of Canada: Canada's child immigrants 1925

Bristol Emigration Society	1894–1906
British Public Schools Association for and placing immigrants on farms in Nova Scotia	1928–31
Canadian Catholic Emigration Society	1899–1905
Children's Aid Society	1892–1907
Church of England Waifs and Strays Society	1893–1950
G. Bogue Smart, Chief Inspector of British Immigrant Children (reports, pamphlets)	1899–1933
Inspection of British Immigrant children	1874–1937
Inspection of Workhouse Children	1894
Juvenile Immigration	1902–18

Lady Aberdeen: inquiries re Barnardo boys charged 1896
Liverpool Catholic Children's Protection Society 1892–1902
Macpherson Home – emigration of children – reception, placement 1893–1925
Middlemore Homes, Halifax 1893–1907
Orders-in-Council re Inspection of immigrant children 1906–28
Re death of a Barnardo boy 1897

National Archives of New Zealand
Department of Immigration, Annual Reports 1924–30
Child Migration Scheme 1949–53
Evacuation of children and refugees from England 1940–45
Parkhurst Boys 1842–53
Third Report of Guardian of Boys from Parkhurst Prison 1844

Alexander Turnbull Library
Nelson Examiner 4 November 1843
New Zealand Gazette and Wellington Spectator 13 December 1843
New Zealand Government Gazette 1843

State Library of New South Wales
The Mitchell Library

Dr Barnardo's in Australia
Cuttings books, 1921–9, 1963–6
Minute books, 1923–41

The Library Board of Western Australia
Battye Library:
Kingsley Fairbridge letter book
Letter book of Superintendent of juvenile immigrants to Colonial Secretary 1843–7
Letter book of Superintendent of juvenile immigrants to Colonial Secretary 1847–52
Passenger manifest of *Charlotte Padbury*, Freemantle, 1883
Research notes 107, Juvenile Emigration

Official Publications and Reports

Great Britain
Select committee on State of Mendicity in the Metropolis. First Report, 1814–15, PP III; Second Report, 1816, PP V
Report from the Select Committee on the Police of the Metropolis 1828, PP VI
First Annual Report of the Poor Law Commission, 1835, PP XXXV
Report from the Governor of the Cape of Good Hope to the Secretary of the

Colonies relative to the condition and treatment of children sent out by the Children's Friend Society, 1840, PP XXIV

Second Report from the select committee of the House of Lords appointed to inquire into the execution of the Criminal Law, especially respecting juvenile offenders and transportation, 1847, PP VII

Report to the President of the Local Government Board by Andrew Doyle, Local Government Inspector, as to the emigration of Pauper children to Canada, 1875, PP LXIII

Letter addressed by Miss Rye to the President of the Local Government Board, 1877, PP LXXI

Reply of Mr Doyle to Miss Rye's Report on the emigration of pauper children to Canada, 1877, PP LXXI

Report of the Departmental Committee on the Education and Maintenance of pauper children in the Metropolis, 1896, PP XLIII

Report by the Departmental Committee appointed to consider Mr Rider Haggard's report on agricultural settlements in British colonies, 1906, PP LXXVI

Report of the Overseas Settlement Committee, 1923, PP XII, 1927, X

Report of the delegation appointed to obtain information regarding the system of child migration and settlement in Canada, 1924–5, PP XV

Canada

Parliament of Canada

First Report of the Select Committee of the Parliament of Canada on Immigration and Colonialisation, 1875

Sessional Papers, Ontario

Reports of the Commission of Immigration and Colonialisation 1873–1935

Report of the Department of Neglected and Dependent Children 1893–1935

Special Report on the immigration of British Children 1897–8

Parliamentary Debates

Great Britain, House of Commons

Juvenile Population, 6 June 1848

Emigration of Orphan Children, 28 May 1850

Western Australian Parliament

Debate on the proposal to import trained boys and girls, 2 September 1896

Serials

Dr Barnardo's:

Annual Reports 1881–1965

Night and Day 1877–1965

Ups and Downs 1895–1949

Church of England Waifs and Strays Society:
Annual Reports 1882–1924
Our Waifs and Strays 1884–1906

Fegan Homes:
The Christian Shield 1877, 1879

Home of Industry:
Occasional Emigration Papers 1869–76

Manchester and Salford Boys and Girls Refuges:
Annual Report, 1886

National Children's Home:
Annual Reports, 1879–1924
The Children's Advocate 1871–87

National Association for the Promotion of Social Science:
Transactions 1857–84

Ragged School Union Magazine 1847–57

Big Brother Movement, British Youth Migration to Australia, Golden Jubilee 1925–75

INDEX

Boards of Guardians of various localities have been grouped under the heading 'Boards of Guardians', stories of individual emigrant children under 'case histories', and names of emigrant ships under 'ships'.

16–17, 21, 46